Internet Censorship

Books in the **Contemporary World Issues** series address vital issues in today's society such as genetic engineering, pollution, and biodiversity. Written by professional writers, scholars, and nonacademic experts, these books are authoritative, clearly written, up-to-date, and objective. They provide a good starting point for research by high school and college students, scholars, and general readers as well as by legislators, business-people, activists, and others.

Each book, carefully organized and easy to use, contains an overview of the subject, a detailed chronology, biographical sketches, facts and data and/or documents and other primary source material, a forum of authoritative perspective essays, annotated lists of print and nonprint resources, and an index.

Readers of books in the **Contemporary World Issues** series will find the information they need in order to have a better understanding of the social, political, environmental, and economic issues facing the world today.

Internet Censorship

A REFERENCE HANDBOOK

Bernadette H. Schell

ABC-CLIO

Santa Barbara, California • Denver, Colorado • Oxford, England

Library of Congress Cataloging-in-Publication Data

Schell, Bernadette H. (Bernadette Hlubik), 1952–
    Internet censorship : a reference handbook / Bernadette H. Schell
    pages cm. — (Contemporary world issues)
    Includes bibliographical references and index.
    ISBN 978–1–61069–481–0 (hardback) — ISBN 978–1–61069–482–7 (ebook) 1. Internet—Censorship. 2. Internet—Access control. 3. Internet—Government policy. 4. Cyberspace—Government policy. 5. Internet—Law and legislation—United States. 6. Freedom of information. 7. Cyberspace—Social aspects. 8. Internet—Social aspects. I. Title.
    ZA4201.S34   2014
    004.67′8—dc23   2014005277

ISBN: 978–1–61069–481–0
EISBN: 978–1–61069–482–7

18 17 16 15   2 3 4 5

This book is also available on the World Wide Web as an eBook. Visit www.abc-clio.com for details.

ABC-CLIO, LLC
130 Cremona Drive, P.O. Box 1911
Santa Barbara, California 93116-1911

This book is printed on acid-free paper ∞

Manufactured in the United States of America

5   DATA AND DOCUMENTS, 209

This book takes a novel approach to the presentation and understanding of a controversial topic in society: Internet censorship. When mainstream society heard about the Internet in the earlier stages of its development, there was much jubilation, because this "Information Superhighway" was supposedly created to help citizens around the world to have fast access to nearly an endless amount of information—without leaving their homes and just by clicking the mouse on their computers.

However, in recent times, there has been growing concern expressed by individuals in the online global society about Internet censorship—whereby governments are increasingly trying to control citizens' online activities, restrict the free flow of information, and infringe on the rights of online users. Stated simply, the battle over maintaining Internet freedom is heating up. Moreover, the methods used to control Internet content by governments are also becoming increasingly sophisticated. At a time when about a third of the world's people are actively engaged online, tactics previously employed by extremely repressive regimes are now being employed by governments once considered to be more open and supportive of Internet freedom. Some of these tactics involve causing premeditated connection disruptions or paying professional commentators to consciously manipulate online discussions.

There is little doubt that most countries restrict access to content on the Internet at some basic level, such as restricting access to Web pages with offensive content or preventing children from viewing content that could result in psychological or physical harm. According to Reporters Without Borders, an organization formed to promote free expression and the global safety of journalists who are committed to freedom of information, some countries such as Belarus, China, Cuba, Egypt, and Iran have very strong censorship policies, while other countries like the United States and Estonia are quite open to the concept of freedom of information.

This book explores the various levels of Internet censorship, from the usage of Web filters to national policies or laws aimed at preventing the flow of information. Also, two sides of the controversy over Internet censorship are explored in depth. First, there are those who believe that some amount or considerable amounts of censorship are acceptable. Second, there are those who believe in and actively play the role of information freedom fighter—with some being more credible in society's eyes than others.

This book has seven chapters, containing the following points of interest. Chapter 1 provides basic background and history on what is meant by Internet censorship, broadly speaking. The chapter opens with an interesting discussion on censorship versus national security—and why there will never be total freedom of the press or a total lack of press and Internet censorship. The discussion then moves to the controversies around adequate information release by governments versus Internet censorship, with a focus on the present-day headline-making cases of WikiLeaks, Private Manning, and Edward Snowden. The main differences between the Internet and intranets are then described. The remainder of the chapter details the growth of the Internet in the United States—from its rather humble beginning to its rapid growth in the 1990s and beyond. The chapter closes with present-day concerns about Internet censorship.

Chapter 2 outlines the unique problems, controversies, and solutions regarding information freedom fighters and Internet censorship. The chapter opens with a quote from Reporters Without Borders regarding the important point that freedom of information is the foundation of any democracy, yet almost half of the world's population is still denied it. The discussion then moves to a more fulsome exploration of the countries generally having strong censorship laws and policies—and why they can justify doing so—compared to those countries advocating for a more open system of information sharing and disclosure, such as the United States and Estonia. Next, the discussion covers the important concept of cultural and legal jurisdictional factors influencing the digital divide, with a particular emphasis on criminal liability on the coincidence of four key elements. The chapter closes with a review of global trends in Internet censorship, with a summary of expert opinions on the factors that may be involved in the next phase of the Internet's evolution in terms of equalizing rather than emphasizing a universal digital divide.

Chapter 3 continues on this expert opinion discussion on Internet freedom and censorship, with views expressed by experts in the fields of criminology, political science, philosophy, and psychology.

Chapter 4 provides sketches on contributors to both the Internet freedom fighters and the Internet censorship sides of the debate. Concepts covered include the hacker cell Anonymous, WikiLeaks and its founder Julian Assange, the hearing and sentencing of U.S. private Bradley (a.k.a. Chelsea) Manning, and the activities of controversial whistleblower Edward Snowden. Also included are proponents of the freedom of speech in its many forms, including the American Civil Liberties Union, the Citizen Lab at the University of Toronto, the Electronic Frontier Foundation, Freedom House, the OpenNet Initiative, Reporters Without Borders, and The Censorware Project.

Chapter 5 provides a series of annotated tables, graphs, charts, and figures regarding the trends in types of Internet censoring that have occurred in the recent past and the present. There is also a discussion of the geographical differences in trends, such as those found in the United States, as compared to those in China and Iran. Special topics in this chapter include an overview of Internet usage and penetration rates by region, a closer look at the *Freedom on the Net 2012* findings, tactics used by the highly censoring countries, and special forms of legislation passed in the United States and elsewhere for dealing with emerging trends in the Internet's evolution as they relate to critical privacy, security, trust, and censorship issues.

Chapter 6 provides an annotated bibliography of print and nonprint resources for further research, including books dealing with information freedom and censorship and the Internet's evolution shakers and movers, as well as short videos made in recent times to capture special events and topics pertaining to Internet censorship.

Chapter 7 summarizes some key events associated with the Internet's evolution, starting with its humble beginnings, moving into its adolescent years, and culminating in its adult years—from 1990 through to the present.

The book closes with a glossary containing brief definitions of key terms on Internet censorship, freedom fighting, and Internet evolution.

Internet Censorship

You have no moral right to rule us, nor do you possess any methods of enforcement that we have true reason to fear.
—John Perry Barlow, "A Declaration of the Independence of Cyberspace," at the World Economic Forum, Davos, Switzerland, 1996

Internet Censorship Defined

Internet censorship, at a basic level, occurs when governments try to control citizens' online activities, restrict the free flow of information, and/or infringe on the rights of online users. Stated simply, since about 2005, the battle over maintaining Internet freedom versus censorship of perceived offensive online content has been heating up worldwide. Each year, the government attempts to control Internet content. Annually, the means that governments use to control Internet content are becoming more and more sophisticated. Furthermore, tactics once used by repressive regimes are now being used by governments deemed to be more prone to content openness and Internet freedom. Some of these more aggressive means include causing planned connection disruptions or giving monies to

Apple president John Sculley, flanked by Apple co-founders Steve Jobs (left) and Steve Wozniak (right), unveils the new Apple IIc to more than 3,000 dealers and software sector representatives in San Francisco, California on April 24, 1984. (Bettmann/Corbis)

professional commentators to sway discussions in particular directions in chat rooms. (Freedom House, 2013).

Censorship versus National Security, and Why There Will Never Be Total Freedom of the Press or a Total Lack of Press and Internet Censorship

In the developed nations, there has been an ongoing tug of war over time between a government's allowing for censorship in the media (and more recently online) when concerns arise about national security, and giving the press full freedoms to publish in the media (and more recently online) what they deem fit for public consumption without recognizable censorship rules in place.

For example, in the First Amendment to the U.S. Constitution, a number of freedoms are cited, most notably freedom of the press. Clearly, in an effort for the founders of the United States to distinguish their new government from that of England— where there was a long history of censorship of the press in order to defend national security—the First Amendment was often referred to as the creation of a "fourth institution" outside the government as an additional check on the three official branches— the executive, the legislature, and the judiciary. The latter was created to maintain checks and balances between those advocating for more freedoms compared to those who saw threats to national security, particularly in times of war—when this freedom is often set aside for what government officials say is clearly a means of defending national security (Goodale, 1997).

Up until the Korean War and later (including the War in Iraq), the media and press were perceived to be helpful in educating citizens in the United States and elsewhere in understanding the basic conflict issues between the warring nations. In recent years, however, scholars have raised a very basic question regarding what is appropriate information sharing with "Joe public"; namely, *how much* censorship is deemed to be appropriate in defending national security while still permitting adequate freedoms to reporters in support of the First Amendment (Ingle, 2007)?

Academic Doris Graber (2003), for example, noted that justifying press censorship can be especially difficult, labeling it "the high-stakes dilemma." She went on to say that in one sense, press freedom is particularly important in times of national crisis like a war or a terrorist attack, but that the risks to security can result when, say, there is a "leak" of information that was intended to be strictly confidential. Thus, restrictions on what reporters can share with others have developed over time, increasing with recent developments in technology, like mobile phones and the Internet.

Accepting that technology has advanced world culture and narrowed the gap between the *haves* and *have-nots* along the access digital divide, Graber forcefully argues that in today's world, the reality is that there is someone—such as a reporter or a hacker group or some business—who will go against the moral grain, depart from established military protocols, and share sensitive information either in print or over the Internet for the whole world to see.

One such historic case making global news occurred in March of 2003, when Geraldo Rivera allegedly engaged in rogue reporting, thus endangering U.S. soldiers in Iraq. Apparently, Rivera told his photographer to tilt his camera downward in the sand so that he could draw a map of both Iraqi and U.S. military movements (Plante, 2003). Sadly, Rivera took the confidential information he was privy to and intentionally tried to transmit that information live to Fox News in the United States, but unintentionally, he shared it with the rest of the world because of technology advancements at that time. U.S. government officials took a hard line on Rivera's action, maintaining that what he did could have caused great harm to the troops. He was escorted out of Iraq and immediately lost contact with the 101st Airborne Division, with whom he had been stationed in trust.

However, censorship was targeted not only at the press during the Iraq war (or other recent wars), for U.S. troops themselves have been under tight disclosure rules in the field.

Apparently, Internet "kill switches" (mechanisms used to shut down or disable machinery, programs, or devices to, say, protect data on a mobile device from being altered or stolen) were utilized on U.S. military information networks in Iraq so that if there was an attack on the forces there, or if there were a number of casualties or some other newsworthy events, a senior military officer had the jurisdiction to literally "pull the plug" on the communications networks so that soldiers and reporters alike could not transmit confidential information outside of the zone. However, military officers realized that cell phones in the field were more difficult to control, because the phones sent signals through local Iraqi communication networks—which fell outside of the domain of the kill switches (Wielawski, 2005). Imagine the horrors if the very personal information about a dead soldier was shared with the world before it was communicated with family members.

Adequate Information Release by Governments versus Internet Censorship: WikiLeaks, Manning, and Snowden

The other side of the coin, of course, is acknowledging the *adequate* amount of information that the U.S. government actually allows to be disclosed to the public, at the time of war. While information freedom fighters (reporters, hackers, dissidents, or others) tend to view *any* kind of censorship as evil, the U.S. government has stated openly that it intends to be fair and reasonable to reporters embedded with soldiers in the field. Business press releases are written ahead of the time that they are actually transmitted to the public; an analogy exists in the battle zone.

In the Iraq War, as a case in point, a military officer could share with reporters planned attacks in any given region—but it was stipulated conclusively that the information cannot be released to the public until a stated time, such as after a said crisis or battle had transpired. Sometimes, this directive can be especially challenging, given increased access by many to the Internet—including reporters in the field. Consequently, rules for censorship and disclosure that may have been constructed within the past five years must be continually revised in the United States and elsewhere to reflect emerging developments in global military confrontations on land and through the Internet (known nowadays as cyber wars). To be sure, *censorship both on land and online is a subject that whenever addressed in any public debate will have clear supporters as well as clear opponents* (Ingle, 2007).

WikiLeaks and Information Freedom Fighter Julian Assange

As the Internet continues to evolve and as military conflicts continue to emerge in various parts of the world, the debate between the freedom fighters and the "appropriate censorship" of harm-inducing highly secret information rages on. Over the past seven years such a debate has continued regarding the concerns over the leaking of secret U.S. military documents and the role of the hacker activist group WikiLeaks. Julian Assange founded this group back in 2006 to provide an outlet to cause regime change and open information sharing to expose injustice and abuses of power (Greenberg, 2010). The Web site has published materials related to the Church of Scientology, Guantanamo Bay, military strikes, and classified documents around the world. The Web site is perhaps most famous for the acquisition and publication of 251,000 American diplomatic cables that range from unclassified to secret documents (Greenberg, 2010). A U.S. Army soldier named Bradley Manning, who downloaded the materials while stationed in Iraq, obtained this information. He then provided the materials to WikiLeaks, who chose to release these materials in batches over two years with the cooperation from major news outlets like *The New York Times* and *Der Spiegel* (Harrell, 2010).

The release of these cables caused massive controversy and embarrassment for the U.S. government, due to the sensitive nature of the information. In fact, a distributed denial of service (DDoS) attack (hack) was launched against the WikiLeaks

Web site shortly after the first release—taking it off line. Subsequently, the companies that provided funding and infrastructure for WikiLeaks, such as PayPal, pulled their support. As a consequence, hacker cells worldwide began DDoS hack attacks against the financial service providers to punish them for their actions. The controversy over these documents led some in the United States to call for the arrest of Assange, and even his execution in some cases (O'Brien, 2010).

But Julian Assange, forever the man seeking headlines globally as an information freedom fighter, was himself "on the lam" in 2012 and remains there in 2013. The WikiLeaks founder took refuge in the Ecuadorian embassy in June 2012, to avoid extradition to Sweden, where he is wanted for questioning by authorities about sexual assault allegations. His real fears, it seems, stem from the fact that Assange thinks Sweden would extradite him to the United States to face charges related to WikiLeak's disclosure of the huge treasure of the classified U.S. military and diplomatic documents associated with Manning (Paramaribo, 2013).

But, it seems, while Assange remains on the run, his online rants have now moved jurisdictions. Deciding that he would run for a Senate seat in his homeland of Australia in September 2013—but lost by 3,000+ primary votes—while still being "holed up" at his place of refuge in Ecuador, Assange set up a WikiLeaks party and released onto the Internet a video making fun of Australian politicians. In response, Ecuadorian president Rafael Correa chastised Assange, noting that as a matter of courtesy, Ecuador would not bar Assange from exercising his right to be a candidate in Australia, so long as he didn't make fun of Australian politicians or its people over the Internet (Paramaribo, 2013).

Information Freedom Fighter U.S. Private Bradley Manning

The case of U.S. soldier Bradley Manning illustrates the delicate relationship between national security during war and the role of the Internet and hackers in overriding established rules of information disclosure to the public. On day one of the trial, which began in the United States on June 4, 2013, Private Manning confessed to being the source for the vast archives of secret military and diplomatic documents made public by WikiLeaks. An official with the military argued on that day that Manning systematically harvested hundreds of thousands of classified documents and then dumped them onto the Internet—into the hands of the enemy as well as Joe public—material that he knew would put the lives of fellow soldiers at risk. Manning's defense lawyer told the judge that Private Manning had, in fact, tried to ensure that the several hundred thousand documents that he released would not cause harm; he was, after all, *selective* about what he gave to WikiLeaks. Manning's motivation? Apparently, to make the world a better place, his defense lawyer argued (Savage, 2013).

On day two of the trial, the link between hackers and the release of confidential information during war—and, in fact, the biggest leak of classified information in U.S. history—became even more explicit. Military prosecutors called to the witness stand an admitted computer hacker named Adrian Lamo, who had befriended Manning and then turned him over to army investigators. Lamo, who at age 22 was charged at the Manhattan Federal Court in 2004 with cracking into the internal computer network of *The New York Times* (see Schell and Martin, 2004), said that Manning had contacted him online in May 2010, from his base in Iraq, seeking guidance from Lamo on encrypted online chats. Lamo said that in his view, Manning saw him as a kindred "idealist" who believed in freedom of information and free speech. Manning apparently wanted to show the American public the reality of war in Afghanistan and Iraq. During these early days of the trial, the prosecution said that there apparently was nothing on Manning's seized laptop that indicated he had a hatred of America (Simpson, 2013).

These disparate views at both ends of the continuum of the freedom fighter and the need for censorship and information sharing underscore the oddity at the heart of the trial, which was projected to last as long as three months. Early on in Manning's trial, the press underscored that if found guilty of violating the Espionage Act and aiding the enemy, Manning could serve a life sentence (Savage, 2013).

By mid-June 2013, prosecutors presented evidence that Private Manning's leaks compromised sensitive information in a range of categories—including techniques for neutralizing improvised explosives, the naming of an enemy target, and the naming of criminal suspects, as well as troop movements. Equally as interesting at this time was the argument made by U.S. First Amendment lawyer James Goodale, author of *Fighting for the Press: The Inside Story of the Pentagon Papers and Other Battles*, that a Manning conviction on any one of the eight espionage counts he was facing or on a federal computer fraud charge would in many ways enable the U.S. government to charge other information-freedom-fighting civilians like WikiLeaks founder Assange (Dishneau, 2013).

By mid-August 2013, when Private Manning himself took the stand, he began with an apology to the American people, noting (Dishneau and Jelinkek, 2013, p. A14): "I'm sorry that my actions hurt people. I'm sorry that it hurt the United States." While he admitted that he understood what he was doing and the decisions that he made, he affirmed that he did not believe at the time that his actions would cause harm. In his defense, an Army psychologist noted that Manning's private struggle with gender identity in a hostile workplace put incredible pressure on the young solder. Consequently, Private Manning's gender identity disorder, along with narcissistic personality traits, his post-adolescent idealism, and his lack of friends in Iraq, caused him to "reasonably conclude" that he could change the world—positively—by leaking classified information over the Internet.

Then on Wednesday, August 21, 2013, a military judge sentenced Private First Class Bradley Manning to 35 years in prison for providing more than 700,000 government files to WikiLeaks—the longest sentence handed down in a case involving a leak of U.S. government information released to the public. Though Manning could have been sentenced for up to 90 years in prison, he was spared. Despite the fact that Manning could be eligible for parole in as few as eight years, as he stood in the courtroom dazed, a handful of supporters in the room labeled Manning as "a hero" in the war for information freedom fighting (Savage and Huetteman, 2013).

NSA Contractor Edward Snowden

On Sunday, June 9, 2013, a 29-year-old past undercover CIA employee named Edward Snowden announced that he was the main source of recent disclosures in the United States about top secret National Security Agency (NSA) surveillance programs that track phone and Internet messages around the globe with the objective of thwarting terrorist threats. Snowden, a tech specialist who was contracted for the NSA and was also employed by the consulting firm Booz Allen Hamilton, affirmed to the press that he disclosed secret documents in *The Washington Post* and *The Guardian* because of the unfairness of the systematic surveillance of innocent citizens by the U.S. government, noting that President Barack Obama failed to follow through on his pledges of transparency. Fleeing the United States and taking refuge in Hong Kong, Snowden said in June 2013 that allowing the U.S. government to intimidate its people with threats of retaliation for revealing wrongdoing is clearly contrary to the public interest. He publicly announced that he would seek asylum from any country that believed in free speech and was opposed to victimizing global privacy (Blake, Gellman, and Miller, 2013).

Within 24 hours of Snowden's public confession, Dianne Feinstein of California, who heads the Senate Intelligence

Committee and supports the notion of Internet surveillance, potentially including phone numbers, email messages, images, video, and online communications transmitted through U.S. providers, accused Snowden of committing an "act of treason," positing that he should be prosecuted accordingly—amidst German- and European-expressed concerns about the U.S. government's surveillance practice. At this point, Snowden told the media that he may seek asylum in Iceland, known for its strong free-speech protections and having a penchant for providing safe headquarters for the outspoken and the outcast. Furthermore, privacy rights advocates argued vehemently that President Obama had gone too far, while The American Civil Liberties Union and the Yale Law School immediately filed legal action to force a secret U.S. court to make a public disclosure of its justification for the scope of the surveillance, calling the programs "shockingly broad" (Jakes, 2013).

On June 11, 2013, bothered by allegations that Britain colluded with the U.S. intelligence agencies to collect data on its citizens, the British government stayed silent on the suggestion that it had been given information from the U.S. surveillance program called Prism that was collected on foreigners abroad from high-tech companies like Google, Facebook, Microsoft, Apple, and Yahoo! Meanwhile, the Hong Kong government, acknowledging that Snowden was staying in a hotel safely within their jurisdiction, said that his case would be handled in accordance with the laws of Hong Kong—which meant that Edward Snowden would probably be able to delay extradition to the United States to face some serious charges but not avoid it altogether (New York Times Service, 2013).

Then, on Sunday, June 23, 2013, a global cat-and-mouse game involving Snowden and the U.S. authorities ensued, as the latter tried to catch "the leaker" before he reached what many thought would be his next safe haven: Ecuador. It was on this day that Snowden unexpectedly left Hong Kong and took a flight to Moscow (Barrett and Chen, 2013). And on

July 1, 2013, Ecuadorian president Rafael Correa said that even if Snowden wanted to seek asylum in Ecuador, he was under the care of the Russian authorities, admitting that the fugitive could not leave the Russian airport without consent of the Russian government (Weissenstein, 2013). By July 2, 2013, Russian president Vladimir Putin said that "if Snowden wanted to go elsewhere, and that country wanted him, then maybe Snowden could eventually leave—but only on the condition that he must cease his work at inflicting damage to our American partners, as strange as it may sound from my lips" (Roth and Barry, 2013, A3).

On August 13, 2013, Edward Snowden thanked the Russian government after being granted temporary asylum for one year. He was able to work in Russia during this time period and was safely out of the reach of U.S. prosecutors—at least for a year. Immediately, U.S. lawmakers called for some form of tough retaliation against Russia, perhaps a boycotting of the Winter Olympic Games to be held in Sochi. Meanwhile, the politicians in the United States were still hoping to put Snowden in prison for espionage (Myers and Kramer, 2013).

But the story does not end here. By October 8, 2013, the Snowden connection had brought into the fray new government players. On this day, the president of Brazil accused Canada of cyber war, after allegations that Canadian hackers hired by their government tried to steal state secrets from the South American country's mining and energy ministry in 2012—a disclosure that threatens to create a lasting rift between Canada and Brazil, now the world's sixth-largest economy and a crucial bilateral partner for Canada.

Here's the interesting likely link between the latter case and Snowden. Journalist Glenn Greenwald is an American journalist based in Brazil. During the summer and fall of 2013, he publicized over the Internet and through media-leaked documents the extent of the electronic eavesdropping campaign under the code name Prism that is being conducted by the

U.S. NSA. Apparently, the bulk of top secret documents given to this journalist and filmmaker Laura Poitras in Hong King was provided by Edward Snowden.

Now comes "the rub." One of the NSA's closest allies is Canada's electronic eavesdropping agency, known as Communications Security Establishment Canada (CSEC)—which has remained relatively unscathed in terms of international scandals to this point. Then on October 6, 2013, Brazil's top news program *Fantastico*, in partnership with Greenwald, featured on their show CSEC-stamped documents from June 2012 (likely leaked by Snowden?), suggesting that Canadian government hackers used a program called Olympia to hack into smart phones and computers affiliated with staff at Brazil's Ministry of Mines and Energy to steal proprietary information. As a result, Brazil officials said, not surprisingly, that they are proposing new laws aimed at *more* state control of resources. This case links the critical elements of security, trust, privacy, and censorship in a networked world (Nolen, Freeze, and Chase, 2013).

What the Internet Is as Compared to an Intranet

Generally speaking, an internet (lower case) is a network connecting computer systems. "The Internet" that we are all familiar with today dates back to 1969, when it was pioneered in the United States. Then, the Internet was a high-speed network built by the U.S. Department of Defense as a digital communications experiment that linked hundreds of defense contractors, universities, and research laboratories. This powerful computer network belonging to the U.S. Advanced Research Projects Agency, or ARPA, allowed for highly trained artificial intelligence (AI) researchers in dispersed locations to transmit and exchange critical information with incredible speed. (AI is a branch of computer science; AI experts have been known for making computers behave as if they were human beings, by modeling computers on human thoughts.

AI is also related to the solving of complex problems using computers.)

To keep the United States and its citizens physically safe, especially in times of crisis, government agents working in isolated pockets could continue to transmit critical information over the ARPAnet rather than to have agents physically move from one geographic location to another to have an information exchange. This "networked" tribe arrangement that was developed back then continues to exist in the more sophisticated online world today, allowing people to connect remotely.

Nowadays, the Internet refers to a collection of networks connected by routers. The Internet is the largest network in the world and comprises backbone networks such as MILNET, mid-level networks, and stub networks (Schell and Martin, 2006). Though the pioneering ARPAnet was dedicated to the U.S. military and selected contractors and universities partaking in defense research, without question, the ARPAnet hugely advanced the emerging field of information technology (IT) (Holt and Schell, 2013).

No single factor produced the powerful Internet that society enjoys today. Groundbreaking events in hardware (the mechanical parts composing the computer and computer networks) and in software (the programming language running the network and doing the necessary computations) were necessary for progress on this front to be made.

As noted, right from the beginning, the Internet has been designed to be a huge network interconnecting many smaller groups of linked computers. The Internet never had a physical or tangible entry, such as a door on a house that provides entry to the rest of the building. Even in 1969, the Internet was designed to be a decentralized, self-maintaining group of redundant links between computers and computer networks. The beauty of the Internet even at its infancy was that it was able to send data rapidly without human intervention and with the unique capability to reroute data if one or more links were damaged or unavailable. Therefore, from a military defense perspective, even if a portion of the network were to be destroyed during a war or through an act of terrorism, with a redundant system, critical data could still reach its intended destination (Holt and Schell, 2013).

By design, data travel along networks not as "whole" information or messages but as very small information packets. Even in ARPAnet's early days, the Internet used packet-switching protocols to allow messages to be subdivided into smaller packets of information. These packets could be sent rather independently to the required destination and be automatically reassembled by the destination computer. Although packets containing information for a larger message often travel along the same path to get to the final destination, some of them could be rerouted along a different path if one or more routers along the route became overloaded. In addition, computers can communicate with one another through the use of a common communication protocol known as the Internet protocol (IP). All applications utilized on the Internet are designed to make use of this protocol and have been since the mid-1960s (Holt and Schell, 2013).

Large research-intensive universities were the early adopters of the Internet, but soon technical wizards with an entrepreneurial spirit realized that online advertising, commercial software applications, and vastly marketable hardware could generate services and tools desired by the general public. This was made manifest though the emergence of the World Wide Web. Though the term *Web* is often used by those in mainstream society to signify the Internet, the World Wide Web (WWW) is just one of the applications using the Internet as a base infrastructure (Schell and Martin, 2006). The www protocol became immensely popular after Tim Berners-Lee developed the HTTP, or hypertext transfer protocol, in the early 1990s, allowing users to access and link information through a simple and intuitive user interface known as the Internet browser.

Readers may often hear about *intranets*, which should not be confused with an internet. By definition, an information system internal to an organization or institution that is constructed with Web-based technology is known as an intranet. The primary usage of an intranet is to keep employees informed about upcoming events; to post online company policies and procedures, including proper online etiquette; and to distribute software or application updates to employees (Holt and Schell, 2013).

Often termed a *portal*, intranets were initially commonly found in large firms having in excess of 15,000 employees, so that employees could access the intranet Web site using a browser. (Technically speaking, a browser interprets HTML—also known as hypertext markup language—the programming language used to code Web pages into words and graphics so that online users can view the pages in the intended layout and rendering.) With improved and more affordable intranet software designed by the Microsoft Corporation and other firms since about 2005, intranets are nowadays found in small- and medium-sized companies as an effective, cost-saving means of communicating online with employees. Moreover, intranets are typically run on a private local area network (LAN) instead of on public servers.

The Internet's Colorful History: Internet Development, Hacking Exploits, and (Eventually) Concerns about Internet Censorship

The Internet's Humble Beginnings: The 1940s through the 1960s

The Internet that we know and admire today started from very humble beginnings and had little to do with issues surrounding censorship. In the late 1940s and 1950s, computers were made with about 10,000 vacuum tubes, and they occupied over 93 square meters of space. Given this reality, computers back then were prone to overheating and exploding.

Moreover, the vacuum tubes could leak, the metal-emitting electrons in the vacuum tubes burned out, and the thousands of vacuum tubes required huge amounts of energy to function.

As a result of significant improvements in computer hardware technology—especially with the development of transistors by John Bardeen and Walter Brattain in 1947 and 1948—and with the development of integrated circuits by Jack Kilby and Robert Noyce in 1958 and 1959—many of the problems with vacuum tube technology were resolved and led the way to the development of smaller computers with greater power. With the development of integrated circuits, instead of making transistors one by one, several transistors could be made at the same time and on the same piece of semiconductor. Since the 1960s, the number of transistors per unit area has been doubling about every one-and-a-half years—thus increasing computing power significantly. This huge progress in circuit fabrication is called Moore's law, named after Gordon Moore, a pioneer in the integrated circuit field and the founder of the Intel Corporation (Schell, 2007).

Back in the 1960s, the question of how to hook up and share the data between computers remained. The revolutionary packet-switching technique invented by Leonard Kleinrock gained popularity among the increasing number of computer users, and Paul Baran at the Rand Institute began researching how to use packet switching for secure voice over military networks. Another critical event occurred in 1969, when Dennis Ritchie and Ken Thompson developed the computer software standard operating system known as UNIX. Back then—as it is now—UNIX was considered by IT folks to be a thing of beauty, for its standard user and programming interfaces advanced computing, word processing, and networking.

The Internet's Adolescent Years: The 1970s and 1980s

Back in 1970—when the civil rights and women's rights movements were in full steam in the United States—only an estimated 100,000 computers were in use there, and only a few of them were "networked." Most were found in large companies, government offices, or research-driven universities. Unlike today, when one can do a lot with a tablet, computer users then had to keypunch data cards, carefully carry them in boxes to maintain the data card order, and then dump them into the computer for processing. In 1971, Ray Tomlinson, one of the forefathers of the Internet, who worked on ARPAnet, gave to society one of the greatest online communications gifts in Internet history: email. He also chose the @ symbol for email—and this was exciting for the few "connected" netizens (citizens on the Internet). In the Internet's adolescent years, however, there was little talk, if any, about the perils of Internet censorship. Most media headlines focused more on the development of the Internet and on the early exploits by hackers.

In 1972, the National Center for Supercomputing Applications created the telnet application for remote login, making it easier for users to log into a remote machine. This same year, David Boggs and Robert Metcalfe invented Ethernet at the Xerox Corporation in California, making it possible to connect computers in a LAN. In 1973, the file transfer protocol (or FTP) was developed, simplifying the transfer of information between networked machines. Also in this time frame, American computer hardware specialists still believed that the bigger the computer, the more powerful it would be. But Canadian mathematician Mers Kutt had an innovative thought that went against the tide; he argued that smaller is better! In 1973, he founded Micro Computer Machines, releasing onto the North American market the world's first personal computer (PC). Holding only 8 kilobytes of memory, this pioneering PC cost $5,000 and got its power from a small chip rather than from vacuum tubes (Schell, 2007).

In 1975, Americans Steve Jobs, Ronald Wayne, and Steve Wozniak founded the Apple computer company, using the simplistic and user-friendly BASIC computer language in their machines—and setting the footprint for the soon-to-blossom home use computer market. Also in 1975, Americans Bill Gates and Paul Allen founded the Microsoft Corporation, producing innovative software products that would quickly capitalize a global market. A year later, secure transactions using the Internet had their roots planted when Whitfield Diffie and Martin Hellman created the Diffie-Hellman public key algorithms, used in many secure protocols on the Internet (Schell, 2007). (An algorithm is a set of rules and procedures for solving a mathematical or logic problem, much like a cookbook assists cooks in solving meal preparation problems; thus, a computer program is actually an elaborate algorithm.)

Though many inventions in the 1970s pushed the Internet into its adolescent years, what was still missing in the virtual world was a networking "social club." To this end, in 1978, two men from Chicago—Randy Suess and Ward Christensen—created the first computer bulletin board system, serving as the forerunner to Internet chat rooms. Also by the end of the 1970s, the transmission control protocol (TCP) was split into the TCP and IP.

The start of the 1980s marked the beginning of the *affordable* PC era. IBM marketed their stand-alone PC, and the Commodore 64 computer (known to many computer hackers as "the Commie 64") was released for public consumption. Also, the TRS-80 computer was released at this time—when fewer than 300 computers were linked to the Internet!

In 1982, California IT pioneers Scott McNealy, Bill Joy, Andy Bechtolsheim, and Vinod Khosla started the Sun Microsystems company, based on the assumption that UNIX running on relatively inexpensive hardware would be a grand solution for a wide range of applications. The simple mail transfer protocol was published—which relates to how email is transmitted between host computers and users. In 1983, the Telnet protocol was published, allowing individuals familiar with UNIX to log onto other computers on the Internet (Schell, 2007).

In 1984, computer hacker Eric Corley (with the online moniker Emmanuel Goldstein) started the still hugely popular *2600: The Hacker Quarterly* (an exciting medium for hackers interested in technical and political issues in the virtual world). Also, Fred Cohen introduced the term *computer virus* into the mainstream to indicate a cyberspace vandal that could corrupt or erase information stored on computers.

In 1985, the first Web site domain name was registered and assigned (known as www.Symbolics.com). Also, the Free Software Foundation (FSF) was started by Richard Stallman; then and now, FSF members—strong advocates for information freedom—have been committed to giving computer users permission to use, study, copy, change, and redistribute computer programs to promote the development of free software. In 1985, the term *hacker* was introduced into the U.S. mainstream to indicate a tech-savvy individual who enjoyed learning the details of computer systems and how to stretch their capabilities; there was no negative or criminal meaning attached to the term *hacker* at this time. One year later, the term *criminal hacker* was alluded to in the British press, when Robert Schifreen and Steven Gold broke into a text information retrieval system operated by BT Prestel and left a message for his Royal Highness the Duke of Edinburgh on his network mailbox; from that time onward, reporters have latched on to the negative connotation (Schell, 2007).

In 1986, U.S. Congress passed the controversial Computer Fraud and Abuse Act, meant to prevent fraud and associated criminal activities aimed at or completed with computers. In 1998, the world first realized the kind of damage that Internet worms could cause when a U.S. graduate student by the name of Robert Morris Jr. accidentally unleashed onto the Internet a worm that he developed while studying at Cornell University; this malware later became known as "the Morris worm." In 1988, largely as a response to the Morris worm, the Computer Emergency Response Team (CERT) and the CERT Coordination Center were created at Carnegie Mellon

University, with the function of coordinating communications among homeland security experts during emergencies. In 1988, Kevin Mitnick, a famous U.S. hacker, was imprisoned and then a number of times afterward for his hacking exploits into various business networks. In 1989, Herbert Zinn was the first minor to be convicted for violating the U.S. Computer Fraud and Abuse Act of 1986, after he cracked the network at American Telephone and Telegraph and that of the U.S. Department of Defense, destroying files estimated to be worth about $175,000 (Schell, 2007).

The Internet's Adult Years: 1990 to the Present

1990 to 1999

The period from 1990 through 1999 was marked by Internet adult-like issues such as a recognizable increase in the variety and damages caused by cybercrimes, threats to Internet freedoms and free speech, and the censorship of content appearing on Web sites. Indeed, the year 1990 was a very significant one in terms of the Internet's reaching adulthood, primarily because of its development on a worldwide scale—and because concerns began to emerge globally not only about various cybercrimes but about threats to freedom on the Internet and the expression of free speech.

On the technical side, in 1990 Tim Berners-Lee and Robert Cailliau developed the protocols that became the World Wide Web, and in the early 1990s, the Internet growth on a "homeowner" scale could be attributed to the fact that an increased number of tech-savvy individuals could afford to buy PCs similar in power and storage to those of the clunky and easily overheated computer systems of the 1980s. The bad news for home PC owners was that the software was still quite expensive, for the products sold by Microsoft to businesses and government offices tended to be beyond the price point of most homeowners in the United States (Schell, 2007).

By 1993, more than 1 million computers were linked to the Internet. In 1994, two Stanford University students named David Filo and Jerry Yang created the now-popular search engine Yahoo!—meaning "Yet Another Hierarchical Officious Oracle." One year later, political activism using the Internet—known as hacktivism—became real to those in mainstream American society after hacktivists squashed the U.S. government's highly controversial Clipper proposal, which would have placed strong encryption (the technical process of scrambling information into something unintelligible) under the government's control.

In 1995, Jeffrey Bezos launched the first online bookstore—the now incredibly successful and more broadly based electronic online store named Amazon. This same year, Microsoft released its Windows 95 software product—making it more in the affordable range for home PC owners (Schell, 2007).

In 1996, the World Wide Web had grown to 16 million hosts, and in this year, the National Information Infrastructure Protection Act was enacted in the United States, amending the Computer Fraud and Abuse Act of 1986, which enhanced the powers of the state. In 1997, ARIN, a for-profit organization, began to assign IP address space for North America, South America, sub-Saharan Africa, and the Caribbean. In 1998, many entrepreneurs launched Internet service providers (ISPs) to sell or give online access to many around the world—a business endeavor that has created some of the world's wealthiest individuals. Also in 1998, the Digital Millennium Copyright Act was passed in the United States as a means of coping with emerging digital technologies and their unlawful disabling or bypass by tech-savvy individuals (Schell, 2007).

The year 1998 was important from a censorship point of view as well, for a number of Web sites were developed in the fight against Internet censorship. Hatewatch members monitored the activities of groups advocating "hate speech" on the Internet in the United States and England (arguing that the best means to control bigotry was to expose it), and the Citizens Internet Empowerment Coalition, owned by U.S. Internet publishers, online users, and Internet service providers, fought for—as the CIEC Web site suggests—"the future of the First Amendment and the future of free expression in the Information age." Furthermore, EPIC, or the Electronic Privacy Information Centre, a large U.S.-based public interest research centre, was formed to have the public become attentive to emerging civil liberties related to new technologies.

On the other side of the coin, the Web site linked to the content-censoring Internet Watch Foundation, belonging to an industry-led group, addressed the problems of what they deemed to be "illegal, harmful" material on the Internet, especially that involving child pornography (Barkham, 1999).

In 1999, the Melissa virus was created by David Smith and released on the Internet, infecting millions of computer systems in the United States and Europe and is said to have caused $80 million in damages to computers worldwide. Also, the Gramm-Leach-Bliley Act of 1999 was passed in the United States to provide limited privacy protection against the sale of individuals' private financial information.

In April 1999, Malaysia, in a move that promoted Internet censorship, made front-page headlines after its government passed the controversial Communications and Multimedia Act, believed to be the first law in the world attempting to impose blanket control over the broadcasting, IT, and telecommunications industries. In short, this law regulated *any* information that could be seen on television screens or computer screens. Opponents feared that the new law would restrict freedom of speech, for any person providing offensive or false material in these media could be put behind prison bars for up to a year (Harrison, 1999).

2000 to 2009

In the 2000 to 2009 period, as more home users were able to purchase PCs, words like computer "viruses" and "worms" became familiar to citizens connected to the Internet. Also netizens began to realize that not only were females active online but they had the advanced capabilities to create viruses from computer languages like C sharp. And by 2005, intense fears of Internet censorship surfaced when Chinese authorities started closing over 10,000 Internet cafes to safeguard their citizens from viewing material deemed to be offensive or harmful. By 2009, not only was cyber warfare a virtual world reality, but U.S. president Obama himself faced censorship when he visited Shanghai to talk to students about free speech and the costs of censoring the Internet.

In 2000, the virtual world became obsessed with data losses feared to result from Y2K computer glitches—which, in the end, were proved foundationless. Also in this year, Canada's "Mafiaboy," Michael Calce, became a familiar hacker family word in North America after he admitted to exploiting Internet servers on the high-profile Web sites of Amazon, eBay, and Yahoo!, causing legitimate online purchasers to be unable to access these sites to complete their transactions—and causing tons of harm to the businesses.

In 2000, *Outcast,* a radical Internet magazine, seen as a threat to freedom of speech on the Internet, was declared the first victim of a libel case. Then, *Outcast,* a "queer affairs" online publication, had its Web site closed by its ISP (Netbenefit) after a complaint about inappropriate material posted there, although the ISP later remarked that they had closed the Web site with great reluctance. A week earlier, Demon Internet, a British ISP, had agreed to pay hefty damages and legal costs to Laurence Godfrey, a physicist who claimed that he had been defamed by two anonymous messages posted on the Web site. Consequently, ISPs in the United Kingdom and elsewhere became concerned about the operational implications of these two cases. If the latter case had not been settled out of court, it could have set a legal precedent about whether ISPs are subject to the same libel laws as other media (Wells, 2000).

In 2001, computer viruses and worms virtually crawled into the mainstream news, because so many home, office, and government agency computers and networks were invaded. The Code Red worm compromised several hundred thousand computer systems worldwide in less than 14 hours, overloading the Internet's capacity and costing an estimated $2.6 billion in damages. Also, a *Los Angeles Times* article spread fears about an imminent cyber apocalypse after mal-inclined hackers attacked a computer system controlling the distribution of electricity in California's power grid—a cyberattack that was said to originate in China's Guangdong province and routed through China Telecom.

The year 2001 also brought global controversies on the Internet censorship front. Many theorists argued that while one of the greatest assets of the Internet is that it provides an open forum for users anywhere in the world to state their views, supposedly free from censorship by governments, businesses, or institutions, the Internet is, nevertheless, a freedom forum that should not be abused by some to serve a particular purpose that poses harm to others. Such were the arguments that arose following the decision of a federal appeals court in San Francisco that upheld the right of anti-abortion groups to publish online what many netizens believed was a "hit list" of physicians performing abortions. These theorists argued that while the first amendment of the U.S. Constitution guarantees free speech, it does not mean that online users can say anything without reference to the consequences. The case in question involved 3 of 7 doctors murdered in the previous 10 years who were cited on the "hit list," along with 17 attempted murders of doctors who were known to terminate unwanted pregnancies. Many reporters did not support the actions of the online "pro-lifers" who published the list, because their actions could potentially lead to the deaths of fellow humans. They concluded that while the U.S. Constitution does give "the right to bear arms," there appears to be too much emphasis on "online freedom *to*" and not enough emphasis on "online freedom *from*" (Keegan, 2001).

In 2002, female cyber criminals started making media headlines; for example, a 17-year-old female hacker from Belgium, known by the online moniker Gigabyte, claimed to have written the first-ever virus in the programming language C# (pronounced "C sharp").

The year 2002 was important regarding another issue regarding Internet freedom of expression and censorship. Google took on Chinese authorities after they tried to limit media coverage of a horrible disaster: the mass poisoning of more than 200 students and workers in Nanjing, China. Chinese authorities attempted to put filters on online posts related to the disaster for about 10 days, and Google fought back by allowing the posts—a move perceived worldwide as a "defeat" for Internet censors. However, this was only a partial victory for Google and the online freedom fighters, for if Chinese online users attempted to search for anything related to "Falun Gong" or "Falun Dafa"—the names for the spiritual sect that Chinese authorities banned in 1999—the Google search would come back empty (Gittings, 2002).

In 2003, stronger legal measures were passed in the United States as a means of combating online child pornography. President George W. Bush passed the PROTECT (Prosecutorial Remedies and Other Tools to End the Exploitation of Children Today) Act of 2003, which implemented the AMBER alert communication system for kidnapped children and redefined *child pornography* to include images of children engaging in sexually explicit conduct with adults, as well as computer-generated images indistinguishable from those of real children engaging in such acts.

Also in 2003, the U.S. government, through the Department of Homeland Security, advanced steps to tighten security in cyberspace, when it strengthened the role of the U.S. Computer Emergency Response Team, or U.S.-CERT.

In 2003, the U.S. Senate passed the CAN-SPAM Act to regulate interstate commerce, which placed limitations and penalties on the transmission of spam (defined as *junk mail*, delivered to online users without their permission).

Elsewhere around the globe, Internet "control" by government authorities continued to be called into question—even in jurisdictions believed to be favorable to Internet freedom fighters. For example, on September 12, 2003, British ministers moved forward with plans to ensure that communications companies—including ISPs—retained records of *every* telephone, Internet, and email user—despite strong opposition from industry and civil liberties groups. The data to be retained included the names and addresses of subscribers, calls made and received, Web sites visited, sources and destinations of emails, and mobile phone data—even information determining the whereabouts of individuals. U.K. government officials argued that because the "voluntary" code of practice had been delayed for about 18 months owing to opposition from the communications industry, it felt compelled to push forward with tough legislation. The Home Office's new list of public bodies given access to the data included those with serious crime-fighting roles, such as the U.K. Atomic Energy Constabulary, the Scottish Drug Enforcement Agency, the Maritime and Coastguard Agency, the Financial Services Authority, the Police Ombudsmen in Northern Ireland, and the Police Ombudsmen in Northern Ireland. (Millar, 2003).

In 2004, some large U.S. companies like the Recording Industry Association of America began legally pursuing citizens for swapping songs using the Internet without paying royalties to the artists; more worms like MyDoom were released on the Internet, causing losses estimated to be about $2 billion worldwide. In 2004, the *Computer Industry Almanac* estimated that the worldwide number of Internet users topped 1 billion, with the United States alone accounting for about 185 million online users (Schell, 2007).

In late 2004 and early 2005, fears of Internet censorship began to appear when Chinese authorities, apparently worried about online content perceived by them to be "immoral" or "violent" in nature, closed more than 12,000 Internet cafes to prevent their citizens from viewing the offensive material. Also in 2005, a Chinese entrepreneur named Robin Li took on the Western value search engine businesses like Google and built a search engine named Baidu.com, which retained the strong censorship values of Chinese authorities in a jurisdiction that clearly allows for a fresh mix of capitalist economics with authoritarian communist politics. In just four years, Li grew his market share to such a degree that his site rapidly overtook Google and Yahoo! as the leading Chinese search engine. Baidu's Web site was navigated by 90 million online users daily from a Chinese online population of 100 million (Watts, 2005).

In 2005, under pressure from U.S. citizens, the FBI abandoned its custom-built and highly controversial Internet surveillance technology named Carnivore, designed to read email and online communications of suspected terrorists and cyber terrorists. The year also saw the breakout of cyber wars (an information war launched in cyberspace; see also Schell and Martin, 2006).

For example, in March 2005, a cyber war started between Indonesia and Malaysia over a dispute regarding the Ambalat oil fields in the Sulawesi Sea. Officials in Kuala Lumpur were apparently upset over an intrusion into its waters by an Indonesian naval vessel after Indonesian president Yudhoyono ordered the military to present itself in the Sulawesi Sea jurisdiction under dispute. Just 24 hours later, the Web site of Universiti Sains Malaysia was under cyberattack and plagued with aggressive anti-Malaysian messages having an Indonesian twist. Two days after this cyberattack, documents seized from members of the Lashkar-e-Toiba terrorist group killed in an encounter with Indian police indicated that they had planned a suicide hack attack on the network of companies producing software and computer chip design outlets in the Karnail Singh area of the Indian city of Bangalore—which houses high-profile companies like Intel, Texas Instruments, and IBM. Their motive was to cyberattack these companies to hinder the economic engine of India. The companies said that they have not only tight entry requirements in these highly secure environments but also well-designed disaster recovery plans in the event of such an attack (Schell, 2007).

The year 2006 began with headlines talking about the emergence of botnets—large numbers of computer programs commandeered by hackers and marshaled for personal gain. Botnets now—just as back then—are often used to overwhelm Web sites with streams of data by feeding off vulnerabilities in computers running Microsoft Windows operating systems. Machines vulnerable are generally those whose owners did not install security fixes or patches for the vulnerabilities, and "zombie" machine owners are typically unaware that malicious programs have been installed on their computers and that they are being "owned," or controlled by crackers in a remote fashion (Schell, 2007).

By year-end 2006, there were more Internet censorship stories. Iran shut down citizens' access to some of the world's most popular Web sites, like Amazon, YouTube, Wikipedia, and *The New York Times*. ISPs followed the Iranian government's instructions to filter these sites. The clampdown was demanded by senior judiciary officials in a campaign to impede "corrupting" foreign films and music and to purge Iran of Western cultural influences. Attempts by online users to open the filtered Web sites were met with a page, "The requested page is forbidden." In 2006, Iran was among 13 countries branded "enemies of the Internet" by Reporters Without Borders, citing state-sanctioned blocking of Web sites and the widespread intimidation of and imprisonment of bloggers by government authorities (Tait, 2013).

In September 2007, reports of Internet censorship surfaced in other parts of the globe. The Burmese junta tried to shut down Internet and telephone links to the outside world after a stream of blogs and mobile phone videos captured dramatic scenes on the streets of Burma. Immediately, cyber cafes were closed by the authorities, and mobile phones were disconnected. Less than 1 percent of the Burmese population had access to the Internet then, and only 25,000 people had email addresses, but some clever citizens capitalized on loopholes by evading the official firewalls and sought access to "connected and relatively open" embassy, foreign business, or nongovernmental organization networks where Internet access was not so controlled (Pallister, 2013).

In June 2006, Google continued a freedom fighter online battle with China, after Sergey Brin, cofounder of the company, said that company officials admitted compromising company principles by accepting the censorship policies of China, though only after Chinese authorities had blocked the company's service. Brin noted that though the company had compromised their principles, they could, by complying with the rules, provide needed information to Chinese netizens—thus making a positive difference by narrowing the digital divide between the haves and the have-nots. Part of the routine agreed to by Google was to omit politically sensitive information that could be retrieved during searches, such as details of the June 1989 suppression of political unrest in Tiananmen Square (Associated Press, 2006).

In May 2007, an attempt to force Google to stop censoring search results of users in repressive countries was rejected by its shareholders. A proposal submitted to the shareholders called for Google to disclose to users when their search results were being censored and to inform users about data that was being retained. Amnesty, a human rights group that had criticized Google a year earlier for bowing to pressure from the Chinese government to censor search results, supported this measure. The proposal also suggested that action should be taken against censorship in Belarus, Burma, Cuba, Egypt, Iran, North Korea, Saudi Arabia, Syria, Tunisia, Turkmenistan, Uzbekistan, and Vietnam—other countries where the governments restrict content on the Internet (Wearden, 2013).

In 2008, the world heard loudly and clearly about Anonymous, a nebulous collection of hacker cells and splinter groups that seemed to coordinate their hacktivistic efforts with hackers around the globe. The operations commonly used in hacktivism include browsing the Internet for information, constructing Web sites and posting information of a political nature on them, and using the Internet to discuss controversial issues, form coalitions, and plan and coordinate activities (Schell and Martin, 2006).

One particular media-worthy occasion saw Anonymous targeting the Church of Scientology. Besides attacking the church's servers, Anonymous arranged for the church's offices to be surrounded by masked protestors and for a large number of pizzas to appear on the church's doorstep. Apparently, the church's secretive, controlling nature ran counter to the hacker collective's freedom fighter views and values. Of significance to this chapter, the work of Anonymous seems to sit on the somewhat odd Venn diagram overlap of *hacking* and *online freedom fighting* (Tossell, 2012).

By 2008, with the Internet's amazing potential and powers, cyber warfare had become a reality. Georgia and Russia briefly went to war online when DDoS attacks brought down Georgian Web sites and caused considerable economic damage. Even to this day, it is not clear who the perpetrator of the cyberattacks actually was; in the media at that time, however, Russia was the obvious target. These attacks have been analyzed by IT experts, and it seems that they likely came from around the world, not just from Russian hackers. Thus, it seems that rather than acting alone, a loose coalition of third-party actors (not unlike Anonymous)—and likely a diaspora—achieved Russia's ends of causing harm to Georgia. A key point that is becoming increasingly clear globally is that the line between a *digital war* and a *land-based war* is difficult to differentiate. Moreover, instead of acting directly, governments are likely hiring talented hackers from within or outside their jurisdictions to produce results that can build extreme chaos and unpredictability in targeted nations or businesses (Tossell, 2012).

In 2009, Microsoft officials said that they were stunned that hackers had finally found a flaw in their Explorer that had been "in hiding" for almost 10 years; it was exploited to steal online users' passwords, highlighting the biggest fear that software-producing companies have—zero-day attacks or exploits, named such for the number of days a software company has to prepare before a hack attack of significant harm occurs (Tossell, 2012).

In 2009 Internet censorship continued to be a concern. U.S. president Obama criticized, speaking to students in Shanghai, the Internet censorship that was taking place in China since at least 2005. He also spoke about the value of freedom of expression and political participation by netizens—wherever they reside. At the time, Chinese officials rejected the U.S. request that about 1,000 students should attend President Obama's speech and that it be broadcast live nationwide. In the end, only about 400 students were in attendance; also, the speech was streamed only on the White House Web site and broadcast live in China on only a local Shanghai television station. Most Chinese citizens were probably allowed to see only brief extracts of the president's speech, absent of his remarks on Internet censorship (Branigan, 2013).

2010 to the Present

From the period 2010 to the present, the Internet continued to manifest adult-like issues like battles occurring between multi-nationals pushing for Internet freedoms in jurisdictions where repressive governments engaged in a combination of Internet censorship and hacking. Also, previously unheard of hacker cells like Anonymous started making mainstream media headlines by exposing confidential governmental information online for netizens around the world to view.

In 2010, a Facebook virus known as Koobface showed the world that social media are also vulnerable to hack attacks. After Koobface infected a computer, it sent a lurid message to the computer owner's Facebook friends, tricking them into downloading malware. Rumor has it that the virus produced over $2 million by commanding infected computers to send clicks, as it were, elsewhere. Also in 2010, a virus called Stuxnet spread around the world through the Internet, but IT experts believe it was created to do one key political job: destroy centrifuges in Iran employed in the country's nuclear program. Actually, the virus caused the centrifuges to shake apart while, on the surface, looking as though they were working normally. Though no country or hacker group has come forward accepting credit for designing this dangerous malware, reporters have widely speculated that the Israeli and American governments were the joint suspects (Tossell, 2012).

In 2010, a major battle began to brew once more between Google and China—this time on the Internet censorship *and* hacking fronts. On January 14, 2010, Google expressed openly in the media that in China they had only 31 percent of the market share, while the Chinese Baidu search engine had a whopping 69 percent. If that wasn't a large enough concern for Google's top executives, the reality that Google's networks had been hacked was. Google executives were worried that talented Chinese hackers had gained entry into the bowels of their network and got hold of the code and secret algorithms that made the company so successful. In fact, Google's chief executive Eric Schmidt had dinner with U.S. secretary of state Hillary Clinton and three other U.S. high-tech executives regarding the dangers of doing business with China, especially if the Internet were involved. The following week, Hillary Clinton made a major speech extolling the virtues of Internet freedom, and President Obama openly addressed in the media citing Internet security as a key national security concern (Fenby, 2010).

On January 14, 2010, VeriSign iDefense Labs, a U.S. Internet security firm, reported that they had traced back the sophisticated cyberattacks against Google's networks and those of about 30 other U.S. high-tech companies to the Chinese government or its proxies (Branigan, 2010). Meanwhile, China denied Google's hacking claims, and by January 25, 2010, Chinese authorities, in an apparent bid to prevent further fallout, declared their willingness to cooperate with the international community to combat crimes in cyberspace (Romana, 2010).

In 2011, Google reportedly had another major cyber problem not necessarily linked to the Chinese government. Hackers had determined how to produce a nasty Trojan horse that fooled Android mobile phone users into thinking that they were installing a regular application but were installing malware that released personal information to a remote server and gave hackers substantial "control" over the phone. From this incident and others that have arisen since 2011, it is clear that new targets have become available for hackers, with the constantly emerging forms of hardware and software technologies. Google responded quickly by sending out a so-called clean-up piece of software, but after noting the "hype" generated around the patch issued by the company, hackers then created a fake clean-up tool that, when installed by Android users, infected their phones with more malware. With smart phone shipments exceeding PC shipments in 2012, there is little mystery in understanding why hackers are keen to target Android phones, which are hugely popular worldwide, with users being able to download applications from anywhere in the world (Tossell, 2012).

January 18, 2012, saw the largest online protest in the history of the Internet. Small and large Web sites "went dark" in protest of two pieces of proposed legislation before the

U.S. House and Senate that could profoundly change the Internet. The two bills—SOPA in the House and PIPA in the Senate—were designed to stop the piracy of copyrighted material on Web sites based outside of the United States. Once word got out about these two bills, many of the Internet giants like Google, Wikipedia, and Twitter argued that the bills, if passed, would stifle innovation and investment in the Internet. Although President Obama's administration had issued public statements with some criticism of these pieces of legislation, the fears among online citizens remained, for they feared that these laws would eventually be passed in some shape or form (Goodman, 2013).

Finally, consistent with the notion that online users would capitalize on the Internet's global potential by pairing hacking *with* claims of Internet freedom fighting, Anonymous, on February 6, 2013, was back in the news, this time again said to be on the side of Internet freedom fighters. They hacked into the U.S. Federal Reserve networks on Super Bowl Sunday and released the login credentials and personal information belonging to over 4,000 U.S. banking executives—a newsworthy event that the Anonymous hacker cell announced on Twitter. Anonymous said that they launched Operation Last Resort in honor of Aaron Swartz, a bright young U.S. technologist and Internet freedom fighter who committed suicide before he was to appear in court on hacker-related charges. Operation Last Resort was supposedly an effort by Anonymous to force the U.S. government to reform computer law, especially regarding the disproportionate prosecution and imprisonment practices levied against hacktivists and other Internet freedom fighters (Stone, 2013).

Summary

From its humble beginnings to its continuing evolution in adulthood, it is clear that the Internet has made tremendous changes in citizens' lives around the globe. On the positive side, governments can transmit their most critical services over the Internet so that citizens do not have to leave their homes to get important information. Businesses can convert their intellectual property, business processes, and assets into data that can be sent over the Internet. Citizens can communicate in social networks or buy things over the Internet without leaving their homes, and their smart phones can seamlessly track their whereabouts. And as world crises occur "in the field," reporters embedded on the battle grounds can communicate online with citizens around the world to help them get a clearer understanding of the root causes of the military engagement.

On the negative side, netizens as well as government agents can bring down targeted Web sites, and perhaps cause considerable harm to targeted nation's economies. Hacker cells like Anonymous can crack government or business networks to unleash nation safety–critical information or industry's proprietary secrets—all in the name of Internet freedom fighting. And governments determined to maintain control over Internet content can place stringent "rules of engagement" on businesses wanting to build market share within their jurisdictions. It is 2013–14, and it is an unpredictable but wonderfully evolving cyber world.

The Global Growth of Internet Usage

Adoption of the Internet in Developed Nations

In just over 40 years since the ARPAnet was invented and the seeds of the Internet were planted, there is little question that the developed world has become totally dependent on the Internet for routine daily activities. Almost all the nations of the world, whether developed or emerging, are aware of the Internet's value for growing and maintaining their economies and for potentially safeguarding their citizens. Think for a moment about all that is done on the Internet—paying bills, filing tax returns, playing games with players around the globe, reading electronic books, communicating with friends through social networking sites, and buying things like vacation tickets, all without leaving home.

The use of technology has had a substantive impact on how individuals spend their time and interact with others. According to 2012 estimates, from ComScore, Inc., Canadians are spending more time online than any other country, including highly wired societies like the United States, China, and South Korea. According to these estimates, the average American spends about 38.6 hours a month online, while the average Canadian spends about 45 hours a month online, with the majority of time spent on social networking sites like Facebook (Holt and Schell, 2013).

More recent Canadian online activity trends indicate that about 75 percent of the households use paid Internet services, almost 60 percent of working Canadians file their personal taxes electronically rather than through land mail, and about 67 percent of Canadian adults bank online. Canadian businesses rely heavily, as well, on the digital infrastructure; currently, about 87 percent of businesses use the Internet—with online sales in Canada totaling about $63 billion in 2011. The Canadian federal government is also reliant on the Internet to "stay connected" with its citizens; in 2011, they offered at least 130 online services to assist consumers and businesses, including such diverse services as taxes, Employment Insurance, and student loans (Comrie, 2011).

This voracious hunger for all things Internet has had a positive impact on advertisers and media companies as well—with digital advertising spending targeted toward Internet-active Canadians alone surpassing $2.5 billion in 2011 (Ladurantaye, 2012).

The massive revenue generated online, coupled with citizens' dependence on the Internet, suggests that if our digital infrastructure were unavailable or compromised by malicious actors or hackers, society may grind to a halt. All of these services would become inoperable, which is frightening especially given that critical infrastructures like public transportation, health care, and public safety are operated, in part, by the Internet.

But before going too far down this dark path, let's continue to examine the growth of the Internet in recent years in developing nations (Holt and Schell, 2013).

Adoption of the Internet in Developing Nations and the Emergence of Internet Censorship

The Internet has clearly had a tremendous economic and political impact on the developing nations, particularly in China, India, Russia, and Pakistan. Compared with the development of the Internet in developed nations—where companies, like Yahoo!, succeeded because they got involved early on in the Internet's history, had plenty of financing to hire top professionals in research and development, and had supportive governments—the "buy-in" in developing nations came later and with significantly less government encouragement.

In China, for example, Baidu, which emerged as a growing success story in 2005, had been at odds with the Chinese government during the early years about censorship issues enforced by the government on search engines. Today, however, Baidu implements China's rigorous censoring schema to stay active and in business. Although relatively unknown outside of China until 2005, Baidu was founded by two Chinese gurus who had previously worked for U.S. technology firms. By 2012, Baidu dominated China's search engine market, with nearly 80 percent of the market share in China, compared to Google's 17 percent (Tsuruoka, 2012).

Also by 2012, China had an estimated 1 billion cell phone users and 550 million Internet surfers. In March of that year, a Chinese news Web site reported that highly successful Apple plans to introduce Baidu as a search engine option for all Apple devices using its mobile operating system in China as early. Considering the large market share in China for anything online and high-tech, this decision, if true, would provide for a lucrative business opportunity for foreign companies like Apple to expand their huge profits even more using its mobile operating system in China, which occurred in June, 2012 (Tsuruoka, 2012).

Other developing nations have gone after Web site companies on their soil that they consider to be violating their laws. In February 2012, Google India said that they removed Web pages deemed to be offensive to Indian political and religious leaders to comply with a court verdict that raised censorship fears in the world's largest democracy. This action followed government pressure for 22 Internet giants to remove from their Web sites photographs, videos, and text deemed to be "anti-religious" or "anti-social"—such as pictures showing Congress party leader Sonia Gandhi and pigs running through Mecca, Islam's holiest city. A New Delhi court gave Facebook, Google, YouTube, and Blogspot, as well as other Web sites, two weeks to present plans for policing their networks. The government also alleged that for India's 100 million Internet users, U.S. Internet standards are just not acceptable. This case highlights the anxiety India faces in balancing religious and political sentiments with their hope that the Internet will help spur the economy and increase the standard of living for 1.2 billion people (Associated Press, 2012).

Assessing the Present-Day Internet Economy on a Global Scale

In March 2012, the authors of the Boston Consulting Group report (Boston Consulting Group, 2012) attempted to estimate the present-day value and positive impact of the Internet on the global economy. While continued Internet growth in most advanced nations' economic sectors has been projected to be "slow to no growth" now and in the years to come, an Internet-powered economy represents a bright light that needs to be capitalized on by developing nations, in particular. The Internet sector offers one of the world's few unfettered growth areas, according to this report. While policy makers often cite gross domestic product (GDP) growth rates of about 10 percent per year in developing markets, across the G20 nations, the value of the Internet economy is projected to almost double, to $4.2 trillion, over the next four years, from $2.3 trillion in 2010–2011, representing a compounded annual growth rate of 10.8 percent over 2010–2016. Though tracking the value of the Internet on developed and developing economies is, indeed, a complex and difficult task, the report attempted to measure the Internet economy by incorporating key variables like online consumption, investment, government spending, and net exports of all Internet-related goods and services (Grant, 2012).

Using this quantifier, the Internet is said to have contributed about $49 billion to Canada's GDP in 2010–2011, representing about 3 percent of the country's economic growth. The Internet's contribution is projected to grow to $76 billion by 2016, representing a compounded annual growth rate in Canada of 7.4 percent during the 2010–2016 time period. If the Internet were currently a measured sector in Canada, it would be viewed as being a greater contributor to the Canadian economy than agriculture, utilities, or hospitality (Grant, 2012).

Other developed nations are projected to have slower Internet growth by 2016—as in the United States, which, according to the report, is projected to have a compounded annual growth rate of 6.5 percent. In contrast, Italy is projected to have a compounded annual growth rate of 11.5 percent. With a ramping up of efforts by governments and small and medium businesses, affirm the authors, the projected compounded annual growth rates for the Internet sector may touch very high levels in many of the developing nations. For example, the projections for Argentina, India, and Mexico are estimated to be 24.3 percent, 23 percent, and 15.6 percent, respectively. The projection for China is estimated to be 17.4 percent over this period (Grant, 2012).

What is more, according to the Boston Consulting Group report, using the Internet is not only good business for companies, but it intensifies sales growth rates. In multiple countries, including China, Germany, Turkey, and France, small and medium enterprises (SMEs) that have chosen to engage actively with clients on the Internet have reported three-year sales growth rates that are up to 22 percentage points higher than those of companies with low or no Internet presence. There is little question, the authors concluded, that, globally, SMEs that embrace and capitalize on the Internet are not only growing faster than SMEs that choose to do otherwise but also creating more jobs compared to the SMEs that do not. In short, by encouraging businesses to turn to the Internet to stimulate transactions, developing and developed nations can improve their competitiveness and growth prospects (Boston Consulting Group, 2012).

Moreover, the authors give some insights regarding the value placed by online consumers on Internet usage; they asked consumers how much they would have to be paid to live *without* Internet access. In the G-20 countries, consumers said that they would need to be paid $1,430 each. However, the "to-be-paid" value did tend to vary among consumers by country: in Turkey, the value was $323 each; in South Africa, $1,215 each; in Brazil, $1,287 each; and in France, $4,453 each. The aggregate value across 13 of the G-20 countries was found to be $1.9 trillion, or approximately 4.4 percent of their GDP. Indeed, these results are highly revealing, given that they demonstrate how intensely connected the Internet consumers' daily lives have become almost everywhere around the globe (Boston Consulting Group, 2012).

Gaining Authorized and Unauthorized Access to the Internet—and How Hacking May Be Related to Internet Censorship

Authorized Access and Various Modes of Communication

Given that the Internet has no entry door, per se, how do Internet users gain access legally? A number of ways exist. One of the earliest ways was through a computer network linked directly to the Internet at an educational institution, business, or government office. The IT department would issue account numbers and passwords to legitimate users.

As more citizens purchased PCs during the 1990s—which had become moderately priced by then—and beyond, users commonly paid a fee to an ISP. In exchange, the user received a software package, a user name, a temporary password, and an Internet access number. Equipped with a modem, the user logged on to the Internet, browsed Web sites, bought things online with the click of a mouse, watched movies online, and sent and received electronic mail (email). In recent years, ISPs have offered high-speed Internet services using DSL (a general term for any local network loop digital in nature) or cable-modem technology. ISPs are connected to one another through network access points.

The most common ways to communicate legally and legitimately with other Internet users include the following (Holt and Schell, 2013):

- **Email:** Here, online users can send messages to one another in real time. Compared to encrypted email, which is secure, unencrypted email is not secure, meaning that its contents may be accessed, viewed, and even altered by someone with computer access.
- **Listserv:** A Listserv is like an online subscription to some topic of interest to users. Registered users receive messages posted by others and post messages for others to read. The kind of software managing Listserv is known as a mail exploder, a program that runs on the server where the list resides. This program also gives instructions to online users about how to automatically unsubscribe. A Listserv may be classified as *open access* or *restricted access*. A moderated Listserv has someone who actually approves of (read *censors*) the messages posted before sending them on to registered users.

- **Newsgroups:** These provide Internet users with articles posted to multitudes of discussion groups. Articles are arranged by topic and distributed through an electronic bulletin board system called Usenet. When a user having access to a Usenet server posts an article, the server forwards the article to adjacent Usenet servers, making the article available to all Usenet sites having access to that newsgroup. While some Usenet newsgroups are moderated, others are not.

- **Internet Relay Chat:** These are servers running software known as Internet relay chat, allowing multiple users to "talk online" and in real time by choosing from many activated discussion channels. The message typed on one user's computer will appear almost immediately on another user's computer monitor. To maintain privacy and to keep real identities unknown to those in chat rooms, users will often go under a false name (known as a moniker), like Fishgirl.

- **Social Networking** Web Sites: By connecting to these sites using the Internet, users can share in an online environment their ideas, events, photos, and activities of personal interest across political, economic, and geographic borders. The technology used to support social networks via computer-mediated communications was utilized in early online services like America Online and was also involved in Usenet, ARPAnet, and Listserv. Now, these programs may utilize various algorithms and are potentially integrated into powerful and very popular search engines like Google or Baidu. A study completed on 2009 by the Pew Internet and American Life Project found that interest in social networking sites grew exponentially post-2000 during the adulthood phase of Internet development, and that the number of adults using social networks had quadrupled between 2005 and 2009. About 90 percent of adults using social networking sites do so to remain in touch with people that they already know, whereas about half of teenagers and adults are looking for new friends (Leggatt, 2009).

- **Telnet:** This is a terminal emulation program, or one based on that protocol, allowing users to log on to the Internet. Put simply, Telnet is an Internet application permitting a user's PC to act as a terminal to a remote system. Many users connecting to the Internet, however, do not use Telnet because it requires knowledge of the UNIX operating system. For example, a professor at one university can use Telnet to make use of the extraordinary computing power of a super-computer at some other university or a string of universities if that professor is familiar with UNIX. A real-world example is Canada's Shared Hierarchical Academic Research Computing Network—the largest high-performance computing consortium in Canada, now comprising 17 universities, colleges, and research institutes (SHARCNET, 2012).

- **Remote Retrieval:** This pertains to how Internet users search for and retrieve information located in remote computers. There are several ways that this process can be completed. One way is to use the FTP to transfer files between systems over the network, particularly from a host (a server) to a remote computer (client). Another way to search and retrieve is to use the gopher protocol, released in 1991 and designed to share documents online. The third way is to use HTTP. Although information is stored in individual HTTP servers worldwide, the connection of these computers to the Internet through W3C, or World Wide Web Consortium, protocols (those used to exchange information) allows the linked information to become part of a single body of information. In other words, the Internet describes a network of HTTP servers using hypertext links to find and access files. For this reason, all Internet site addresses begin with http://.

Unauthorized Access to Networks and the Types of Harm Caused by Hack Attacks

Given the massive amount of information that may be generated by the citizens of Internet-embracing nations, coupled with the huge number of devices presently connected to the Internet, chances are there is somebody connected to the Internet who wants to "bend" it to meet one's own selfish needs. In the section on the history of the Internet, there are numerous examples of network attacks conducted for selfish and self-promotional reasons, as well as for acts of retaliation. Nowadays, when we hear about online users getting access to data or information on the Internet for which they do not have authorization, the label *hacker* immediately comes to mind. The ability to hack is a skill, involving the manipulation of technology in some way, shape, or form—and that this skill set can range from rudimentary to advanced.

The term *hacker* has taken on many different meanings in the past 25 years, ranging from computer-savvy individuals professing to enjoy manipulating computer systems to stretch their abilities to the malicious manipulators bent on breaking into computer systems through deceptive or illegal means with the intent to cause harm (Steele et al., 1983). Both definitions are correct, as the term *hacker* has been applied to both malicious and benevolent online users, alike. This confusing reality is a consequence of the evolution of hacking in tandem with the technological development of the Internet over several decades.

To differentiate between malicious and benevolent hackers, individuals within the hacker community—known as the Computer Underground (CU)—began to use the term *cracker* to recognize individuals who engage in criminal or unethical acts using hacking techniques. This term was meant derisively, suggesting that a cracker is different from a hacker and should be treated accordingly. The use of the term *cracker* is not common outside of the hacker culture or the CU, but it is extremely important to our understanding of hacking and cracking, the abuse of the Internet's privileges and opportunities by those connected in the virtual world, and the way in which cracking, in particular, is viewed by those who use their tech-savvy skills to cause harm to others, motivated largely by personal gain or revenge.

Black hat hacking, or cracking, is commonly viewed as a crime committed against a computer or a network using another computer for hacking exploits, which often result in deception or in harm to property or data owned by governments, businesses, or individuals. Cracking can fall into various forms of cybercrime, based on the target of the attack and the outcome it produces for the victim in terms of property damage, economic loss, or personal harm.

Hacker exploits that target computer systems or data can be viewed as acts of trespass, deception, or theft through a variety of cracking techniques such as the following (Schell and Martin, 2004; Holt and Schell, 2013):

- **Flooding:** A form of cyberspace vandalism resulting in denial-of-service (DoS) to authorized users of a Web site or system.
- **Virus and Worm Production and Release:** A form of cyberspace vandalism causing corruption, and possibly erasing, of data.
- **Spoofing:** The cyberspace appropriation of an authentic user's identity by non-authentic users, causing fraud or attempted fraud in some cases and critical infrastructure breakdowns in other cases.
- **Phreaking:** A form of cyberspace theft or fraud (or both) consisting of using technology to make free long-distance telephone calls.
- **Infringing Intellectual Property Rights and Copyright:** A form of cyberspace theft involving the copying of a target's information or software without consent.
- **Phishing:** A form of fraud where the offender sends prospective victims an email from a financial institution or service indicating that the user will be cut off from services if

the user does not respond in a timely fashion. The information provided is then stolen and used by the offender.

In recent years, as noted in the section on Internet evolution, hacking exploits have resulted in harm to persons or governments. During the adult phase of Internet development, there were a number of cases cited where harm was perceived to be caused by cyber wars, even though the perpetrators may have argued that their motivations were positive and not destructive (Brenner, 2008; Denning, 2011). When Indian border guards, for example, tortured a Bangladeshi cowherd who had crossed territorial lines in December 2011, the Dhaka government issued an official protest to the incident. In today's high-tech world, there is actual video footage of this incident, apparently taken by one of the guards. The video went "viral" through the Internet. When the Dhaka government later continued to play down the incident, patriotic young citizens took matters into their own hands. They launched what they labeled a "cyber war" aimed at official and commercial Web sites in India. The hackers claimed to have hit more than 30,000 Web sites in 10 days, defacing them with Bangladeshi flags, images of civilians killed or tortured by Indian border forces, and lists of demands for the Indian government. The government and businesses claimed significant economic and social upheaval harms.

Indian hackers began to retaliate, and at this point, the cyber war became the headline focus in the Bangladeshi media. The media generally treated the cyber war as being caused by a bold civilian response to the lack of appropriate government action, likely motivated by a fear of its more powerful neighbor. Web experts have stated that the hacking war actually began three or four years ago, with occasional flare-ups caused by tech-savvy citizens in India, Bangladesh, and Pakistan (Nolen, 2012).

By law, some acts of online protest, such as hacktivism, tend to be categorized as technical non-offenses, even though, as we have seen from the examples cited above, harm can be caused (Schell, 2007). There is little question that in recent times, governments worldwide seem to be taking hacktivism very seriously. Since first recognized for their hacktivism around 2008, when they targeted the Church of Scientology, Anonymous, in 2013, as a case in point, has become a national security concern as recognized openly by the U.S. government and others (Blue, 2013).

How Hacking May Be Related to Internet Censorship

Though in April 2010 world leaders met in Washington, D.C., to discuss the dangers of nuclear war, the present-day reality is that, as the world—developed and developing—becomes increasingly reliant on the Internet and connected to it and through it, cyber war is another real threat that is more security compromising than nuclear war. What's more, when high-tech giants like Google are likely targets of cyberattacks (witness those in 2010), how safe is the United States, or any country, for that matter, from large-scale cyberattacks? While in 2010, possible Chinese hackers attacked Google's servers in the name of political activism, what will happen tomorrow? Will the targets of hack attacks actually become networked critical infrastructures that are so essential to keeping the world economy and society running smoothly (Lynch, 2010)?

Beyond the anxieties around cyber wars and threats to critical infrastructures now and in the future, might there somehow be a link between hacking and Internet censorship—such that perpetrators of hacking may often profess that they are completing their exploits because they are in favor of freedom of information and opposed to Internet censorship. First, we need to acknowledge that all countries, not just China or Russia, are engaged in cyber espionage—including NSA's Prism program—either to gain military advantage over another nation or to steal some proprietary information belonging to industry. Even on the domestic front in China, government agencies and industry networks are being hacked so that the perpetrators can spread malware to try to steal identity numbers and virtual money from various targeted online venues, such as multiple-player games. Because of China's dependency on Microsoft products (about 90 percent of the Chinese government offices uses Windows)—and given that a lot of this software is pirated (so that vulnerabilities are not patched)—Chinese government networks are, indeed, vulnerable to hack attacks. Hacking networks occur all over the world, even if legislation is in place to act as a deterrent. Despite what the media says about China, the fact is that like the United States and Canada, China, too, has anti-hacking laws. There, it is not uncommon for hackers to spend three years in prison and be fined tens of thousands of dollars for illegal hack attacks (Lynch, 2010).

From a pragmatic and theoretical point of view, clearly defining the link between hack attacks and Internet censorship in countries is very challenging. Maybe the logical way to approach this challenge is to accept that what in one jurisdiction (say, in China) is a hacktivistic act (technically, a criminal non-offense) may in another jurisdiction be perceived as a criminally motivated targeted hack attack (say, by Google executives or government officials in the United States). Thus, the United States would likely argue that the perpetrators should be subject to criminal sanctions.

This variation in interpretation of online exploits also helps explain how some officials in one jurisdiction can feel justified about censoring content on the Internet, while officials in another jurisdiction may be opposed to such online censorship. Put another way, what is perceived to be an expression of freedom of speech in one jurisdiction may be perceived as a violation of community standards of tolerance in another jurisdiction—thus, the need for enforcement of Internet censorship rules and regulations.

And on a sobering closing thought, we need to accept that hackers—whether they live in China or the United States—are not all cut from the same cloth or have the same motivations for hacking. In all jurisdictions worldwide, there are the script-kiddies—typically teens hacking for fun or to see what they can accomplish. There are also cyber criminals—those who hack networks for financial gain. Then there are the patriotic hackers—those who hack targeted Web sites for political motivations. Finally, there are hackers in the military who are hired to think about how they can use their skills effectively in an actual military exercise or conflict as a means of safeguarding their country and its citizens (Lynch, 2010).

Online Users' Concerns about Censorship and the General State of Online Censorship in 2012

Concerns by Global Citizens about Online Censorship

As noted at the start of this chapter and as was evident from the section on the adult phase of Internet development, in particular, governments (some more than others) are increasingly trying to control citizens' online activities, restrict the free flow of information, and infringe on the rights of online users—all in the name of keeping the country and its citizens safe from various harms—morally, politically, or otherwise. These efforts by governments around the world—as manifested in China and Iran over the last decade, in particular—have contributed to present-day concerns of online users regarding excessive online censorship by certain governments and their strong push for compliance to "rules of engagement" by ISPs.

Moreover, there is a digital divide between those who are wealthy enough to obtain access to the Internet and those who cannot afford to do so—a form of *unintentional* censorship. Even in developed nations, there is a portion of the poor, and particularly those who live in the inner cities, whose access to the Internet is limited because of lack of affordability. In fact, in 2013, it is estimated that about 21 percent of Canadian households *do not* have access to the Internet, the cost of service and computer purchase often cited as major barriers. Current figures show that only slightly more than half of the poorest Canadian households—those with incomes of $30,000 or less—have Internet access, according to Statistics Canada (Trichur, 2013).

Let's be clear: besides these financial barriers separating the Internet haves from the have-nots, not every government is agreeable to having its citizens roam the Internet freely, because there are alleged moral or political concerns and harms that must be accounted for. Consequently, some government officials feel an ethical and moral need to censor Web sites and the content contained therein. And when officials decide what online content needs to be viewed and, when necessary, blocked as a means of reducing harm, they typically call on ISPs and forms of legislation to assist in this regard.

Early in 2010, when President Obama was in Shanghai to speak out against online censorship, Secretary of State Hillary Clinton gave a now-famous speech about the importance of Internet freedom and of telecommunications industry freedom fighters. She called on them to help *balance* the fragile freedom fighter versus censorship scales worldwide, as noted in her words below (Masnick, 2010, 1):

> For companies, this issue is about more than claiming the moral high ground. It really comes down to the trust between firms and their customers. Consumers everywhere want to have confidence that the Internet companies they rely on will provide comprehensive search results and act as responsible stewards of their own personal information. Firms that earn that confidence of those countries and basically provide that kind of service will prosper in the global marketplace. *I really believe that those who lose that confidence of their customers will eventually lose customers.* No matter where you live, people want to believe that what they put into the Internet is not going to be used against them. And censorship should not be in any way accepted by any company anywhere. And in America, *American companies need to make a principled stand. This needs to be part of our national brand. I'm*

*confident that consumers worldwide will reward companies
that follow those principles.*

The General State of Online Censorship by Governmental View: Placements on the Freedom Fighter versus Censorship Scales

What could be said about the countries filtering online content? What are the various means by which country officials require ISPs to do the job for them? Perhaps the easiest way to find out is through the OpenNet Initiative, which documents attempts by nations to mold the Internet. That institution lists IP blocking, domain name system tampering, uniform resource locator blocking using a proxy, keyword blocking, and DoS attacks as the most frequent kinds of filtering employed by censorious countries and enforced by ISPs wanting a piece of the online market share. (See Schell and Martin, 2006, for further definitions of these technical terms.)

State-directed censorship, as we have discussed throughout this chapter, is occurring heavily in countries like China and Iran, and it is conducted at the Internet backbone (defined as a high transmission line providing networking opportunities to high-speed Internet service providers globally)—thus adversely impacting open access for online users throughout these countries. China's powerful Internet restrictions, for example, are generally called the Great Firewall, because they are installed on the international Internet gateway of mainland China. As a result, "troublesome" IT invaders with questionable Western values— such as Google+, Twitter, Facebook, and YouTube—are banned. Nonetheless, clever hackers have found vulnerabilities even in the Great Firewall and have exploited them to help online users not only transmit but receive information perceived to be not acceptable by government authorities. A case in point would be President Obama's Google+ account, which was hit with various online posts from Chinese Internet users in February 2012, after vulnerabilities in the Great Firewall were discovered and exploited, thus permitting netizens to access the Google+ social network and send important messages to President Obama (Karasidis, 2012).

Back in 1993, Internet pioneer John Gilmore remarked, "The net interprets censorship as damage and routes around it," and, says IT security writer Bruce Schneier (2008), we believed Gilmore. Three years later, cyber libertarian John Barlow proclaimed a declaration of the independence of cyber space at the World Economic Forum at Davos, Switzerland. At that time, Barlow said to governments, "You have no moral right to rule us, nor do you possess any methods of enforcement that we have true reason to fear." And back then, many people in the room shared his sentiments, for, in their view, the Internet empowered people, giving them access to an information highway that could not be stopped, blocked, or filtered. Give online users access to the Internet, it was believed, and they could, virtually, have access to every piece of information. Back then, it was also thought that the governments that relied on censorship to control their citizens were, for all intents and purposes, doomed. Fast forward to 2008. Things were very different then from how they were back in 1996. At least 26 countries—primarily in the Middle East, North Africa, Asia-Pacific, and the Soviet Union—chose to selectively block their citizens' Internet access. Equally as depressing, a significant number of countries legislated control over what could be said or not said online or downloaded (Schneier, 2008).

When it comes to Internet openness or censorious behavior by government agencies, countries generally place a three-pronged information-censoring continuum, and ISPs wanting to get, grow, or maintain market share within these jurisdictions must comply to

- closed networks,
- some surveillance of Web site content because of existing legislation,
- transparency regarding requests to ISPs for removing content on Web sites.

Going by this continuum, Iran is clearly a closed network. In 2012, this country decided to literally cut itself off from the global Internet, claiming that foreign powers are intentionally trying to arrest its closed network development, citing the reality that in 2010 there was a computer worm that caused Iran's centrifuges to fail at its main uranium enrichment facility—likely planted by Israel and the United States. However, despite Iran's best intentions to develop a closed network, reporters at Al Jazeera have said that Iran's proposal may actually find proponents in some rather odd corners. Given that Iran's supreme leader Ayatollah Ali Khamenei, for example, has his own Web site in 13 languages and his own personal accounts on Twitter and Instagram (a photo-sharing Web site), he may take extreme offense to any interruption to Iran's global Internet access—for lack of access is very likely to cause harm regarding his communications with followers (Karasidis, 2012).

Freedom House, an independent watchdog organization monitoring online freedom and censorious geographic locations worldwide, has, for example, cited South Africa as a minimal Internet surveillance location because political content online tends not to be censored and bloggers tend not to be jailed for what they say. However, this status may change if the proposed Protection of State Information Bill is passed, making it illegal to publish on paper or online particular state-owned confidential information. Furthermore, if the General Intelligence Laws Amendment Bill is passed in South Africa, bulk online content monitoring could become legalized, thus hampering freedoms currently allowed to bloggers, Internet users, and online whistle-blowers.

Finally, government agencies have not been transparent in their requests to ISPs and search engine companies to censor "offensive" or "politically sensitive" content. For example, though seeing themselves as a solid freedom fighter corporate citizen, in September 2012, Google officials temporarily blocked the film *Innocence of Muslims* in Libya and Egypt. Legal experts have suggested that, like other censorious governments for restricting Web site content, Libya and Egypt officials had concerns about the harm caused by defamation, pornography, hate speech, threats to national security, religious offence, and infringement of copyright and trademark law. Within the past decade, Google's decisions regarding online censorship have clearly indicated that though the company is not a court the legal authority to decide what information should be allowed or not be allowed to online viewers, company officials decide officials decide whether to comply with a government's request taking into account the said country's rules (Karasidis, 2012).

In closing, it is clear that online censorship is growing in scale, scope, and sophistication around the world. Without doubt, the regulation of the Internet has continued to grow over time—a reality that is not surprising, given the importance of this medium economically and socially. As John Palfrey of the Berkman Center for Internet and Society affirmed back in May 2007, "As Internet censorship and surveillance grow, there's reason to worry about the implications of these trends for human rights, political activism, and economic development around the world" (Berkman Center for Internet and Society, 2007, 1).

Conclusion

This chapter detailed the humble beginnings of the Internet in the United States and then discussed the good things and the bad that have occurred once the Internet reached its adolescent and adult phases of development. The endorsement of the Internet by businesses, government agencies, and citizens grows even more intense annually, making it a major revenue-generating machine on a global basis. Yet, despite all of the opportunities for citizens globally that have resulted from the Internet's growth—from buying airline tickets to watching movies or social networking with friends without leaving home—for every opportunity flagged with good intentions, there are opportunities flagged with mal-intentions and harms to society. The balance of the chapter described legitimate ways to gain access to the Internet as well as illegal ways, as well as the prevailing debates between the online freedom fighters and the Internet content censors.

References

Associated Press. "Google 'compromised principles' over China." 2006, http://www.guardian.co.uk/technology/2006/jun/07/news.searchengines (accessed June 7).

Associated Press. "Google's following of India's standards hikes fear of censorship." *The Globe and Mail*, February 7, 2012, p. A10.

Barkham, P. "Censorship on the Internet links." 1999, http://www.guardian.co.uk/technology/1999/feb/03/freespeech.internet (accessed February 3).

Barrett, D., and T.-P. Chen. "U.S. scrambles to snare Snowden as he flees Hong Kong." *The Globe and Mail*, June 24, 2013, pp. A1, A11.

Berkman Center for Internet and Society. "Survey of government Internet filtering practices indicates increasing Internet censorship." 2007, http://cyber.law.harvard.edu/newsroom/first_global_filtering_survey_released (accessed May 18).

Blake, A., and B. Gellman. "NSA secrets leaker revealed." *Las Vegas Review-Journal*, June 10, 2013, pp. 1A, 4A.

Blake, A., Gellman, B., and G. Miller. (2013). "NSA secrets leaker revealed." *Las Vegas Review-Journal*, June 10, pp. 1A, 4A.

Blue, V. "Anonymous re-hacks US sentencing site into video game asteroids." 2013, http://www.zdnet.com/anonymous-re-hacks-us-sentencing-site-into-video-game-asteroids-7000010384/ (accessed January 28).

Boston Consulting Group (BCG). "Clicks grow like BRICS: G-20 Internet economy to expand at 10 percent a year through 2016." 2012, http://www.bcg.com/media/

PressReleaseDetails.aspx?d=tcm:12-100468 (accessed March 19).

Branigan, T. "Google attacks traced back to China, says US Internet security firm." 2010, http://www.guardian.co.uk/technology/2010/jan/14/google-attacks-traced-china-verisign (accessed January 14).

Branigan, T. "Barack Obama criticizes internet censorship at meeting in China." 2013, http://www.guardian.co.uk/world/2009/nov/16/barack-obama-criticises-internet-censorship-china (accessed January 25).

Brenner, S. W. *Cyberthreats: The Emerging Fault Lines of the Nation State*. New York: Oxford University Press, 2008.

Comrie, G. R. "Cybersecurity: Protecting digital infrastructure through CIE." *Engineering Dimensions*, 32 (2011): 41.

Denning, D. E. "Cyber-conflict as an Emergent Social Problem," In T. J. Holt and B. Schell (Eds.), *Corporate Hacking and Technology-Driven Crime: Social Dynamics and Implications* (pp. 170–186). Hershey, PA: IGI-Global, 2011.

Dishneau, D. "Leaks revealed tactics, evidence suggests." *Las Vegas Review-Journal*, June 12, 2013, p. 8A.

Dishneau, D., and P. Jelinkek. "WikiLeaker sorry 'actions hurt people.'" *The Globe and Mail*, August 15, 2013, p. A14.

Fenby, J. "Google blazes a trail with China rift." 2010, http://www.guardian.co.uk/commentisfree/libertycentral/2010/jan/13/google-china-politics-censorship (accessed January 13).

Freedom House. "New Report: Governments grow increasingly repressive online, activists fight back." 2013, http://www.freedomhouse.org/article/new-report-governments-grow-increasingly-repressive-online-activists-fight-back (accessed January 22).

Gittings, J. "Sense and censorship." 2002, http://www.guardian.co.uk/technology/2002/sep/17/news.china (accessed September 17).

Goodale, J. C. "The first amendment and freedom of the press." *Issues of Democracy, 2* (1997): 4.

Goodman, A. "The Sopa blackout protest makes history." 2013, http://www.guardian.co.uk/commentisfree/cifamerica/2012/jan/18/sopa-blackout-protest-makes -history (accessed January 29).

Graber, D. A. "Styles of image management during crises: Justifying press censorship." *Discourse & Society 14* (2003): 539–557.

Grant, T. "Canada lags peers in 'Internet economy.'" *The Globe and Mail*, March 19, 2012, p. B3.

Greenberg, A. "An interview with WikiLeaks' Julian Assange." 2010, http://www.forbes.com/sites/andygreenberg/2010/11/29/an-interview-with-wikileaks-julian-assange/5/ (accessed December 16).

Harrell, E. "Defending the leaks: Q&A with WikiLeaks' Julian Assange." 2010, http://content.time.com/time/world/article/0,8599,2006789,00.html (accessed December 1).

Harrison, F. "Malaysia casts legal eye over Net." 1999, http://www.guardian.co.uk/technology/1999/apr/02/freespeech.internet (accessed April 2).

Holt, T. J., and B. Schell. *Hackers and Hacking: A Reference Guide*. Santa Barbara, CA: ABC-CLIO, 2013.

Ingle, T. "Censorship vs national security." 2007, http://voices.yahoo.com/censorship-vs-national- security-686138.html (accessed December 3).

Jakes, L. "U.S. spying raises fresh anger." *Las Vegas Review-Journal*, June 11, 2013, pp. 1A, 6A.

Karasidis, A. "Online censorship in 2012." 2012, http://mg.co.za/article/2012-11-20-looking-back-on-2012-online -censorship/ (accessed November 28).

Keegan, V. "Caught in freedom's net." 2001, http://www.guardian.co.uk/technology/2001/mar/30/news.freespeech (accessed March 30).

Ladurantaye, S. "A country of clickers: Canada tops in Web usage." *The Globe and Mail*, March 2, 2012, pp. B1, B5.

Leggatt, H. "Number of adults using social networks quadrupled since 2005." 2012, http://www.bizreport.com/2009/01/number_of_adults_using_social_networks_quadrupled_since_2005.html (accessed March 30).

Lynch, E. M. "Adam Segal discusses US-China relations in a cyber world." 2014, http://chinalawandpolicy.com/tag/patriotic-hackers/ (accessed January 29).

Masnick, M. "Hillary Clinton: Then and now on Internet freedoms and censorship." 2010, http://www.techdirt.com/articles/20101207/12043712168/hillary-clinton-then-now-internet-freedoms-censorship.shtml (accessed December 7).

Millar, S. "Blunkett revives plan to let agencies trawl phone and net users' records." 2003, http://www.guardian.co.uk/technology/2003/sep/13/freespeech.politics (accessed September 13).

Myers, S., and A. Kramer. "Snowden thanks Russia after being granted temporary asylum for a year." *The Globe and Mail*, August 2, 2013, p. A3.

New York Times Service. "Hong Kong not the safe harbor Snowden expects, expert says." *The Globe and Mail*, June 11, 2013, p. A11.

Nolen, S. "Torture spurs India-Bangladesh hacker war." *The Globe and Mail*, March 2, 2012, p. A11.

Nolen, S., C. Freeze, and S. Chase. " 'Cyberwar' threatens Brazil rift." *The Globe and Mail*, October 9, 2013, pp. A1, A16.

O'Brien, M. "Republican wants WikiLeaks labeled as a terrorist group." *The Hill.com*, November 29, 2010.

Pallister, D. "Junta tries to shut down Internet and phone l inks." 2013, http://www.guardian.co.uk/world/2007/sep/27/burma.technology (accessed January 25).

Paramaribo, S. "Ecuador rebukes Assange for mocking Australian politicians in video." *The Globe and Mail*, August 31, 2013, p. A20.

Plante, C. "Military kicks Geraldo out of Iraq." 2003, http://www.cnn.com/2003/WORLD/meast/03/31/sprj.irq.geraldo/ (accessed March 31).

Romana, C. "China denies Google hacking claims." 2010, http://abcnews.go.com/International/china-google-hacking-claims-groundless/story?d=9654628 (accessed January 25).

Rosencrance, L. "Spammer sentenced to nine years in jail." 2004, http://www.pcworld.com/article/118493/article.html (accessed November 5).

Roth, A., and E. Barry. "Russia denies Snowden extradition." *The Globe and Mail*, July 2, 2013, p. A3.

Savage, C. "Leaker portrayed as 'good-intentioned' and a traitor." *The Globe and Mail*, June 4, 2013, p. A3.

Savage, C., and E. Huetteman. "Manning's 35-year sentence 'the longest in a leak case.'" *The Globe and Mail*, August 22, 2013, p. A3.

Schell, B. *Contemporary World Issues: The Internet and Society*. Santa Barbara, CA: ABC-CLIO, 2007.

Schell, B., and C. Martin. *Contemporary World Issues: Cybercrime*. Santa Barbara, CA: ABC-CLIO, 2004.

Schell, B., and C. Martin. *Webster's New World Hacker Dictionary*. Indiana: Wiley, 2006.

Schneier, B. "Schneier on Security: Internet Censorship." 2012, (accessed April 7).

SHARCNEC. "FAQ." 2012, https://www.sharcnet.ca/my/help/faq (accessed March 29).

Simpson, I. "Witness at Manning trial focuses on motives." *The Globe and Mail*, June 5, 2013, p. A11.

Steele, G, Jr., D. R. Woods, R. A. Finkel, M. R. Crispin, R. M. Stallman, and G. S. Goodfellow. *The Hacker's Dictionary.* New York: Harper and Row, 1983.

Stone, M. "Anonymous hacks Federal Reserve in fight for Internet freedom." 2013, http://abcnews.go.com/International/china-google-hacking-claims-groundless/story?d=9654628 (accessed February 6).

Tait, R. "Censorship fears rise as Iran blocks access to top Web sites," 2013. http://www.guardian.co.uk/technology/2006/dec/04/news.Iran (accessed January 25).

Tossell, I. "The ABCs of cybersecurity." *The Globe and Mail Report on Business 28* (10) (May 2012): 55–60.

Trichur, R. "Helping the poor catch the net." *The Globe and Mail*, June 3, 2012, p. B3.

Tsuruoka, D. "Apple said using Baidu as search option in China." 2012, Investor's Business Daily, Inc., http://news.investors.com/articleprint/605708/201203 271250/aapl-reportedly-adds-bidu-search.aspx (accessed March 27).

Watts, J. "The man behind China's answer to Google: Accused by critics of piracy and censorship." 2005, http://www.guardian.co.uk/technology/2005/dec/08/piracy.news (accessed December 8).

Wearden, G. "Google sticks by censorship policy." 2013, http://www.guardian.co.uk/technology/2007/may/11/searchengines.newmedia (accessed January 25).

Weissenstein, M. "Ecuador President says Snowden can't leave Moscow." *The Globe and Mail*, July 1, 2013, p. A7.

Wells, M. "Freedom fear on Web site closure." 2000, http://www.guardian.co.uk/technology/2000/apr/03/freespeech.internet (accessed April 3).

Wielawski, I. M. "For troops, home can be too close." 2005, http://www.nytimes.com/2005/03/15/health/psychology/15fami.html?r=0 (accessed March 15).

Freedom of information is the foundation of any democracy.
Yet almost half of the world's population is still denied it.
Reporters Without Borders (2012)

As the Reporters Without Borders Web site acknowledges, in a democracy, freedom of expression and open access to information will likely always be perceived by citizens to be one of their greatest freedoms. What would the world be like, for example, if journalists—who are bent on finding and sharing *the truth* with citizens of the world—were not allowed to report facts on global incidents in the making, abuses against women and children in various societies, or environmental issues related to saving our planet? The positive reality is that in some countries where such abuses occur, the perpetrators halt their heinous acts once these facts are revealed to the world by reporters— commonly over the Internet as well as in print. The negative reality is that in some countries where such abuses exist, the way government in power copes is to severely restrict access to the Internet or shut it down altogether.

There is little doubt that most countries restrict access to content on the Internet at some basic level, such as restricting citizens' access to Web site pages with what is deemed by

---

The WikiLeaks homepage, featuring a picture of founder Julian Assange, on December 24, 2010. (Jjspring/Dreamstime.com)

government officials to be "offensive" content that exceeds community standards or preventing children from viewing certain Web site pages that parents feel might be harmful. According to Reporters Without Borders (2012), the organization formed to promote free expression and the global safety of journalists who are committed to freedom of information, some countries such as Belarus, China, Cuba, Egypt, and Iran have very strong censorship policies, while other countries like the United States and Estonia are quite open to the concept of freedom of information—whether in print or over the Internet.

After the 9/11 terrorist attacks in the United States, some IT-enabled stealth surveillance and censorship issues have surfaced. For example, on June 7, 2013, a leaked document (later linked to Edward Snowden) published in the media indicated monumental U.S. government surveillance of Americans' telephone records—hundreds of millions of calls, actually—in the first apparent hard-core evidence of massive data collection with the goal of combating terrorism under powers granted by Congress after the 9/11 attacks. The legal issue at the center of the controversy was a court order in Britain, requiring the communications company Verizon to hand over on a daily basis the records of *all* landline and mobile telephone calls of its customers, both within the United States and in other countries. Also publicly announced was that the National Security Agency and the FBI tapped directly into Google, Facebook, and Apple servers—under a code name Prism—to extract a targeted user's emails, chats, file transfers, and even search histories. Apparently, targets of Prism include major global players like Microsoft, Yahoo!, Google, Facebook, Paltalk, AOL, and Apple. The program, started in 2007 under President George W. Bush, has grown tremendously during President Barack Obama's presidency (Cassata and Benac, 2013).

Within 24 hours of this news release, President Obama assured Americans that no government agency was "listening" to their telephone calls, and that only non-U.S. citizens were targeted—which certainly suggests that Canadians and the

Chinese are a potential target of IT surveillance, censorship, and data analysis. Information gathered in such surveillance programs—as in the case of the Verizon warrants—is known as *metadata*, which by definition means information about information. Using metadata, intelligence agencies can, for example, try to pinpoint fraud by looking at connections between customers and, say, filed claims for unusual patterns (Clark, 2013).

On the eve of a two-day California summit in early June 2013, the primary agenda for the meeting—President Obama was to meet with Chinese president Xi Jinping to talk about Chinese cyber spying on U.S. business and government agency networks—took second-place priority relative to the questions raised about the extent of the U.S. government's domestic and non-domestic surveillance and data-spying efforts. The major U.S. tech companies affirmed, however, that they do not provide any government agency with "direct access" to their servers (Holland, Spetalnick, and Ruwitch, 2012).

Moreover, as noted in Chapter 1, in recent times, there has been a growing concern among individuals in the online global society about Internet censorship—whereby governments are increasingly trying to control citizens' online activities, restrict the free flow of information, and infringe on the rights of on-line users. Stated simply, since about 2005, the battle over maintaining Internet freedom has been heating up practically, legally, and morally. Moreover, the methods governments use to control the Internet are becoming increasingly sophisticated. At a time when about a third of the world's people are actively engaged online, tactics previously employed by extremely repressive regimes are now being employed by governments once considered to be more open and supportive of Internet freedom. Some of these tactics involve causing premeditated connection disruptions or paying professional commentators to consciously manipulate online discussions. As noted in Chapter 1, restrictions on Internet freedoms are frequently strengthened during times of war or terrorist attacks, even by more open-policy governments such as the United States.

Chapter 2 opens with an overview of what the *Computer Industry Almanac* says about PC, mobile phone, and Internet usage for various countries over the past few years. Next, we discuss cultural and legal jurisdictional factors influencing the digital divide, along with some additional legal insights into the handling of the controversial Internet-related Manning-WikiLeaks case. Following a discussion of this case, I outline the important differences between the concepts of information freedom and Internet censorship, along with jurisdictional issues pertaining to criminal liability on the coincidence of four key elements. The discussion then moves on to recent trends in Internet censorship (as noted in the *Freedom of the Net 2012* report) that seem to support online global citizens' fears and concerns regarding Internet censorship. Next, there is a more fulsome discussion on various online activities that are continually under the microscope of government authorities—either because of their strong support for Internet openness or because of their tactics used to reinforce Internet censorship; the jurisdictions discussed include the United States, Azerbaijan, Russia, China, Iran, Pakistan, and Egypt. Next, we look at how various countries and nation-states use Web filters, business-government policies, and laws aimed at preventing the flow of information over the Internet. Finally, we discuss some expert opinions on what factors may be involved in the next phase of the Internet's evolution, in terms of determining ongoing Internet censorship and information freedom.

A Look at PC, Mobile Phone, and Internet Usage Globally

PC Usage

According to the *Computer Industry Almanac* (2012), the number of PCs in use reached over 1.6 billion units worldwide at the start of 2012. The United States had the PC usage lead, with over 50 percent more PCs in use than second-placed China. In fact, the United States accounts for over 19 percent of all PCs in use, with only 4.5 percent of the worldwide population. As alluded to in Chapter 1, however, the PCs-in-use growth rate is expected to slow over the next five years, as growth bursts are now being seen in iPads and other tablet computers. Ironically, the United States was projected to have more PCs in use than people by the start of 2013. The appeal and rapid growth of mobile PCs (which include iPad and other tablet computers) is the major reason for present and future PC expansion in the United States and elsewhere.

In terms of PC usage on a global scale (*Computer Industry Almanac*, 2012), for the top 15 countries, having 70.5 percent of the global market share, the breakdown in market share by country at the start of 2012 was as follows: (1) United States: 19.4 percent; (2) China: 12.2 percent; (3) Japan: 6.12 percent; (4) Germany: 4.47 percent; (5) India: 3.56 percent; (6) United Kingdom: 3.41 percent; (7) Russia: 3.34 percent; (8) France: 3.34 percent; (9) Brazil: 3.01 percent; (10) Italy: 2.79 percent; (11) South Korea: 2.55 percent; (12) Canada: 1.96 percent; (13) Mexico: 1.71 percent; (14) Spain: 1.42 percent; and (15) Australia: 1.22 percent. Other countries had the remaining 29.5 percent of the market share. Thus, the top 15 countries place in the PC-usage-"haves" category, and the remaining countries, relatively speaking, place in the PC-usage-"have-not" category.

Mobile Phone Usage

The mobile phone market took off like wild fire in 2011 due to the Smartphone boom; the *Computer Industry Almanac* (2011) projected that by the year's end worldwide sales of mobile PCs would reach almost 227 million units, a huge increase from 2005, when only 63 million mobile PCs were in use. Again, the major growth factor is the huge marketability of the iPad and similar tablet devices. Moreover, sales of mobile PCs by 2015 are projected to account for about 71 percent of the PC market share. Again, the industrialized countries tend to fall into the haves category, while the non-industrialized countries tend to fall in the have-not category. In the front-running United States, mobile PC usage as a percentage of PC usage has grown from 19 percent in 1995 to over 63 percent in 2011 and is projected to be over 74 percent by 2015.

Internet Usage

By the start of 2009, according to the *Computer Industry Almanac* (2010), (1) China held the largest market share in terms of Internet usage (17.03 percent), followed by (2) the United States (13.41 percent) and (3) India (6.85 percent). The top 15 countries had 67.07 percent of the Internet usage market share—representing the have category. The remaining market share, by country, was as follows: (4) Japan (5.61 percent); (5) Germany (3.31 percent); (6) Brazil (2.80 percent); (7) United Kingdom (2.58 percent); (8) Russia (2.36 percent); (9) France (2.35 percent); (10) Italy (2.19 percent); (11) Indonesia (2.10 percent); (12) South Korea (2.10 percent); (13) Mexico (1.51 percent); (14) Canada (1.49 percent); and (15) Spain (1.38 percent). During this time, countries in the have-not category had the remaining share of about 33 percent.

According to the *Computer Industry Almanac* (2010), by the start of 2010, the worldwide number of Internet users exceeded 1.83 billion—up from only about 2 million in 1990, when the Internet was reaching its adulthood phase of evolution. Five years later, in 1995, there were 45 million Internet users. By the year 2000, there were 430 million Internet users worldwide, and by 2005, there were about 1.09 billion. There is little question that Internet adoption increased worldwide as the Internet continued to evolve throughout its adult stage. Using these projections, the *Computer Industry Almanac* suggested that by the end of 2010, over 2 billion users would be connected to the Internet. Much of the current and future growth, they added, would come from the BRIC countries of Brazil, Russia, India, and China. They also projected that, over the 2010s, many Internet users will be supplementing their PC Internet usage with smart phones and other such mobile devices. In the developing countries, it was projected that many new Internet users will come from the mobile and smart phone markets.

Cultural and Legal Jurisdictional Factors Influencing the Digital Divide

Cultural Adaptation Factors

In short, in terms of PC, mobile phone, and Internet usage, there is a digital divide between the haves and have-nots, with cultural and socioeconomic factors being the determinants. A recent newspaper article, for example, talked about the harsh reality that for India's "down and out" people on the wrong side of the digital divide, life can look better on Facebook than it looks in real life. The story involved a young student named Raju Shaikh, who lives in a Delhi shelter for homeless boys, sharing a history of violence, fear, and hunger. Though the shelter is crowded and noisy, Raju has created a new and exciting life through his Facebook accounts. On one Facebook account, Raju posts pictures of himself chilling with his friends, and he lists songs and movies that he likes. On a second account, Raju falsely mentions that he is studying software engineering at New York University, and through this channel, he chats with "friends" online, though he has not met any of them in person yet (Nolen, 2012).

There are also demographic and legal jurisdictional adaptation factors that come into play in defining this digital divide. For example, demographic variables, including gender and life stage, have been reported to have an impact on Internet user access and adoption, particularly in the developing nations (Vaagan and Koehler, 2005). Moreover, Internet access is far greater for citizens living in cities than in rural areas—with Internet cafes (i.e., storefronts with Internet connections for fee-paying customers) being quite popular in more densely populated areas of even developing nations. Also, in the developing nations, the well-educated college and university population and those citizens with greater economic means are more likely to have Internet access than are those without advanced education or wealth. Even during the early days of ARPAnet development, access to the Internet was restricted to university students and faculty working on U.S. homeland security issues; U.S. citizens did not have access.

Even in today's somewhat more liberated world for women (especially in the developed world), gender remains a key variable regarding Internet access. Young males are more likely to gain access to a computer at earlier ages and to be more interested in such high-tech activities like hacking and networking as compared to young females (Schell, Dodge, with Moutsatsos, 2002). For example, in a study conducted by Schell and Melnychuk (2011) on male and female hacker conference attendees, the mean age that males ($n = 66$) became interested in technology was 11 years, whereas for females ($n = 68$), the mean age was 15.5 years. Furthermore, the mean age that males ($n = 61$) became interested in hacking/IT security was 18 years, whereas for females, the mean age ($n = 57$) was 23 years.

Finally, life stage factors are important in terms of Internet access. Individuals born after 1950 are more likely to seek access to the Internet than those born earlier, because the former are more likely to have been exposed to computers at a younger age; therefore, they are less likely to feel overwhelmed by the opportunities that Internet access can provide (Schell, 2007).

Legal Jurisdictional Adaptation Factors and the Key Elements of Liability in Conventional and Online Crimes

There is little question that Internet access to and adoption by citizens in developed and developing nations can result in both personal and national economic growth. However, it has become equally clear that as the Internet continued to evolve into its adulthood, Internet access and adoption by the masses have led to both positive and negative outcomes. Sometimes, the latter result in harm to property or persons, or both. As these harm-inducing cases have been brought to court in the United States and elsewhere, interesting legal jurisdictional questions have arisen, as well as a basic understanding of the key elements of liability in both conventional and online crimes. Moreover, generally speaking, when more than one jurisdiction becomes involved in cases involving online crime, the legal complexity of the case increases exponentially.

In the various Internet-exploit cases cited in Chapter 1, when harm was caused—as in the Google hacking/censorship case regarding Chinese authorities—a cybercrime had *technically* occurred. However, the prosecution and the defense typically have different views about who is liable for the cybercrime—and why.

For conventional crimes to occur, Anglo-American law bases criminal liability on the coincidence of four key elements, as outlined by Susan Brenner (2001):

- A culpable mental state (the *mens rea*)
- A criminal action or a failure to act when one is under a duty to do so (the *actus reus*)
- The existence of certain necessary conditions or *attendant circumstances*. With some crimes, it must be proven that certain events occurred, or certain facts are true, in order for an individual to be found guilty of a crime.
- A prohibited result, or harm.

In a conventional crime such as bigamy, or multiple marriages, all four of these elements must combine for the imposition of liability. To start, an individual must enter into a marriage knowing either that he or she is already married or that the person whom he or she is marrying is already married. The prohibited act is the *redundant* marriage (the *actus reus*). The culpable mental state (the *mens rea*) is the perpetrator's knowledge that he or she is entering into a redundant marriage. The attendant circumstance is the existence of a previous marriage still being in force. Finally, the prohibited result, or harm to persons, is the threat that bigamous marriages pose to the stability of family life. Put simply, crimes—whether they occur on land or online—involve conduct deemed to be unacceptable by society's standards. Thus, society, through its laws, imposes criminal liability (Schell and Martin, 2004).

A U.S. Legal Jurisdictional Case

The following case is an illustration of these four elements converging in the instance of a U.S. case involving the Internet, the WikiLeaks hacker cell and its founder Julian Assange, businesses who supported the WikiLeaks Web site and the fight for Internet openness and freedom of information, and Private Bradley Manning (who while on duty in Iraq in 2009 and 2010 as a U.S. intelligence analyst had access to high-security government and military documents). Manning chose to transmit these secret documents to WikiLeaks founder Julian Assange over the Internet while he was stationed in the field. Assange then chose to transmit the said documents over the Internet for citizens and maybe even the enemy to view.

As noted in Chapter 1, the court-martial of Bradley Manning in 2013 is believed to be the most significant whistle-blower case since Daniel Ellsberg leaked the Pentagon Papers. And although Bradley Manning pleaded guilty to 10 offenses that could get him 20 years in prison, military prosecutors on the first day of his court-martial were steadfast in insisting that he not only aided the enemy with the use of the Internet (i.e., a cybercrime) but also violated the Espionage Act. At the end of Manning's trial, he was sentenced to 35 years, but likely eligible for parole in 8.

Interestingly, on the second day of the court-martial at Fort Meade, Maryland, a hacker by the name of Adrian Lamo (who in 2004 was charged for a hack attack cybercrime) affirmed that Private Manning contacted him online in

May 2010, from base in Iraq, seeking guidance on encrypted on-line chats, so there was a strong implication that premeditation on Manning's part had, indeed, occurred (Simpson, 2013).

Regarding the four critical elements of criminality liability, is Manning guilty of *both* a cybercrime and violations of the Espionage Act? Or is he an innocent man who went through pretrial abuse (i.e., forced nudity inspections while in solitary confinement) and harassment over his sexual identification issues, but is nevertheless the responsible bearer of his "legal duty" to expose war crimes—and thus not guilty of any crime? Given the importance of this case in American history, legal experts had earlier projected that the court-martial could last up to three months, which it did. From what had been published on the case by the media, here were the arguments used by the prosecution and the defense.

To begin, the prosecutors used a Civil War court-martial argument to advance their position that Manning intentionally sent (the *mens rea*) hundreds of thousands of classified documents to the WikiLeaks Web site, thus aiding al-Qaida and causing harm to U.S. soldiers in the field (the *actus reus*). In order for the four elements to be upheld, the prosecutors must have proven without a reasonable doubt that Manning knew al-Qaida members would see what WikiLeaks published (*attendant circumstances*) and that this was *a prohibited act*. In other words, harm was or could be done. The prosecution said during the pre-trial, for example, that the government planned to introduce evidence that al-Qaida members, including Osama bin Laden, *saw* the war logs and the State Department cables that Manning allegedly sent to WikiLeaks—and that harm actually occurred. The prosecution also noted that military courts in the past have recognized that publishing critical information in a newspaper can indirectly send information to the enemy—thus constituting the act of "aiding the enemy" (Dishneau, 2013).

Defense lawyers argued that the Civil War era cases involved coded messages disguised as advertisements, and that all of the modern cases of espionage have actually involved military members who have given the enemy information directly. The defense went on to argue that there has been no case in the full history of military jurisprudence dealing with someone giving information to a legitimate journalistic outlet (like WikiLeaks?)—and then having them publish it online, whether the enemy viewed it or not. The evidence disclosed by Adrian Lamo, the online-confidant-for-Manning-turned U.S. government confidant, was that Manning *intentionally* chose to leak the content through the Internet, because he wanted the people of America and around the world to see the truth. Moreover, Manning, like other freedom fighters of his time (such as Aaron Swartz), apparently believed that information should be free (Dishneau, 2013).

Furthermore, in July, 2012, Manning's defense attorney filed a 110-page motion requesting that all charges against the soldier be dismissed, based on Article 13 of the Uniform Code of Military Justice, which bans punishment or penalty other than arrest or confinement upon the charges pending against someone who is detained. The defense further argued that it does not believe that there has ever been such an egregious case of unlawful pretrial detainment as that of Private Manning, who was subjected to an equivalent of solitary confinement for over eight months, with emails indicating that at least one three-star general ordered unbearable conditions for Manning, including his being subjected to nudity during repeat inspections (London, 2012).

The defense further argued that Manning was just "doing his legal duty" of reporting war crimes while on duty in Iraq. Recall that Manning was charged with crimes for sending hundreds of thousands of classified items and videos, such as the "collateral murder" video depicting a U.S. Apache attack helicopter killing 12 civilians and wounding 2 children on the ground in 2007 in Baghdad. The helicopter then fired on and killed the rescuers of the wounded, and a U.S. tank drove over one of the bodies, allegedly slicing the man in half. From a legal perspective and under Article 85 of the first protocol to the Geneva Conventions, these acts constitute three war crimes. Moreover, argued Manning's defense lawyers, Section 27-10 of the U.S. Army Subject Schedule No. 27-1 stipulates that it is the *obligation* of solders to report all violations of the law of war. At his earlier guilty plea hearing, Manning had, in fact, maintained that he had spoken to his superiors and asked them to investigate the video and other "war porn" but that his superiors refused to do so. Manning said that he was very disturbed by the maimed children, the soldiers shown in the video who appeared not to value human life, and their blatantly referring to the targets as "dead bastards." So, in essence, argued his defense, Manning was only 22 years old and he *courageously* committed the legal duty acts for which he stood criminally accused. To counter charges that he violated the Espionage Act, the defense further argued that the prosecution must prove "beyond a reasonable doubt" that Manning had "reason to believe" that the files he transmitted to WikiLeaks over the Internet "could be used to harm the United States or aid a foreign power" (Cohn, 2013, p. 2 of 4).

At the hearing, when he pleaded guilty to 10 charges, Manning announced, "I believed if the public, particularly the American public, could see this, it could spark a debate on the military and our foreign policy in general as it applied to Iraq and Afghanistan." Manning added, "It might cause society to reconsider the need to engage in counterterrorism while ignoring the situation of the people we engaged with every day." These are hardly the words of someone who thought that his Internet transmissions could harm the United States or aid a foreign power, noted his attorneys. But that was the critical issue left to the powers that be at the court-martial—who, in the end, found that the prosecution's arguments were the more credible (Cohn, 2013, p. 2 of 4).

A Multi-jurisdictional, Competing, and Complex Legal Case

Though the U.S.-jurisdictional case of Bradley Manning had its challenges from both the prosecution and the defense perspectives, Internet crimes involving cross-border jurisdictions make for much more difficult prosecution than singular jurisdiction cases and, often, competing rulings and remedies by the courts.

So, what about Julian Assange? Is he guilty of a cybercrime, and in which jurisdiction should he be tried? Also, what law did he allegedly violate?

Julian Paul Assange is the editor-in-chief and founder of the whistle-blowing Web site WikiLeaks. During his youth in Australia, he was involved with the hacker group known as the International Subversives and he used the online name "Mendax." In 1991, he was caught by the police after hacking into the systems of the communications company Nortel. He was also affiliated with hack attacks against universities and U.S. government systems, and was charged with 31 counts of hacking and related cybercrimes. In 1995, he pleaded guilty to 25 counts but was released with a small fine and no additional time behind prison bars. In fact, the judge for this case indicated that Assange's hack attacks were not malicious but rather a consequence of his intelligence and tech-savvy curiosity. Thus, the judge ruled that Assange did not merit more substantive punitive sanctions.

In 2006, Assange founded WikiLeaks to provide, according to the WikiLeaks Web site, a means of causing regime change and to advocate for open information sharing to expose injustice and abuses of power. Though the Web site published controversial materials related to the Church of Scientology and Guantanamo Bay in its earlier years, perhaps WikiLeaks' biggest call to universal fame came with the publication of the American diplomatic cables on the Internet by Bradley Manning in 2009 and 2010 (Koring, 2012). Subsequently, the companies that provided funding and infrastructure for WikiLeaks, such as PayPal, pulled their support.

In December 2011, news broke that military investigators had uncovered evidence of what appeared to be a direct link between Manning and Assange, after a U.S. government digital forensic expert examined the computer of Manning and retrieved communications between the two men. Although Assange has always denied having direct contact with Manning—though he has never revealed how the materials that Manning stole happened to come into the possession of WikiLeaks—a file included in the computer investigation included this line: "You can currently contact our investigations editor directly in Iceland at 354.862.3481: 24 hour service: ask for Julian Assange." Though these revelations seem to provide some evidence suggesting that Assange had lied about his contact with Manning while he was in Iraq, the bigger question for the courts is whether this fact strengthens any potential American legal charges against Assange regarding the Manning case. Until this time, it seemed as though Assange would be relatively untouchable, because there was no direct evidence that he had been in contact with Manning prior to, or subsequent to, the data theft. Going by this evidence, there is a strong suggestion that Assange was likely affiliated with Manning *prior to* the data theft, perhaps even coaching him about what to look for in the confidential files of interest. If this is the case, the prosecutors could be looking at Assange's likely liability, as well as Manning's, under the Espionage Act or similar laws (Mataconis, 2011).

Taking a closer look at Assange's guilt or freedom prospects, there is quite a difference between a case where Assange was *just the recipient* of documents from some anonymous third party who had gotten the secret documents from Manning and a case where Assange was *actively* in contact with Manning before, during, and following the theft of the said classified documents. In the first case, the defense could argue that Assange was merely acting as a journalist and was not guilty of any crime. In the second case, Assange would have some major legal liability to contend with, for his guilt in aiding and abetting an act of espionage becomes more apparent (Mataconis, 2011).

That said, lawyers maintain that U.S. authorities could face tremendous legal hurdles if they tried bringing criminal charges against Assange, assuming in the first place they could get

Assange out from his current hideaway in the Ecuadorian embassy (and although he is likely fearing extradition to the United States to face espionage-related charges).

Three specialists in espionage law have argued that prosecuting someone like Assange on espionage charges would require evidence that the defendant was not just in contact with representatives from some foreign power but that he also *intended* to provide them with secrets. No such evidence has surfaced in the case of this Australian-born former computer hacker who is now an international celebrity, visited by such notables as Lady Gaga, while he remains "in hiding." Attorney General Eric Holder warned that the U.S. Justice Department had "an active, ongoing criminal investigation with regard to this matter . . . [and] to the extent that we can find anybody who was involved in the breaking of American law and who has put at risk the assets and the people I have described, they will be held responsible . . . They will be held accountable." However, Mark Stephens, a London lawyer retained by Assange to represent him should a trial be set in motion, responded, "Until I see a specific allegation, then it is difficult for me to respond." Stephens also remarked that given that Manning made unauthorized disclosures of secret documents while employed for the U.S. government, there is a much stronger legal foundation of a criminal case against him than that made for Assange (Reuters, 2010).

Apart from the legal debate just outlined, other experts believe that the argument against an Espionage Act prosecution of Assange should not be built upon a denial on his part that he spoke with Manning. Rather, the fact that Assange communicated with Manning—directly or indirectly, through an intermediary, or both—should be embraced and protected, because *the pair's ability to communicate* is the tenet that deserves protecting in a free society, whether that communication occurred in person or through the Internet. It is curious that Floyd Abrams, one of the leading legal authorities on the First Amendment and U.S. Constitutional Law appearing before the U.S. Supreme Court, defended the *New York Times* in the Pentagon Papers case in 1971. This case was very controversial at the time because the paper published secret reports on U.S. involvement in Vietnam from 1945 to 1967. However, Abrams feels that it would be far more difficult arguing that Assange is not guilty of violating the Espionage Act on the basis that the WikiLeaks Web site is journalism and, therefore, should be judged by the standards of the First Amendment (Khatchadourian, 2011).

What Abrams likely had in mind was a line from some very early WikiLeaks correspondence expressing the notion that such information leaks could, indeed, "bring down many administrations that rely on concealing reality—including the U.S. administration." But, one needs to ask whether what Assange and WikiLeaks did was really with criminal sentiment— or was the act of disclosure on the Internet simply fair expression of one's rights under the First Amendment in a society that values freedom of information, regardless of the mode in which it is delivered (Khatchadourian, 2011).

The Differences between Freedom of Information, Internet Freedom, and Internet Censorship

According to an extensive report released by Freedom House in 2012, brutal attacks against bloggers in some Internet-connected nations, politically motivated surveillance of online content, proactive manipulation of Web content by some governments, and emerging restrictive laws aimed at regulating free speech online are just some of the diverse threats against information and Internet freedom that have emerged since 2010. But the story is not all bleak. Increased pushback by civil society, technology companies, and independent courts, who believe in defending information freedom and in fighting against Internet censorship, have resulted in a variety of notable victories (Freedom House, 2012).

Freedom of Information Defined

Freedom of information generally refers to a citizen's right to access information held by the government. In many developed countries such as the United States and Canada, this freedom is supported as a constitutional right. In the United States, for example, the Freedom of Information Act (FOIA), Title 5, United States Code, Section 552, was signed into law on July 4, 1966, by President Lyndon B. Johnson. Afterward, the FOIA was amended a number of times—in 1974, 1986, and in 1996 with the enactment of the Electronic Freedom of Information Act Amendments of 1996. FOIA requires U.S. federal agencies to make public records available to citizens both electronically and through public reading rooms.

Though the FOIA applies to records created and kept by agencies in the executive branch of the federal government, such as the Department of Energy, it does not apply to Congress, the judicial branch of the federal government, or to state or local governments. Nevertheless, many state governments in the United States have enacted open records law to support freedom of information (U.S. Department of Energy, 2013).

Clearly, the FOIA was created to broaden access to government information to citizens, regardless of whether the medium is online or conventional. The Freedom of Information Act and similar legislation in other countries were established to have transparency, government accountability, public protection against mismanagement or corruption, and general education for citizens. In the United States and elsewhere, related human rights include such protections as freedom of expression, data protection privacy, and freedom of association. More than 70 countries with government representation have approved similar freedom of information legislation. For example, in China, the Freedom of Government Information Law has been in effect since December 28, 2005 (Janssen, 2013).

Internet Freedom Defined

To show their citizens that they "support" Internet freedom, governments around the globe, in varying degrees, have adopted diverse legal and policy decisions to increase access to Internet-based communication technologies for its citizens. Sometimes, their motives for endorsing Internet-based technologies include emphasizing cultural norms or transmitting to the masses key political objectives. One rather convenient way to profess some degree of Internet freedom is to set up a series of Internet cafes so that citizens in more urban areas, at least, have Internet access. Speaking in January 2010, then U.S. secretary of state Hillary Clinton compared the spread of Internet-driven information networks to "a new nervous system for our planet." She went on to say, "[I]n many respects, information has never been so free. [But] we've seen a spike in threats to the free flow of information" (U.S. Department of State, 2010, 1).

Defining *Internet freedom* on a macro system basis is a more difficult problem. From a rhetorical point of view, most global citizens and their government leaders will espouse support for the concept of Internet freedom. But what "freedom" is, per se, means different things to various citizens and governments, primarily because culture plays such a huge factor in defining life and one's priorities in life. This normative divergence plays out in debates over access to information and education, threats to freedom, online content controls, and governance, in general. In short, the concept of Internet freedom holds within it a series of conflicts about how the Internet should function. Consequently, accepting these tensions appears to be a sound approach to take in defining the term *Internet freedom* (Bambauer, 2010).

From this angle, several realistic statements about the premises underlying Internet freedom can be made (Bambauer, 2010):

- First, in order to enjoy the wide range of content available on the Internet 24/7, citizens need to have access to the

Internet. Countries and nation states vary on their access policies for citizens. For example, in the United States, the ability to "go online" is treated more like a market access privilege issue than as an entitlement. Simply stated, if citizens can afford to pay for access to the Internet, they are welcome to do so, but if they cannot afford to have a private account, they are dependent on Web site available to the public—such as those found at libraries or in schools. In contrast, Finland has a policy whereby having a 1 MB connection to high-speed broadband is a basic right for all citizens. Also, France's Constitutional Council has declared that high-speed broadband access is a legal right for all citizens.

• Second, countries and nation states vary on the question, "Free *from whom* or *from what*?" One threat in some countries is that the nation state can actually impinge online liberties in a myriad of ways, ranging from criminalizing online speech or conduct, monitoring messages communicated over the Internet, or blocking material on the Internet altogether. While Americans tend to be focused on preventing unchecked governmental powers by their governments, other countries such as those in Europe are concerned about the vast amounts of personal information about online users that corporations have accumulated—and may misuse. Over the past several years, the latter fear seems to have been substantiated to some degree—accepting, for example, the controversy generated over Google's video service in Italy and Google's Street View geo-mapping projects in numerous jurisdictions that raised concerns about adequate Privacy protections for citizens.

• Third, liability for "inappropriate" Web site content varies from country to country. In some countries, for example, there is a need to prevent impingements on one's freedom generated by other users, such as concerns about the harm that may be done to one's reputations should someone decide to place false and highly defamatory content on Web pages. For this reason, some governments have a policy requiring Internet Service Providers and social networking Web sites to police questionable content so as to avoid liability suits, while other countries have policies that provide immunity for anyone but the author of such content.

• Fourth, there is little question that different countries and nation-states "balance" in a variety of ways "freedom of expression" and "access to information" against "concerns about the harm caused by perceived 'offensive content.'" Generally, there is concern about *harm* done to individual citizens (such as online defamation of someone's character), religious or ethnic minorities, or common and prioritized societal values. For example, the United States views the free exchange of information as "weighty enough" to displace concerns of a competing nature—which helps to explain why so-called "offensive" materials like hate speech and pornography are protected by the US constitution. Having said this, however, the US constitution does prohibit certain online threats like cyber stalking, child pornography, and obscene materials—all perceived to surpass established community standards of tolerance. In contrast, while European countries like France and Germany adhere to and strongly protect "open expression" online, both countries ban online pornographic content. Finally, in Saudi Arabia, where the bulk of citizens are followers of the Sunni segment of Islam, Web sites featuring tenets of the Baha'i faith or the Shia teachings of Islam have their content blocked by government authorities.

Thus, given these four factors, if one were to view Internet freedom as protecting unfettered expression online, this liberty is counterbalanced in various degrees by competing concerns even within countries and jurisdictions. As stated, this counterbalancing of competing factors occurs even in countries having a history of strongly protecting citizens' free speech (Bambauer, 2010).

Finally, countries vary in their perception of *who should actually govern Internet freedom, and how this process should occur.* Clearly, this debate has been ongoing since the Internet "went commercial." Given that the U.S. government created the Internet's initial architecture, known as ARPAnet, to this day the United States maintains some degree of control over the workings of the Internet because of the strong connect between the U.S. Department of Commerce and ICANN (the Internet Corporation for Assigned Names and Numbers)—which is primarily responsible for overseeing the domain name system (Schell, 2007).

The United States has strongly protested against the transfer of ICANN's functions to other entities because of their strong belief that putting the Internet under international control would weaken freedom of expression; in particular, other countries have argued vehemently that moving forward, there needs to be a larger voice in decision making about the Internet's underlying protocols and standards. Many countries believe that the Internet is currently overrun by America's fixation to properly balance privacy, security, trust, and Internet censorship issues. This debate has reared its controversial head in a number of venues, such as the World Summit on the Information Society. While the Australian government has argued for mandatory Internet filtering, other government officials have argued that such filtering is too broad. Perhaps, notes Bambauer (2010), *Internet freedom* is a term that should be abandoned for now, because in a real-world sense, it is too general to be useful.

Internet Censorship Revisited

Internet censorship occurs when governments try to control citizens' online activities, restrict the free flow of information, and infringe on the rights of online users. Since about 2005, attempts to maintain Internet freedom and openness have been challenged in a number of countries. Moreover, the methods used by governments to control the Internet are also becoming increasingly sophisticated, in both developed and developing nations.

If you were to enter this debate, which seems to be recurring worldwide, which side would you argue for—that there are circumstances under which countries or nation-states can legitimately censor the Internet, or that Internet censorship is, without question, evil? In 2010, Professor Derek Bambauer from the Brooklyn Law School and Professor Richard A. Epstein from the University of Chicago entered such a public debate. Bambauer argued the former position, while Epstein argued the latter. Below is a summary of their speaking points to help readers decide which side of the debate they would tend to agree with (Bambauer and Epstein, 2010):

1. **For Censorship (Bambauer)**: Let's face it, the fictional binary world of "Censorship" OR "Freedom" no longer exists, and perhaps even before the Internet came into existence, it never existed. Every country has a long history of spying on their own citizens at times, especially when there is a perceived security threat. Before the Internet's time and now, we have lived in a world of ubiquitous Internet Censorship *and* surveillance. Technological companies and Internet Service Providers have had to face these business challenge questions when setting up their products and services in China, Egypt, Pakistan, Australia, and India. In fact, the United States even requires telecommunications companies to build wiretapping capabilities into their products and services so that they can be utilized during terrorist or other security attacks. So, once "spying" is part of the core functionality of Internet telephony, it is available to snoops in any country or government arm, not just the FBI. What is more, we need to acknowledge that China, Australia, and Ethiopia commit the same

"crime," for they restrict access to content online through laws and technology, and they spy on Internet communications. To the point, there appears to be some justification by countries to censor the Internet; thus, there is a justifiable argument that the key factors determining legitimacy are found in the process by which a country arrives at the decision to filter the Internet and how precisely it blocks content in practice during non-threatening periods.

2. **Against Censorship (Epstein)**: One can suggest that it is difficult to tell which reasons for censoring content are valid because nations tend to filter different kinds of Internet content. For example, the United States government blocks the unauthorized use of copyrights materials [as seen through its passage, for example, of the DMCA]. Yet China restricts political speech, the Mumbai government blocks the speech of extremist Hindu groups, the French government blocks the images of white supremacist groups, and the New Zealand government blocks child pornography. Here are five different governments with five unique agendas for blocking Internet content. It is wrong to suggest that we turn to procedures to determine how various governments make these censorious decisions. From the viewpoint of a classical liberal scholar, I would submit that the world can discover the right principles by looking at the *output* of the process rather than merely guessing about the various ways that different nations make their laws. In my view, there appears to be no sound reason why good laws that emerge, even as if by chance from less democratic processes, should be condemned.

3. **For Censorship (Bambauer)**: My closing argument is that the methodology suggested by you has some merit because it looks at the ends, not the means. But what values should be prioritized in assessing "appropriate censorship"? Do these values, for example, derive from American thinking, or should they be more universal in nature? There is a fear,

for example, that an approach grounded explicitly in U.S. values might result in strong resistance from outside actors, for other governments are often hesitant to yield to Western values because they conflict with their own, or because they want to avoid being labeled by their own citizens as too weak to fight against the Western values being imposed. Not only does a universal approach risk weakening core commitments just to achieve consensus, but, realistically speaking, an approach driven by one country's ideas about information seems totally impractical. Let's face it: Substance-based decisions require technology firms to make very fine-grained decisions about what content is inflammatory and what is critical. For example, should YouTube adhere to the Iranian government's demands to block a video of a 26-year-old female named Neda Salehi Agha Soltan, who was shot in Iran in an anti-government protest on June 20, 2009, on the grounds that this explicit online video showing her death might induce protests? Rather, *a process-based analysis* may provide a clearer mechanism for companies to make faster, cheaper, and (hopefully) better decisions about censoring content. Because Iran's decision-making methods for filtering appear to be arbitrary and lacking in opportunity for participation as well as transparency, it would appear that YouTube should reject any request made by the Iranian government to block content, as in the case of Neda's cold-blooded shooting and the recording of this event.

4. **Against Censorship (Epstein):** My closing point is to admit that I remain a universalist on matters of morals and ethics, for my prior training in Roman law has reinforced the notion that social relations do not differ in fundamental ways across societies. What does differ from one country to another are the formalities and institutions utilized to enforce these fundamentals of social relations. In my view, the U.S. Constitution, for example, has been quite successful because it accepts the universal standards

of sanctity of property and contract that require government control of such undesirable behaviors like aggression and fraud—whether they occur on land or in the virtual world. I would submit that these values are not distinctively American but are present in both Roman and English systems worldwide. Moreover, the American founders did not regard these principles as "distinctively American" but were happy to learn and borrow these principles from others inhabiting other lands.

Recent Trends in Internet Censorship According to the *Freedom on the Net 2012* Report

According to a study entitled *Freedom on the Net 2012: A Global Assessment of Internet and Digital Media*, some recent trends on Internet censorship support the concerns of online global citizens (Freedom House, 2012):

- In some countries, laws have been passed since January 2011 that either restrict online speech, violate online users' privacy, or punish online users for posting content viewed as "objectionable."

- Bloggers and online users are facing arrest for political speech and for content posted on the Internet deemed to be "offensive" to the government.

- Bloggers and online users are tortured, viciously assaulted, or are gone missing in retaliation for posting offensive messages online—particularly if the content is deemed to be "offensive" to the government.

- Pro-government commentators are paid to manipulate online discussions to influence the masses in the direction that the government favors.

- Cyber wars pitting one nation state against another are becoming increasingly more common following real-world events.

- Online citizens, along with some enlightened court decisions, are effectively yielding some positive returns on hacktivistic activities aimed at curbing Internet censorship.

Of course, not all censorship of information on the Internet can be viewed as negative. Parents around the world, for example, use Web filters to limit or block access to their children to specific Web sites that may cause them psychological or physical harm. But let's take a closer look at some of these world events that are causing consternation. *The Freedom on the Net 2012* study looked at barriers to access, limits on content, and violations of online user rights in 47 countries and then rated countries as "free" or "not free." Freedom House monitors the status of freedom in countries that are advocating for democracy, human rights, and Internet openness. *Freedom on the Net 2012* is written by editors affiliated with Freedom House.

One key finding in this report was that Estonia had the greatest degree of Internet freedom among the countries examined, with the United States ranking second. Iran, Cuba, and China were viewed as the most restrictive. According to this report, though China has the world's largest population of Internet users, the authorities seem to operate a highly sophisticated system of Internet censorship, with their Great Firewall becoming notorious for shutting down Internet "chatter" that the government authorities deem to be "sensitive." Earlier in 2012, Chinese censors had completely blocked search terms as a means of preventing online citizens from getting news on prominent human rights activist Chen Guangcheng, who created a "diplomatic storm" when he escaped house arrest and sought refuge in the U.S. embassy in Beijing.

Moreover, major Web portals and social networking Web sites in China—not state-owned—were given the ultimatum of complying with strict government-imposed Internet censorship rules or risk being shut down altogether. In March 2012, after commencing a campaign to remove "rampant online rumors," Chinese authorities ordered China's leading micro-blogging sites (like Sina Weibo) to disable their site's comment feature for three days. Unlike in the United States and democracies elsewhere, in China, bloggers are required to register their real names and not use some moniker disguising themselves. Accepting that this reality is imposed in China, there is no real record of how many online citizens have actually been compliant (Armstrong, 2012; Freedom House, 2012).

Eleven other countries were ranked as not free in the *Freedom on the Net 2012* report, including Belarus, Saudi Arabia, Uzbekistan, and Thailand—all countries that seem to perceive Beijing's influence as an "incubator for sophisticated restrictions" to be a good role model for Internet censorship in other jurisdictions. Moreover, 20 of the 47 countries examined were given a negative trajectory in terms of Internet freedom since January 2011—with Bahrain, Pakistan, and Ethiopia showing the greatest declines. These declines in ranking reflect increased censorship, arrests, and violence used against bloggers by authorities in the Middle East in an effort to silence public calls for democratic reform. What's more, in Saudi Arabia, Ethiopia, Uzbekistan, and China, government authorities tried imposing even more restrictions on Internet content after they saw the key role that the social media played in the Arab Spring uprisings calling for more democracy in Egypt (with the overthrow of government leader Hosni Mubarak) and Tunisia (with the ouster of President Zine el Abidine Ben Ali) (Armstrong, 2012; Freedom House, 2012).

According to the *Freedom on the Net 2012* report, the Saudi government warned online Saudi users about their desire to clamp down on protests and went so far as to discourage protestors from participating in demonstrations via BlackBerry's multimedia messaging service. Word coming out of Saudi Arabia was that the authorities had not only detained but had literally intimidated hundreds of online political activists and online commentators. The authorities had also filtered what they deemed to be "sensitive" political, religious, or pornographic content from entering the Saudi Internet, and they had allegedly gone to great lengths recruiting supporters online to "campaign against" calls for protests. It seems that in Saudi Arabia, Egypt's "revolution for democracy," which saw the 30-year rule of Hosni Mubarak come to an end, was called "the Facebook or Twitter revolution" because of how effectively hacktivists used the social media to spread their message online, even though there were a number of strong censoring countermeasures employed. The government's countermeasures included arresting dissidents, blocking Internet access when they deemed appropriate to do so, and restricting cellular phone networks.

Despite citizens' hopes in Egypt that things would improve, the report noted that it remains to be seen how the incoming president Mohamed Morsi will view Internet censorship following the very controlling era of Mubarak and the interim governing Supreme Council of the Armed Forces (SCAF). Apparently, the Internet, social media, and citizens' mobile phones remained under intense surveillance, bandwidth speeds were on "slow speed" for specific events, and SCAF-affiliated commentators continued to manipulate online discussions. Equally as bad, according to facts gathered by Freedom House, hacktivists and bloggers continued to be beaten, intimidated, or tried in military courts for allegedly "insulting the military power" or "disturbing social peace." Though President Morsi pledged to set free Egyptians who were subjected to unfair imprisonment, their fate and the future of Internet freedom in Egypt remain at high risk (Armstrong, 2012; Freedom House, 2012).

The report accorded 14 countries a positive trajectory rating, with Tunisia and Burma experiencing the largest improvements following dramatic political openings calling for broader institutions of democratic governance and the upholding of Internet freedom. However, a flicker of hope seemed to be blown out quickly by the start of 2013, particularly after the assassination of Chokri Belaid on February 6. Belaid was the leader of a Tunisian opposition alliance that had been highly critical of the ruling Islamist party. As a result of the many and highly volatile changes in government, many young people in Tunisia have become disillusioned by the country's faltering economy, an unemployment rate soaring over 17 percent, and the continued Islamist crackdowns on civil liberties and Internet freedom (Reguly, 2013).

In fact, some scholars have recently noted that with the visible instability of the government and economy in Tunisia, the cradle of the Arab Spring is now becoming a top exporter of Jihadist militants (Ben Bouazza and Schemm, 2013).

Online Activities in Jurisdictions "Under the Microscope": Their Strong Support for Internet Openness and Their Hard-Core Tactics Used to Reinforce Internet Censorship

Countries Supporting Internet Openness

According to the *Freedom on the Net 2012* editors, several countries—including the United States, Azerbaijan, and Russia—have been suggested to be, in various degrees, supporters of Internet openness, whereas other countries are clearly censorious. Let's take a closer look at the kind of detailed information Freedom House maintains and discloses to the public as a means of assessing Internet freedom in various countries (Freedom House, 2012).

The United States of America

The first example we will review is the United States. With a population of 314 million, the United States had an Internet penetration in 2011 of 78 percent. Web 2.0 applications were not blocked, there was no notable political censorship, there were no bloggers or Information and Communication Technology (ICT) users arrested, and status of press freedom was declared to be "free." Also, the Internet freedom status for both 2011 and 2012 was "free." On a scale from 0 through 100, where 0 indicated "most free" and 100 indicated "least free," the overall Internet freedom status for the United States was 13 in 2011 and 12 in 2012. This rating included assessment on "obstacles to Internet access" (the United States received a rating of 4 for both 2011 and 2012); "limits on Internet content" (received a rating of 2 for 2011 and 1 for 2012); and "violations of Internet user rights" (received a rating of 7 for both 2011 and 2012).

By definition, "obstacles to Internet access" assessed the infrastructural and economic barriers to Internet access; the government's attempts to block specific applications or technologies; and legal and regulatory ownership of and control over the Internet and mobile phone access providers. "Limits on Internet content" addressed the extent of filtering and blocking of certain Web sites, as well as other kinds of censorship and self-censorship. This definition included manipulating Web page content, limiting the diversity of online news media, and limiting digital media for various forms of hacktivism. Finally, "Violations of Internet user rights" assessed placing legal protections and restrictions on online activities, watching over the Internet's content, overriding principles of online privacy, doling out penalties for online activities deemed to be "inappropriate" or "offensive," and engaging in imprisoning, physically attacking, or harassing online users whose activities were deemed to be immoral, "offensive," or beyond established community standards of tolerance within a jurisdiction.

Given these combined ratings, in the United States Internet access is "open" and fairly "free," compared to that found in the rest of the world. The U.S. courts seem to have consistently upheld that prohibitions against the U.S. government's regulation of speech are applied to Internet content as well. There are some concerns, however, with regard to the U.S. government's voiced need to increase Internet surveillance through its recent attempts to pass the Stop Online Piracy Act (SOPA) and the Protect IP Act (PIPA) (Kelly, Cook, and Truong, 2012, 569–581).

As noted in Chapter 1, January 18, 2012, marked the largest online protest in the history of the Internet when Web sites of various sizes "went dark" in protest of the two U.S. Bills known as SOPA and PIPA (Goodman, 2013).

Azerbaijan

Azerbaijan is the next country we will review. With a population of 9.3 million, this country had an Internet penetration in 2011 of 50 percent. Web 2.0 applications were not blocked, and there was no notable political censorship. However, unlike the United States, there had been reports that certain Internet bloggers and ICT users were arrested. For this reason, the Freedom House report declared press freedom status to be "not free." The report ranked Azerbaijan at 48 in 2011 and 50 in 2012 on overall Internet freedom status, rating the country on "obstacles to Internet access" at 15 for 2011 and 13 for 2012; "limits on Internet content" at 15 for 2011 and 16 for 2012; and "violations of Internet user rights" at 18 for 2011 and 21 for 2012.

As host of the Internet Governance Forum held in November 2012, the government of Azerbaijan has been extremely keen to promote itself as an ICT innovator, but since that time, it has actually increased its restrictions on Internet freedom. Instead of actively promoting online content, this government has been prone to raid cyber cafes to gather data on user identities, put into prison politically active Internet users on trumped up charges, and harass hacktivists and their family members. Since that time, the government authorities also increased their surveillance capabilities of mobile phones (Kelly, Cook, and Truong, 2012, 53–64).

Russia

The third example we examine is Russia. With a population of 143 million, this country had an Internet penetration in 2011 of 49 percent. Web 2.0 applications were not blocked, and there was no notable political censorship. However, unlike the United States, there had been reports that certain Russian Internet bloggers and ICT users were arrested. For this reason, the Freedom House report declared press freedom status to be "not free." The report ranked Russia at 52 for both 2011 and 2012 on overall Internet freedom status, rating the country on "obstacles to Internet access" at 12 for 2011 and 11 for 2012; "limits on Internet content" at 17 for 2011 and 18 for 2012; and "violations of Internet user rights" at 23 for both 2011 and 2012.

In Russia, the Internet is the last somewhat uncensored public debate platform. However, the disappointing news is that since January 2011, massive distributed denial of service attacks (described in Chapter 1), as well as smear campaigns aimed at decreasing the credibility of hacktivists in Russia, have heightened. Moreover, after online tools played a key role in pulling together anti-government protests that surfaced at the end of 2011, the Kremlin said that it fully intends to tighten its control over Internet content and various forms of communications (Kelly, Cook, and Truong, 2012, 408–421).

Countries Using Hard-Core Tactics to Reinforce Internet Censorship

According to the *Freedom on the Net 2012* editors, several countries—including China, Iran, and Pakistan—seem to be, in various degrees, using hard-core tactics to reinforce Internet censorship.

China

Let's begin with China. With a population of 1.3 billion, this country had an Internet penetration in 2011 of 38 percent. Web 2.0 applications were blocked, there was notable political censorship, and there were reports that certain Chinese Internet bloggers and ICT users had been arrested. For this reason, the Freedom House report declared press freedom status to be "not free." The report ranked China at 83 for 2011 and 85 for 2012 on overall Internet freedom status, rating the country on "obstacles to Internet access" at 19 for 2011 and 18 for 2012; "limits on Internet content" at 28 for 2011 and 29 for 2012; and "violations of Internet user rights" at 36 for 2011 and 38 for 2012.

Though China is home to the world's biggest population of Internet users, it is also one of the most restrictive regimes when it comes to the Internet. Lately, the government seems to be increasingly more restrictive. In terms of human rights violations, in 2011, the government authorities kidnapped dozens of hacktivists and bloggers, held them "incommunicado" for weeks on end, and sentenced a number of them to lengthy prison terms. Moreover, the Chinese government has increased controls over popular micro-blogging platforms like Sina Weibo and pressured important companies like Google to increase their censorship of political content. The Chinese authorities have also told businesses using the Internet to register online users' real names and not fake names. Other countries like Belarus, Uzbekistan, and Iran see China as a terrific role model for developing stringent Internet controls in their jurisdictions (Kelly, Cook, and Truong, 2012, 126–151).

Iran

The second country that we'll observe as Internet restrictive is Iran. With a population of 79 million, this country had an Internet penetration in 2011 of only 21 percent. Web 2.0 applications were blocked, there was notable political censorship, and (like China) there had been reports that certain Iranian Internet bloggers and ICT users were arrested. For this reason, the Freedom House report declared press freedom status to be "not free." The report ranked Iran at 89 for 2011 and 90 for 2012 on overall Internet freedom status, rating the country on "obstacles to Internet access" at 21 for both 2011 and 2012; "limits on Internet content" at 29 for 2011 and 32 for 2012; and "violations of Internet user rights" at 39 for 2011 and 37 for 2012.

After the disputed government elections in 2009, the Iranian authorities began to clamp down on Internet censorship. The Iranian authorities employed a wide range of hard-core tactics, including upgrading content-filtering technologies, "cracking" digital certificates to undermine online users' privacy, and taking steps to create a national Internet that would be under the government's strict censoring eye. Rated as likely the world's harshest disseminator of prison sentences for online users' behaviors perceived to exceed the community standards of tolerance, Iran is known to have imposed the death penalty on at least three online bloggers and IT professionals (Kelly, Cook, and Truong, 2012, 262–278).

Pakistan

The third country we review as Internet censorious is Pakistan. With a population of 180 million, this country had an Internet penetration in 2011 of only 9 percent. Web 2.0 applications were not blocked, but there was notable political censorship, and like China, there had been reports that certain Pakistani Internet bloggers and ICT users were arrested. For this reason, the Freedom House report declared press freedom status to be "not free." The report ranked Pakistan at 53 for 2011 and 63 for 2012 on overall Internet freedom status, rating the country on "obstacles to Internet access" at 16 for 2011 and 19 for 2012; "limits on Internet content" at 17 for 2011 and 18 for 2012; and "violations of Internet user rights at 22 for 2011 and 26 for 2012.

Some rather unsettling recent developments regarding the Internet in Pakistan have included a ban on encryption and virtual private networks. There was also a reported death sentence issued for an online user's alleged "blasphemous" text message, and there was a reported one-day block by the government authorities on all mobile phone networks in the Balochistan province. Other steps used by the Pakistani authorities to increase Internet censorship included a plan to filter text messages by keyword, as well as a proposal to develop a nationwide Internet firewall. However, these two ideas were put on hold as a result of effective civil society advocacy campaigns. The thought remains among online users in Pakistan, however, that the government authorities are continuing to make plans to filter key messages by keyword and to develop a nationwide Internet firewall. (Kelly, Cook, and Truong, 2012, 386–399).

The Role of Web Filters and Firewalls, Business-Government Policies, and Laws Aimed at Internet Censorship

Web Filters and Firewalls

In this section, we will discuss how various countries and jurisdictions use Web filters, business-government policies, and laws aimed at preventing the flow of information over the Internet. In earlier days, the Internet was affectionately known as the Information Superhighway because it was supposed to let the average online user navigate quickly through the contents of various Web pages on a myriad of topics. Those were the good old days. Nowadays, depending on the jurisdiction that online users are in, there could be some major roadblocks along the "Information Superhighway" that prevent easy navigation—or any navigation at all.

On the basis of the types and number of controls implemented to engage in Internet censorship, the editors of *Freedom on the Net 2012* classify countries in one of three categories (Kelly, Cook, and Truong, 2012, 3–4):

1. **Blockers**: Here, the government blocks a large number of politically relevant Web sites and certain social media platforms. The government also places considerable resources into hiring people with the right kind of talent and technical capacities to identify "offensive" content that should be

blocked. Countries considered to be "blockers" include Bahrain, China, Ethiopia, Iran, Saudi Arabia, Vietnam, Syria, Thailand, and Uzbekistan. Blocking and filtering are the key tools for implementing Internet Censorship in these jurisdictions, but the authorities have used intense pressure on bloggers and Internet Service Providers, they have hired pro-government commentators to advance their positions, and they arrested online users posting comments deemed to be critical of the authorities.

2. **Non-blockers:** Here, the government is not yet at the stage of systematically blocking politically relevant Web sites, although the authorities may have already restricted online content, especially after noticing the critical role that online tools can play in overturning the political "status quo." Typically, the authorities like to show that they respect "Internet Freedom" and openness, so they tend to use less visible or less traceable censorship tactics. They may engage in, for example, "anonymous" cyberattacks targeting influential news sites at the "right" political moment. Moreover, these jurisdictions may adopt a harsh legal framework around free speech; it is not unlikely, in fact, that online users who post information critical of the government will find themselves charged, detained, or arrested. Countries placing in this category include Azerbaijan, Egypt, Jordan, Malaysia, Venezuela, and Zimbabwe.

3. **Nascent blockers**: Here, the governments appear to be at a crossroad; though the authorities impose politically motivated blocks, the blocks tend to be sporadic, and the blocking system is far from being institutionalized. Countries placing in this category include Belarus, Sri Lanka, Pakistan, and Russia. In Russia, for example, the government authorities officially block content considered to promote "extremism" but because of the range attributable to this term, political Web sites tend to be blocked as well. Moreover, other jurisdictions like Pakistan have given serious thought to

instituting filtering of the Internet nationwide, but because this effort has not yet transpired, Pakistan is presently considered to be a "nascent blocker" rather than a "blocker."

It is quite clear that the motivations for Internet censorship vary from country to country, ranging from the blocking of, say, content unsuitable for and should not be seen by minors (which is what parents also commonly do to prevent their children from viewing Web sites with pornography, gambling, hate speech or chat rooms) to completely controlling a nation's access to information online. There are several software products on the market that can limit or block access to specific Web sites and are known as Web filters. For the home buyer, for example, popular Web filter software include Net Nanny and CYBERsitter, which has 35 filter categories that parents can select from. Individuals against any form of Internet censorship label blocking filters as "censorware" (Strickland, 2013).

Most Web filters use two main techniques to block content (Strickland, 2013):

1. **Blacklists**: Lists of Web sites that the Web filter's creators have designated as undesirable. The list tends to change over time, so most companies marketing this software offer updated lists free of cost. The bottom line is once this software is installed any attempt to visit a blocked site fails.

2. **Keyword Blocking**: With keyword blocking, the software actually scans a Web page as the user tries to visit it. The program quickly analyzes the Web page to determine if certain keywords exist, and if the program determines that the Web page is inappropriate, it blocks users' access to the page.

Another common option for blocking content is installing a firewall. In essence, a computer firewall provides protection from dangerous or undesirable content. Firewalls can be either software or hardware, and their purpose is to act as a barrier between the Internet and the computer network. Firewalls are designed to allow only safe content through and to prevent everything else from entering the network. Implementing and maintaining a firewall requires considerable IT skill, and for this reason, businesses and government agencies employ network administrators. In short, firewalls contain rule sets that either grant or deny traffic flowing into or out of a network; simply put, firewalls are to the perimeter of a network what a moat and wall were to a castle (Schell and Martin, 2006).

Business-Government Policies and Laws for Internet Censorship

There is no question that if companies want to do business in various countries and jurisdictions, they have to be careful to abide by the host nation's policies and laws pertaining to Internet freedom, openness, and censorship. Let's face it: businesses and government agencies alike rely on firewalls as well as Web filtering software. Thus, by using firewalls, both can literally pick and choose which Web pages or even entire domains to block. This way, companies and government agencies can avoid blocking Web sites that employees or citizens need to access legitimately. Even in countries deemed to be "free," when an online user tries to access a restricted Web site, the user will see a message that typically includes the option of petitioning the network administrator to unblock access if that user feels the Web site is wrongfully blocked. Afterward, the network administrator can adjust which Web sites are restricted through firewall settings (Strickland, 2013).

Further, in blocking various Web sites, government agencies rely on cooperation from businesses like telecom and cable companies, for they play a critical role in determining what content customers or citizens can access on the Internet—which is, by the way, an ongoing debate in jurisdictions worldwide. For example, in the United States, there is an ongoing debate over a concept called *net neutrality*, which refers to a so-called level playing ground where Internet service providers (ISPs) allow users to access to all content without favoring any particular Web site. There are, of course, opponents to this concept, and in the United States, telecom and cable companies have successfully petitioned the Supreme Court to dismiss it. Without net neutrality, ISPs can charge content providers a fee for bandwidth usage so that the content providers paying the fee will have greater broadband access. With more broadband access, such Web sites load faster compared to those of competitors who choose not to pay the fee. So, let's say that Yahoo! paid the fee to an ISP but Google chose not to; consequently, the ISP's clients would find that Yahoo!'s search engine loads much more quickly than Google's. Proponents of net neutrality maintain that such preferential treatment is simply Internet censorship. Recently, as we have noted in these first two chapters, search engine companies like Yahoo! and Google have been criticized by censorship opponents for helping restrictive countries like China to maintain control of the Internet. However, although the companies have their headquarters in the United States, they still need to obey local government restrictions elsewhere if they want to do business in any jurisdiction (Strickland, 2013).

Moreover, one would be naïve to think that any country is totally "free" from Internet censorship, for even democratic countries restrict access to content on the Internet at some level. Though labeled "free," even the United States has laws (such as the Children's Internet Protection Act) that impact the kind of information that citizens can access on the Internet, even in public spaces like schools or public libraries. And as we have seen in this chapter, some countries are much more restrictive when it comes to Internet freedom and openness, while other countries promote few Internet content restrictions.

The OpenNet Initiative, an organization dedicated to letting the public know about Web filtering and surveillance policies globally, classifies Web filtering into four categories consistent with the tenets of prevailing laws in any given jurisdiction (Strickland, 2013):

1. **Political**: Content belonging to Web sites that include views counter to the respective country's policies regarding the Internet and allowable content. This category also includes Web site content related to human rights, religious movements, and other causes of a social nature.

2. **Social**: Content belonging to Web sites that focus on sexuality, gambling, drugs, and other social-cultural issues that a country's authorities may find "offensive."

3. **Conflict/Security**: Content belonging to Web sites relating to wars, skirmishes, overt dissent, and other conflicts occurring either within a nation or in some other nation.

4. **Internet tools**: Content belonging to Web sites offering tools like email, instant messaging, and language translation applications and those aimed at circumventing censorship.

Some democratic countries like Australia—deemed by Freedom House to be "free" with an Internet freedom score of 18—and the United Kingdom—also deemed by Freedom House to be "free" with a score of 25—are fairly liberal with their government-business policies and laws, restricting a minimum of Web pages. Yet other countries, such as China and Iran, have more restrictive government-business policies and laws and are deemed by Freedom House to be "not free." As noted, China's advanced filtering system known internationally as the Great Firewall is intensely restrictive, and it can actually search new Web pages and restrict access in real time. This advanced filtering system can also search blogs for subversive content and block Internet users from visiting them. Finally, it is a little-known fact that Cuba has very restrictive Internet policies and laws; there, private Internet access is banned completely, and online users wanting to access the Internet must go to a public access point (Kelly, Cook, and Truong, 2012; Strickland, 2013).

The Internet's Continuing Evolution: A Comparison of Internet Censorship in 2005 and 2012

The Internet's State of Openness in 2005

How far has the battle against Internet censorship come in the past eight years or so? To help us answer this question, Charles Gimon gives us a glance at Internet censorship trends and practices around the world in 2005—five years after the United States passed the Children's Internet Protection Act, which introduced Web filters in schools. Gimon asked this important question: what are other countries doing to censor their citizens, or to protect free speech in their bits of cyberspace? And then he answered it, as follows (Gimon, 2005):

- In many countries, the Internet is still so new that censorship isn't an issue yet. In others, computer networking and email aren't on the same level as they are in North America, East Asia, Europe, or even Chile or Turkey. For example, in Sri Lanka, email is delivered to a Web site outside of Sri Lanka; it then is transmitted through a uucp network over regular telephone lines. When email has to be delivered to a Web site outside of Sri Lanka, it has to go over an expensive long-distance call from Colombo to Stanford University in the United States. Because of the expense of sending email, Sri Lankan email users are strongly encouraged not to send long or "frivolous" emails. Moreover, in Sri Lanka, transferring any image via the Internet—pornographic or not—is forbidden. In fact, the cost of sending or receiving images on the Internet is more effective than the government's having direct interference through, say, Internet Censorship measures.

- Full Internet service has just opened in Beijing, China, but it carries just a little over 1,000 Usenet groups on its news server, and a post sent to Usenet from Beijing warned that "some sensitive newsgroups are locked out."

- In Malaysia, newsgroups carrying discussions or images against the law in this jurisdiction are shut down. In fact, the "Acceptable Use Policy" for the Internet at Jaring, the main Malaysian Internet backbone, states that "members shall not use Jaring network for any activities not allowed under any Law of Malaysia. Given that Malaysian censors are debating whether the children's movie 'Casper' should be permitted into the country, the potential for Internet Censorship here appears to be high."

- In Singapore, the Minister for Information and Arts said in a speech that "the act of censorship is symbolic and an affirmation of the values we hold as a community." Government censors tried to stop un-encoded binaries of any kind from coming into Singapore, certain overseas Web sites were blocked to on-line users in Singapore, and officials talked about the likelihood of suing critics for libel and slander on the newsgroup soc.culture.singapore. And, believe it or not, virtually chewing gum in this jurisdiction could lead to a real-time caning.

- In the United Kingdom, legislation was being discussed that would give Internet providers "common carrier status"— meaning that the Web site would not be responsible for the actions of its users. In New Zealand, a pending Technology and Crimes bill would have punished "every person . . . who casts, transmits, communicates, or receives through any means, any objectionable image, or sound" regardless of whether individuals have knowledge that the said item is "objectionable" or not. And in Canada, graphic information about the infamous Karla Homolka murder trial (involving the sexual assault and cold-blood killing of two Canadian school girls) continued to be available on the Internet, despite a total press ban by a judge presiding on the case. As long as Internet messages were routed through the United States or elsewhere, and as long as the information was stored outside Canada, Internet users could render the Canadian press ban powerless.

The Internet's State of Openness in 2012

Now, flash forward to 2012. What did Freedom House say about how far along many of these jurisdictions have come in terms of Internet freedom? Let's look at some scores and rankings for the present time frame (Kelly, Cook, and Truong, 2012):

- With a population of 21 million people, Sri Lanka still has only a 15 percent Internet penetration. Though, nowadays, the country is considered to be "partly free" with a Freedom House total score of 55, the country does not block Web 2.0 applications, but there is notable political censorship, and bloggers and ICT users are being arrested. For this reason, Sri Lanka's press freedom status remains as "not free."

- Earlier, we noted that China remains one of the most censorious governments in the world, and their Internet freedom status remains as "not free." What is more, if the Chinese authorities do not like the online coverage that other countries' online businesses give news events, present-day China may have its hackers invade those networks. For example, in January and February 2013, Facebook said that their network had been the target of a series of sophisticated hack attacks. Twitter said that they also were hacked during this same period, noting that about 250,000 user accounts were potentially affected. And newspaper Web sites including *The New York Times*, *The Washington Post*, and *The Wall Street Journal* were similarly infiltrated; their network administrators attributed the hack attacks to Chinese hackers targeting their alleged "offensive" coverage of China (Reuters, 2013).

- Malaysia, with a population of 29 million, seems to be improving in terms of Internet freedom. Internet penetration for 2011 was 61 percent. Currently, Web 2.0 applications are not blocked, and there is no notable political censorship. However, because Malaysian bloggers and ICT users are being arrested, the country's press freedom status remains at "not free," and the Internet freedom status for 2012 was "partly free." The total Internet freedom score for 2011 was 41 and was downgraded to 43 for 2012.

- Singapore, New Zealand, and Canada did not receive Internet freedom status ratings in 2012, so we cannot comment further for these countries.

- The United Kingdom did well in 2011 and 2012 in terms of Internet freedom. With a population of 63 million, the United Kingdom had an Internet penetration of 82 percent in 2011. Currently, there is no Web 2.0 applications blockage, there is no notable political censorship, and there are no British bloggers or ICT users being arrested. Therefore, the press freedom status is "free" and the Internet freedom status is marked "free" (with an overall score of 25 for both 2011 and 2012).

Key Tactics That Have Restricted Free Speech and Encouraged Internet Censorship in Countries in Recent Years

Clearly, pushing for Internet openness in various jurisdictions is an ongoing challenge. In the section above, we looked at some changes in a few jurisdictions from which we had data for 2005 and 2012, noting that some "light" at the end of the tunnel of Internet openness was seen in a few jurisdictions, but that many other jurisdictions still had serious obstacles. However, according to Freedom House (2012), there appears to be a shifting set of tactics used by various governments worldwide to control the free flow of information online. Although blocking and filtering the content of Web sites are two of the preferred methods of restricting citizens' access to online content, some countries are increasingly using the following four tools to put the lid on political and social speech deemed "offensive," in excess of established community standards, or as intentionally offending the existing authority structure and its ruling beliefs and policies. These alternative tactics include the following four major categories (Kelly, Cook, and Truong, 2012):

1. Governments introducing vague laws prohibiting certain types of online content
2. Governments proactively manipulating Internet discussions so as to reflect their followings
3. Governments arranging for actual physical attacks to occur against bloggers and other Internet users whose speech is deemed to be "offensive" and "inappropriate"
4. Governments arranging for increased surveillance of citizens' online activities

Governments Introduce Vague Laws Prohibiting Certain Online Content

Dismayed by the details of some recent user-generated content finding its way onto the Internet—such as the confidential U.S. military material posted online by the anonymous hacker cells in cooperation with Private Bradley Manning—governments have tried to pass new legislation to regulate online speech and prescribe harsher penalties for those found violating a so-called established set of rules. Although some governments tout the passage of these new vague laws as a means of maintaining national security and keeping their online citizens safe from, say, online pornographers or spammers, these laws are generally viewed by legal experts and those espousing information freedom and free speech as overly broad. In short, they are so broadly worded that they can easily be used against political opponents—at least those perceived to be so by the authorities.

For example, even in countries like the United States—which has been assessed by Freedom House to be Internet open and supportive of free speech—it took massive online campaigns by civil society groups and technology companies to stop the recent attempts at the passage of the SOPA and the PIPA—which were seen by citizen groups to have an adverse impact on free speech and on the further healthy development of the Internet. These two U.S. bills were designed to stop the privacy of copyrighted material over the Internet on Web sites based outside of the United States. Then, on Wednesday, January 18, 2012 (as noted in Chapter 1), the real world and the virtual world watched the largest protest in the history of the Internet. "Connected" onlookers around the globe, governments and citizens alike, saw the extreme effectiveness of the concurrent "blacking out" of popular Web sites—a protest viewed by Americans as a means of increasing the public's awareness of the two proposed bills. What is more, the world listened when many of the Internet giants, like Google, Wikipedia, and Twitter, argued that these U.S. laws, if passed, would stifle innovation and investment in the Internet—a global concern, even in the developing nations (Goodman, 2013). Needless to say, the tactic of the massive online protest had an immediate effect, for it has since been repeated in countries like Jordan and Italy when the authorities were considering potentially restrictive legislation regarding online activities.

Furthermore, with the 2013 death of 26-year-old American hacktivist Aaron Swartz—who committed suicide just before his hacker trial was to commence—lawyers and Internet freedom activists in the United States have begun to question overly broad older U.S. legislation, such as the Computer Fraud and Abuse Act. According to Freedom House (2012), in largely democratic settings worldwide, the courts have begun to play a key role in defending Internet freedom and in overturning older pieces of legislation that may infringe upon it. For example, in Hungary, the Constitutional Court decided in December 2011 that its restrictive new media regulations would not apply to online news sources and portals, and in South Korea in August 2012 the Constitutional Court issued its third positive decision favoring Internet freedom over a two-year period.

However, in countries where the judiciary is not independent, internal public pressures and international pressures have resulted in executive branch decisions nullifying negative court rulings. For example, in Azerbaijan, Bahrain, China, Egypt, Syria, Russia, and Saudi Arabia, at least each jailed blogger or hacktivist was pardoned or released from detention as a result of high-profile Internet campaigns. There have also been some exceptionally good news as a result of hugely successful Internet campaigns, as in Myanmar (Burma), where dozens of online activists were released after their cases were heard under very restrictive laws which had landed them in jail.

As noted earlier, since 2011, China has emerged as "the major incubator" for employing sophisticated new types of tactics restricting Internet access. For example, a prime method for controlling social media content in China is to restrict access to international networks, while simultaneously forcing domestic counterparts to heavily censor and monitor users' online communications based on Communist Party standards and directives. This censorious activity has been viewed, however, positively in countries like Iran, Ethiopia, Libya, Sri Lanka— whose authorities have apparently asked China for assistance in this regard. Besides China, authoritarian countries like Russia, Tajikistan, and Uzbekistan have in 2011 submitted a proposal to the UN General Assembly calling for an Internet code of conduct which would, for example, legitimize the censoring of any Web site that is perceived by authorities to undermine political and social order.

Governments Proactively Manipulate Internet Discussions to Reflect Their Views

According to Freedom House (2012), countries where progovernment commentators heavily manipulate Internet discussions to reflect the governments' views have included Bahrain, Belarus, China, Cuba, Egypt, Ethiopia, Iran, Malaysia, Russia, Saudi Arabia, Syria, Thailand, Ukraine, and Venezuela. Besides using filters and real-life hackers to censor "inappropriate" online content of citizens, a growing number of governments—such as those just cited—are paying commentators to manipulate online discussions, say in chat rooms. This tactic seems to have spread from 2010 to 2012, with Freedom House seeing an increase in these types of tactics in 14 of the 47 countries studied.

These paid commentators tend not to reveal their "official links" when they do their online posts. Also, it is likely not surprising that the government authorities engaging in these types of tactics tend not to tell their tax-paying citizens that some of their money is being spent in this way. Then, there are the countries like Cuba that seem to hire hundreds, if not thousands, of bloggers to spread online nasty rumors about the personal lives of the country's influential but government-independent bloggers. Exactly how many resources are put into such manipulative tactics worldwide is not known, but an Iranian official apparently revealed to Freedom House that in mid-2011, about 40 companies received well over $56 million to create digital content that was clearly pro-government and that accurately reflected the government's views.

Furthermore, while government-independent bloggers and overly political news Web sites are favorite targets for governments engaging in online manipulation, some hijackings or online impersonations have targeted influential citizens. For example, since August 2011, the blogs and Twitter accounts of at least 24 prominent citizens and government critics in Venezuela have been hacked and hijacked. The professionals targeted have included journalists, artists, writers, and economists. The content posted in their names supports the government's economic policies, criticizes opposition leaders, or issues threats to other online users who are not behaving "appropriately."

Governments Arrange for Actual Physical Attacks to Occur against Bloggers and Other Internet Users Whose Speech Is Deemed to Be "Offensive" and "Inappropriate"

According to Freedom House (2012), countries where critics of the authorities have been victims of physical abuse or have been killed include Azerbaijan, Bahrain, Burma, China, Cuba, Egypt, Indonesia, Iran, Jordan, Kazakhstan, Libya, Mexico, Pakistan, Saudi Arabia, Sri Lanka, Syria, Thailand, Uzbekistan, and Vietnam. According to their study results, Freedom House concluded that in 19 of the 47 countries assessed in 2012, a blogger or Internet user was the victim of torture, brutal assault, or a mysterious disappearance. What is more, at least five reporters or activists were killed in these regions in retaliation for some information that they posted online exposing human rights abuses in that jurisdiction.

For example, in China, after online calls in February 2011 for a Tunisian-like Jasmine Revolution, 20 or more bloggers, lawyers, and other popular online activists were kidnapped—some were detained and sentenced to long prison sentences, while others were held "incommunicado" and then released (Freedom House, 2012). There are consistent stories about the victims being beaten, being deprived of sleep, suffering from bad health with no medical assistance, and being otherwise abused. Furthermore, in Bahrain, the moderator of a popular online forum was killed in police custody in April 2011, within a week of his arrest—with a commission of inquiry later confirming that his death resulted from painful torture. There is also an increasing trend of bloggers and citizen journalists being targeted by security forces when they are reporting from the field, particularly on citizen-related conflicts and political unrest. For example, in Libya and Syria, citizen journalists held in high regard by their online comrades—with some even reaching international prominence—were killed in cold blood by government forces. And in Kazakhstan, a blogger was allegedly assaulted by police holding a gun to his head after he uploaded a video to YouTube showing local residents protesting a government crackdown. Furthermore, in some countries, attacks by non-state actors have occurred without punishment by government authorities; for example, in Thailand, a professor advocating a campaign to stop more restrictive legislation was assaulted by a pair of unidentified people in an incident that human rights groups believe was somehow related to his advocacy.

According to Freedom House (2012), authorities in some jurisdictions use less extreme tactics—intimidation of victims—having more evasive manifestations. In countries like Bahrain, Cuba, Turkey, and Thailand, for example, individuals have been fired from jobs, restricted from universities, or banned from traveling outside of the country after they posted comments criticizing the government. Also, the various forms of intimidation, particularly in China, may extend to the target's family. News Web sites or free expression online groups have been subject to various attack tactics. For example, in Venezuela, the offices of a civil society group actively defending online freedom of expression were burglarized twice, and in Sri Lanka, a fire was set to the offices of a popular online news site that supported the president's main competitor in the 2010 election.

Governments Arrange for Increased Surveillance of Citizens' Online Activities

According to Freedom House (2012), of the 19 countries that passed new legislation adversely impacting Internet freedom in 2011 and early 2012, 12 bolstered their surveillance of citizens' online activities, or their authorities were planning to do so. Accepting that most countries—even democracies like the United States and the United Kingdom—have been known to intercept online communications as a means of, say, preventing terrorist attacks, Freedom House found that in far too many countries surveillance powers are clearly being abused for political objectives. Having said this, in recent times, even in democratic settings, lawyers have effectively argued that issue of warrants and other protocols have not been adhered to before snooping into online users' information.

In the highly repressive yet technically sophisticated countries, authorities have been found to engage in bulk monitoring of online communications—often through a central point.

Various intelligence agencies working for the state can then obtain access to online users' communications across a variety of platforms, including but not limited to mobile phone conversations, email messages, users' browsing histories, text and instant messaging histories, and VoIP discussions. According to Freedom House (2012), the most advanced systems are actually capable of scanning the network traffic in real time; this task is accomplished using preset keywords or email addresses of particular interest to government authorities. Increasingly, voice recognition software is being used in jurisdictions to scan for sensitive keywords or targeted individuals' voices. Moreover, ISPs may be required to keep data and online content on targets and then turn such in to authorities when requested to do so. While in most authoritarian countries authorities can intercept communications or obtain requested information with a judicial warrant, in most democratic countries, a court warrant is required to access online user information.

Given the anonymous nature of the Internet, however, authorities with moderate technological capability are still finding that they face obstacles in tracing a particular message to its author. To overcome this obstacle, a number of countries have recently passed regulations requiring online users to use their real names and not some other moniker. In China, for example, major micro-blogging services had a March 2012 deadline to start implementing real-name registration for their online users if they were not already doing so. Also, Kazakhstan, Saudi Arabia, and Syria recently passed regulations increasing restrictions on user anonymity. In other countries deemed to be more democratic—such as India and Mexico—regulations passed within the last 18 months have increased the authority of security and intelligence agencies to intercept communications even without a court order. However, even when a judge's permission is required by law, approval may at times be granted almost automatically because of a lack of judicial independence. According to Freedom House (2012), for example, Indonesia has nine different laws authorizing surveillance, with each law setting a different standard of accountability—and with only a subset of these laws actually requiring judicial approval.

All of this discussion merely points to the obvious: the growth in surveillance in various jurisdictions (as evidenced by the clandestine mass electronic data mining program launched in 2007 by the National Security Agency in the United States and that Canada set up spy posts to assist the Agency in their efforts) adds to the reality that even in countries advocating for an Open Internet, netizens worry that their privacy is being overtly or inadvertently violated—if not abused by their governments. According to Freedom House (2012), numerous countries have had internationally reported scandals in recent years with political authorities misusing their powers to either spy on opponents or engage in bouts of extortion. As a case in point, in April 2012, Mexico's Geolocation Law went into effect, giving law enforcement agencies and lower-level public servants the ability to get access to mobile phone users' data without a warrant. What is more unnerving is that they are able to access this data in real time. Although this piece of legislation was likely passed to nab drug traffickers and other most-wanted criminals, online citizens, understandably so, feared that the data could and would fall into the wrong hands of authority. This fear is not unfounded, for previously collected data on mobile phone users mysteriously found its way for sale online.

Furthermore, even in democratic jurisdictions, note the editors at Freedom House (2012), where minimal surveillance exists, online citizens fear that the government may pass laws and regulations to increase their surveillance capabilities. These fears were evident in 2012 when the U.K. government announced its proposal to expand its existing surveillance measures by requiring ISPs to maintain the particulars of customers' social networking activities, email messages, Internet calls, and online gaming activities for a year.

In the United States, controversial provisions in the PATRIOT Act once again appeared on the public radar screen in the Spring of 2011, causing concern among online users and information freedom groups. The U.S. Congress hastily passed the anti-terrorist USA PATRIOT Act in 2001, within seven weeks of the 9/11 attacks on the World Trade Center. Since its passage, this piece of legislation has long been the subject of fierce debate over the balance between civil liberties and national security. Besides other measures, the act expanded government search and surveillance authority. After the passage of the PATRIOT Act, Attorney General John Ashcroft sent to some of his government colleagues a draft of the PATRIOT II Act, also known as the Domestic Security Enhancement Act of 2003. Had this piece of legislation been passed, it would have had more than 100 provisions intensifying measures against cyber terrorists. Public outcry killed its passage (Schell, 2007).

Finally, legal ambiguities regarding companies' and governments' data stored in the "cloud" have prompted concerns among experts that increased surveillance capabilities may be looming on the horizon (Kalyani, 2014).

How Can Progress Continue to Be Made in Reducing Internet Censorship?

Is more laws the answer? Or should more effective technological solutions be used? No, say experts, to the first question, because new laws tend to be more restrictive rather than open (Strickland, 2013).

Moreover, regarding technology, there is currently a debate going on between those who believe that technology is a great equalizer and those who fear that even in developed nations, technology may not only fail to produce more Internet openness but actually put an end to the middle class as we know it today. Likely the dividing line is between those who think that the tech revolution will continue to bring in *hyper-change*, carrying with it data transfer speeds beyond our imagination toward ever newer technologically shaped realities *indistinguishable from magic*, and those who think more along the lines of the Luddites, who feared that the Industrial Revolution would result in structural unemployment. For example, Lawrence Summers, former president of Harvard University and former U.S. secretary of the treasury, recently remarked at the World Economic Forum in Switzerland: "As economists like to explain, the system will equilibrate at full employment. But maybe the way it will equilibrate at full employment is there'll be specialists at cleaning the shallow end and the deep end of rich people's swimming pools. And that's a problematic way for society to function" (Freeland, 2013, B2).

So, is totally banking on technology the sole answer for conquering the great divide and Internet censorship? Probably not. Furthermore, as has been obvious over the last 40 years, as the Internet has evolved from its humble beginnings throughout its adulthood, it has become abundantly clear that *humans* make decisions about censorship, not technologies—regardless of their rapid speed of growth. In short, note the freedom fighter experts, although individual heroes continue to fight Internet censorship, either in a premeditated fashion or via happenstance, the bottom line is that there need to be the following factors working in tandem (Strickland, 2013):

1. An increase in a strategic analysis of transitions in the post-communist world

2. A strategic increase in policies worldwide advancing human rights and democracy

3. A strategic direction in terms of action—with an increase in the training and support of human rights defenders, civil society organizations, and members of the media to strengthen reform efforts in countries around the world

A group of hackers, on the other hand, think that they have come up with another solution not commonly considered by lawyers and those in the mainstream for fighting Internet censorship. They plan to fight back with their own satellite communications system. According to a report on the BBC, the plan was outlined in 2012 at the Chaos Communication Congress in Hamburg. Dubbed the Hackerspace Global Grid, the project apparently calls for the launching of a satellite into space and the development of a grid of ground stations on earth to track and communicate with the satellites. Although this strategy sounds a bit like science fiction, it was apparently a response to Internet censorship threats such as proposed legislation like SOPA. Hacker activist Nick Farr said that the first goal of the grid should be to take the Internet out of the control of terrestrial entities. Alan Woodward, a computer science professor at the University of Surrey, however, cautioned that though this grid sounds like an interesting solution to Internet censorship, the reality is that there is an interesting legal dimension in that outer space is *not* governed by the countries over which it floats. So, theoretically, outer space could be a place for illegal communications and Internet censorship to thrive, for any country could take the law into its own hands and disable the satellites (Prince, 2012).

Conclusion

This chapter discussed the trials and tribulations occurring around the growth of the Internet in various jurisdictions, starting from its humble beginnings in the United States and through its evolution in its adulthood—when concerns about Internet censorship began to surface worldwide. The issue of criminal liability was then discussed, with a fulsome coverage of the recent case involving Private Manning's expression of Internet freedom during the Iraq War.

On the basis of the *Freedom on the Net 2012*, some countries were identified in this chapter as "free" and "open," while others were identified as "not free" and censorious. This chapter looked at the various factors involved in the free and censorious ends of the equation, and cited many examples of countries that have taken identifiable stands on why the

Internet should be free or censored—and the measures that they have incorporated to ensure that such is the outcome.

From a worldwide perspective, a debate on how free and how open the Internet should be will, obviously, continue. According to some experts, decreasing Internet censorship on a global basis will require more activism, more increases in strategic policies to advance human rights and democracy, and more strategic action in terms of training and supporting human rights defenders. According to a group of hackers, a satellite network might be able to hold Internet censorship at check. Given that the world is a forever-evolving political and technological sphere, the same can be said about the challenges of the ongoing evolution of the Internet.

Although there is an open commitment to advancing human rights and democracy in some jurisdictions—such as the United States and Estonia—other countries will continue to challenge the degree and transparency of such commitments. For example, on October 23, 2012, The Voice of Russia pronounced, in a 63-page white paper entitled "On the Human Rights in the USA," that the U.S. government, along with private companies in that jurisdiction, seem to be actually *increasing* Internet censorship, not arresting it. The Voice of Russia stressed, as well, that the First Amendment to the U.S. Constitution does not allow authorities to openly crack down on the freedom of speech—which makes the U.S. authorities go about it in crafty other ways—such as exerting control over the ISPs, basically an indirect form of Internet censorship (Voice of Russia, 2012).

References

Armstrong, P. "Big brother still watching: Internet censorship on the up, report says." 2012, http://www.cnn.com/2012/09/27/world/world-internet-freedom-report (accessed September 28).

Bambauer, D. "The enigma of Internet freedom." 2010, http://infousa.state.gov/media/internet/docs/defining-internet-freedom.pdf (accessed June).

Bambauer, D., and R. Epstein. "Who's right? Debating Internet censorship." 2010, http://photos.state.gov/libraries/amgov/30145/publications-english/EJ-defining-internet-freedom.pdf (accessed June).

Ben Bouazza, B., and P. Schemm. Jihadists spring from Tunisian chaos. *The Globe and Mail*, 2013, p. A11.

Brenner, S. W. "Is there such a thing as 'virtual crime'?" *California Criminal Law Review, 4* (2001), pp. 1–12. http://www.boalt.org/CCLR/v4/v4brenner.htm (accessed April 2012).

Cassata, D., and N. Benac. "US tracking millions of calls." *The Globe and Mail*, June 7, 2013, p. A3.

Clark, C. "US surveillance: Secret—and sweeping." *The Globe and Mail*, June 8, 2013, p. A11.

Cohn, M. "Bradley manning's legal duty to expose war crimes." 2013, http://smirkingchimp.com/thread/marjorie-cohn/49869/bradley-mannings-legal-duty-to-expose-war-crimes (accessed June 4).

Computer Industry Almanac. "Worldwide Internet users top 1.8 billion in 2009. China tops 310M Internet users." 2010, http://www.c-i-a.com/pr072010.htm (accessed July 12).

Computer Industry Almanac. "PC sales will top 370M in 2011: Worldwide mobile PC sales to reach 227 M units." 2011, http://www.c-i-a.com/pr072011.htm (accessed July 25).

Computer Industry Almanac. "PCs in-use reached over 1.6B in 2011: USA has nearly 311M PCs in-use." 2012, http://www.c-i-a.com/pr02012012.htm (accessed February 1).

Dishneau, D. "Army likens Manning case to Civil War espionage." 2013, http://www.military.com/daily-news/

2013/01/10/army-likens-manning-case-to-civil-war
-espionage.html (accessed January 10).

Freedom House. "New report: Governments grow increasingly
repressive online, activists fight back." 2012, http://www
.freedomhouse.org/article/new-report-governments-grow
-increasingly-repressive-online-activists-fight-back (accessed
November 11).

Freeland, C. "A tech-powered end to the middle class." *The
Globe and Mail*, February 22, 2013, p. B2.

Gimon, C. A. "Internet censorship around the world." 2013,
http://www.gimonca.com/personal/archive/foreign.html
(accessed February 8).

Goodman, A. "The Sopa blackout protest makes history."
http://www.guardian.co.uk/commentisfree/cifamerica/
2012/jan/18/sopa-blackout-protest-makes-history (accessed
January 29, 2013).

Holland, S., M. Spetalnick, and J. Ruwitch. "US-China talks
'chart the future.'" *The Globe and Mail*, June 8, 2012,
p. A16.

Janssen, C. "Technopedia explains Freedom of Information."
2013, http://www.techopedia.com/definition/24976/
freedom-of-information (accessed February), pp. A12–A13.

Kalyani, M. "NSA surveillance taking a toll on U.S. cloud
computing companies." 2014, https://spideroak.com/
privacypost/cloud-security/nsa-surveillance-taking-a
-toll-on-us-cloud-computing-companies/ (accessed
February 25)

Kelly, S., S. Cook, and M. Truong. *Freedom on the Net 2012:
A Global Assessment of Internet and Digital Media*. New York:
Freedom House, 2012.

Khatchadourian, R. "Manning, Assange, and the Espionage
Act." 2011, http://www.newyorker.com/online/blogs/
newsdesk/2011/05/manning-assange-and-the-espionage-act
.html (accessed May 20).

Koring, P. "Bradley manning testifies at pretrial." *The Globe and Mail*, December 6, 2012, p. A16.

London, E. "Bradley manning defense files motion to dismiss charges over pre-trial abuse." 2012, http://www.wsws.org/en/articles/2012/08/mann-a16.html (accessed August 16).

Mataconis, D. "Direct link between Bradley Manning and Julian Assange discovered?" 2011, http://www.outsidethebeltway.com/direct-link-between-bradley-manning-and-julian-assange-discovered/ (accessed December 20).

Nolen, S. "For India's down and out, life can look better on Facebook." *The Globe and Mail*, February 13, 2012, pp. A1, A18.

Prince, B. "Hackers plan satellite network to fight Internet censorship." 2012, http://threatpost.com/hackers-plan-satellite-network-fight-internet-censorship-010112/ (accessed January 1).

Reguly, E. "The Tunisian revolution is in trouble." *The Globe and Mail*, January 15, 2013, p. A3.

Reporters Without Borders. "Who we are?" 2012, http://en.rsf.org/who-we-are-12-09-2012,32617.html (accessed September 12).

Reuters. "Hard case for US against Wikileaks's Assange: Lawyers." 2010, http://www.theage.com.au/technology/technology-news/hard-case-for-us-against-wikileakss-assange-lawyers-20101201-18g5z.html (accessed December 1).

Reuters. "Facebook hacked 'in a sophisticated attack.'" *The Globe and Mail*, February 16, 2013, p. B8.

Schell, B. *Contemporary World Issues: The Internet and Society.* Santa Barbara, CA: ABC-CLIO, 2007.

Schell, B., and C. Martin. *Contemporary World Issues: Cybercrime.* Santa Barbara, CA: ABC-CLIO, 2004.

Schell, B., and C. Martin. *Webster's New World Hacker Dictionary.* Indiana: Wiley, 2006.

Schell, B., and J. Melnychuk. "Chapter 8: Female and male hacker conferences attendees: Their autism-spectrum quotient (AQ) scores and self-reported adult experiences." In T. Holt and B. Schell (Eds.), *Corporate Hacking and Technology-Driven Crime: Social Dynamics and Implications.* Hershey: IGI Global, 2011.

Schell, B., J. Dodge, and S. Moutsatsos. *The Hacking of America: Who's Doing It, Why, and How.* Westport, CT: Quorum Books, 2002.

Simpson, I. "Witness at manning trial focuses on motives." *The Globe and Mail,* June 5, 2013, p. A11.

Strickland, J. "How Internet censorship works." 2013, http://computer.howstuffworks.com/internet-censorship.htm (accessed February 9).

U.S. Department of State. "E journal: Defining Internet freedom." 2010, http://infousa.state.gov/media/internet/docs/defining-internet-freedom.pdf (accessed June).

U.S. Department of Energy. "What is the Freedom of Information Act (FOIA)?" 2013, http://www.wipp.energy.gov/library/foia/foiadefined.htm (accessed February 6).

Vaagan, R., and W. Koehler. "Intellectual property rights vs. public access rights: Ethical aspects of the DeCSS decryption program." 2005, http://informationr.net/ir/10-3/paper230.html (accessed April).

Voice of Russia. "US steps up Internet censorship—Report." 2012, http://English.ruvr.ru/2012_10_23/US-Internet-censorship-scales-up-report/ (accessed October 23).

The Internet continues to grow by leaps and bounds. As reported in The Telegraph, roughly 250 million people went online for the first time in 2012, according to the International Telecommunications Union, a United-Nations-sanctioned agency. With similar growth anticipated this year, it's projected that 2.7 billion people will be connected to the Internet by the end of 2013. . . Still, 4.4 billion of the world's 7.1 billion people remain unconnected.

Ryan, 2013

This chapter explores a range of pertinent issues related to both sides of the coin regarding Internet freedom and Internet censorship. Perspectives on this intriguing topic include contributions from experts in criminology, political science, psychology, and philosophy. Readers will find the perspectives to be insightful, as they explore how things got the way they did in the past—and how the Internet is likely to evolve.

HACKTIVISM, CYBER WARRIORS, AND CENSORSHIP
Thomas J. Holt

As technology increasingly enables individuals to communicate and connect with others around the world, computer-mediated

Chinese youths work at their computer stations at an Internet cafe in Beijing, China in 2006. (AP Photo, file)

communications like Facebook and Twitter have become a key resource to individuals' expression of dissent with the practices of their own government or those of foreign nations (DiMaggio et al., 2001; Van Laer, 2010; Vasi, 2006). The computers, servers, and resources that undergird the Internet and critical systems across the world also present vulnerable targets that can be harmed with fewer resources than might be needed in the real world (Brodscky & Radvanovsky, 2011; Wilson, 2008). The infiltration of sensitive government networks in order to delete or otherwise destroy important information are an excellent way for attackers to express dissent and cause harm to a government that they view as an enemy, regardless of their rationale (Brenner, 2008; Denning, 2011; Kilger, 2011). Access to such data might also lead an actor to reveal this knowledge to the general public to either embarrass or attack an institution, as with the recent release of diplomatic cables through WikiLeaks (Sifry, 2011). Similarly, actors can use Web defacements to vandalize Web sites and post messages and beliefs (Denning, 2011; Woo, Kim, and Dominick, 2004). Web defacements have become a regular tool for politically motivated hackers and actors to express their opinions and often appear around many hot-button social events (Denning, 2011; Woo, Kim, and Dominick, 2004).

Such Web defacements are often attributed to hackers because of their general involvement in cybercrimes and intrusions into sensitive systems (Holt, 2009; Jordan and Taylor, 2004). This, however, is an oversimplification, as actors may use hacking techniques in order to complete various attacks. Individuals who use hacking techniques to promote an activist agenda or express their opinion are typically referred to as hacktivists (Denning, 2011; Jordan and Taylor, 2004). Such an attack may be illegal, but it does not create a high degree of fear or concern among the larger community of citizens that hactivists may hope to reach with their messages (Jordan and Taylor, 2004). Individuals who use hacking techniques in order to cause fear among civilian populations and economic harm or disruption of vital services may be classified as cyber terrorists because of the analogous relationship their actions have with real world terror (Brenner, 2008; Britz, 2010; Brodscky and Radvanovsky, 2010; Denning, 2011).

A third, and more recent, group emerging in this space is actors who engage in attacks but have no ties with or sponsorship from a nation or military group (Denning, 2011; Kilger, 2011). Such actors can leverage technological resources as a force multiplier to engage either in nonviolent actions like protest or in serious forms of violence such as targeted attacks against infrastructure with a greater magnitude than what may otherwise be possible through real world protest and political action (Brenner, 2008; Jordan and Taylor, 2004; Kilger, 2011). The faceless, borderless nature of the Internet also allows individuals to efficiently mask their real identity and reduce their likelihood of detection (Brenner, 2008; Denning, 2011). These conditions have given rise to the "civilian cyber warrior" who can operate with no state sponsorship to attack various resources within the individual's own government or a foreign nation, a task made easier by the power differential provided by the Internet and various forms of computer-mediated communications like Twitter (Denning, 2011; Kilger, 2011).

Though these groups vary on the basis of their interests and intentions, they all benefit from the open nature of the Internet and the value of free information sharing. The general hacker community, and hacktivist groups in general, supports the idea that information should be freely accessible to all, and that government and industry stymie creativity and attempt to censor the Web (Holt, 2009; Jordan and Taylor, 2004; Levy, 2001). Hacktivist groups use their skills to openly promote vulnerabilities in hardware and software as well as hacking techniques to ensure that information is made available for everyone (Jordan and Taylor, 2004). In fact, hacktivist groups like the Cult of the Dead Cow have created tools like Torpark to give users a Web-browser that can circumvent nation-level firewalls used to stifle free exchange (Denning, 2011).

The open promotion of information flow thereby enables the activities of malicious hackers and cyber terrorists because they can use attack tools against various resources. Modern hackers need not have significant knowledge of technology to engage in cyberattacks, as tutorials and forums enable information sharing for use against various targets (Denning, 2011; Holt, 2009; Jordan and Taylor, 2004). Specifically, the global jihad movement has also leveraged a range of forums across the globe written in multiple languages to discuss justifications for the resistance to Western occupation of Iraq and the general lack of respect Western nations show for Islamic value systems (Britz, 2010; Denning, 2011). Hackers in support of al-Qaida have posted various resources to facilitate cyberattacks; for example, Youni Tsoulis published a hacker tutorial titled "The Encyclopedia of Hacking the Zionist and Crusader Web sites" (Denning, 2011). This guide provides detailed information on vulnerabilities in U.S. cyber infrastructure, as well as techniques to engage in data theft and malware infections.

Many actors interested in causing harm to various targets can seek malicious software that is free or available at a low cost through cybercrime markets. For instance, the group Anonymous uses a simple point-and-click denial of service tool called the Low Orbit Ion Cannon, which may be downloaded for use in attacks against government and industry targets (Correll, 2011; Poulson, 2011). The group espouses that governments are stifling the free flow of information and media companies are unfairly restricting access to materials and that therefore a response from frustrated citizens is required.

There are, however, few studies considering who may engage in an attack as a cyber warrior. Recent research by Holt and Kilger (2012) used a scenario-based survey mechanism with a sample of college students to identify any correlates for individual willingness to engage in various forms of cyberattack. They found few correlates for willingness to engage in cyberattacks, except for willingness to engage in protest activities in the real world. Thus, there may be a relationship between protest and civil disobedience online and off-line (Holt and Kilger, 2012). Further research using demographically diverse samples could help to determine the influence of attitudinal and behavioral factors on actors' willingness to engage in virtual and real world acts of violence (Holt and Kilger, 2012; Kilger, 2011).

References

Brenner, S. W. *Cyberthreats: The Emerging Fault Lines of the Nation State.* New York: Oxford University Press, 2008.

Britz, M. T. "The Internet as a Tool for Terrorists: Implications for Physical and Virtual Worlds." In T. J. Holt (Ed.), *Crime On-Line: Correlates, Causes, and Context* (pp. 159–185). Raleigh, NC: Carolina Academic Press, 2010.

Brodscky, J., and R. Radvanovsky. "Control systems security." In T. J. Holt and B. Schell (Eds.), *Corporate Hacking and Technology-Driven Crime: Social Dynamics and Implications* (pp. 187–204). Hershey, PA: IGI-Global, 2011.

Correll, S. P. "An interview with Anonymous." *PandaLabs Blog.* 2011, Accessed June 12, 2012. http://pandalabs .pandasecurity.com/an-interview-with-anonymous/.

Denning, D. E. "Cyber-conflict as an emergent social problem." In T. J. Holt and B. Schell (Eds.), *Corporate Hacking and Technology-Driven Crime: Social Dynamics and Implications* (pp. 170–186). Hershey, PA: IGI-Global, 2011.

DiMaggio, P., E. Hargittai, W. R. Neuman, and J. P. Robinson. "Social implications of the Internet." *Annual Review of Sociology,* 27 (2001): 307–336.

Holt, T. J. "The attack dynamics of political and religiously motivated hackers." In T. Saadawi and L. Jordan (Eds.), *Cyber Infrastructure Protection* (pp. 161–183). New York: Strategic Studies Institute, 2009.

Holt, T. J., and M. Kilger. "Examining willingness to attack critical infrastructure on and off-line." *Crime and Delinquency*, 58 (2012): 798–822.

Jordan, T., and P. Taylor. *Hacktivism and Cyber Wars.* London: Routledge, 2004.

Kilger, M. "Social dynamics and the future of technology-driven crime." In T. J. Holt and B. Schell (Eds.), *Corporate Hacking and Technology Driven Crime: Social Dynamics and Implications* (pp. 205–227). Hershey, PA: IGI-Global, 2011.

Levy, S. *Hackers: Heroes of the Computer Revolution.* New York: Penguin, 2001.

Poulson, K. "In 'Anonymous' raids, Feds work from list of top 1,000 protesters." *Wired Threat Level*, 2011, Accessed June 18, 2012 http://www.wired.com/threatlevel/2011/07/op_payback/

Ryan, A. "Talking points: Logging in." *The Globe and Mail*, October 10, 2013, p. L10.

Sifry, M. *WikiLeaks and the Age of Transparency.* New York: OR Books, 2011.

Van Laer, J. "Activists online and offline: The Internet as an information channel for protest demonstrations." *Mobilization: An International Journal*, 15 (2010): 347–366.

Vasi, I. B. "The new anti-war protests and miscible mobilizations." *Social Movement Studies*, 5 (2006): 137–153.

Wilson, C. *Botnets, cybercrime, and cyberterrorism: Vulnerabilities and policy issues for Congress.* Congressional Research Service Report RL32114. Washington D.C.: Congressional Research Service, 2008.

Woo, H., Y. Kim, and J. Dominick. "Hackers: Militants or merry pranksters? A content analysis of defaced Web pages." *Media Psychology*, 6 (2004): 63–82.

Dr. Thomas J. Holt is an associate professor in the School of Criminal Justice at Michigan State University.

INTERNET CENSORSHIP AND THE EUROPEAN UNION: EXTERNAL COHESIVENESS VERSUS INTERNAL DISHARMONY

Michael Johns

The European Union (EU) may be seen as one of the great political experiments of the twentieth century. If one were to dismiss the EU as a failure on the basis of the financial crises in Greece, Cyprus, Spain, and elsewhere, that would be a mistake. What the EU represents is the coming together of 28 countries and over 500 million people to create an international organization that exerts enormous influence on the world stage. Even given the relative decline of the Euro, the combined weight of the EU economies and their collective trading practices makes the EU one of the economic powers in the world today—if not the most powerful. As the EU has evolved over time from merely a trade agreement into its current form it has attempted to use this economic power to influence non-EU members politically and socially.

A recurring issue for the EU is that while it attempts to speak with one voice on external matters, it faces challenges posed by its various member-states to ensure that cohesiveness. Whether the issue surrounds discrimination or the protection of minorities the EU has often argued for one thing and done the other. Currently, the EU is facing this exact problem when trying to address the issue of Internet censorship. This brief section will examine the EU's policies to encourage greater openness of the Internet and also highlight the challenges it faces from among its own member-states.

For some, it may seem odd that this is an issue for the EU at all. Many see the EU as simply a trade organization based on the freedom of movement of goods, services, and people. While this may have been the original intent of the founders of the EU, it has progressed far beyond its initial mandate. It is now responsible for the standardization and coordination of issues that go well beyond traditional understandings of trade. The EU is now involved in the creation of policies on fiscal, political, and social issues—with questions surrounding Internet censorship blurring many of these lines.

As the EU has expanded in size and influence it has also begun to try to export its values and principles to nations the EU trades with. Because of the attractiveness of the European market and the collective influence of the 28 member-states, the EU is often successful in placing conditions on potential trading partners that go far beyond the traditional rules of trade. Recently, the EU has looked to make issues surrounding Internet censorship as one of the conditions for trade. Going beyond their trading partners, the EU has also worked to promote the global freedom from censorship of the Internet through policies and mandates coming from the European Commission and endorsed by the EU Parliament. The crux of this new emphasis on Internet censorship is the 2011 initiative from the European Commission called No Disconnect, which tied access to information online (what the EU calls ICT—information and communication technology) to issues of human rights. The policy had four main goals:

1. Developing and providing technological tools to enhance privacy and security of people living in non-democratic regimes when using ICT.

2. Educating and raising awareness of activists about the opportunities and risks of ICT. In particular, assisting activists to make best use of tools such as social networks and blogs while raising awareness of surveillance risks when communicating via ICT.

3. Gathering high quality intelligence about what is happening "on the ground" in order to monitor the level of surveillance and censorship at a given time, in a given place.

4. Cooperation. Developing a practical way to ensure that all stakeholders can share information on their activity and promote multilateral action and building cross-regional cooperation to protect human rights.

The No Disconnect policy has been subsequently expanded with initiatives seeking to add teeth to the ideals promoted above. In 2012, the European Commission pushed further to announce that it would be creating the European Capability for Situational Awareness (ECSA). The ECSA, once fully operational, would serve as a global watchdog for Internet censorship and would provide information on violators not only to the agencies of the EU but also to journalists, activists, academics, and other state governments. The ECSA will "attempt to pull together, aggregate, and visualize up-to-date intelligence about the state of the Internet across the world. It will show content filtering, blocking, or other disruptions to the Web" (www.slate.com). By providing some of this information publically, the ECSA hopes to bring attention on to the states that infringe on freedom of the Internet and engage in online surveillance; it would also put pressure on the technology firms that provide the software that allows these states to act. Also in 2012, the European Parliament adopted a resolution put forward by Jules Maaten that called for the EU to fully attach conditions on Internet censorship to access to EU trade. Maaten's proposal stated that the EU should "deal with all restrictions to the provision of Internet and information society services by European companies in third countries as part of its external trade policy and to consider all unnecessary limitation to the provision of those services to be trade barriers" (http://www-cs-faculty.stanford.edu/~eroberts/cs181/projects/international-freedom-of-info/europe_4.html). While the EU has yet to formalize this proposal, it is clear the direction it is heading. Outside of the EU's border, it will no longer accept Internet censorship, excessive online monitoring, or any attempts to limit access to the Internet. Moreover, this proposal applies to trading partners, including companies such as Yahoo! and Google, who work inside and outside of the EU, and any dictatorial government around the world.

It is becoming obvious, then, that the EU is moving toward a greater emphasis on the freedom of the Internet when dealing with the world abroad; however, it may prove more difficult to do the same within its own borders. While it has been able to start developing protocols for dealing with non-democracies— as their infringements of freedoms are easier to identify—it has not had the same influence on the 28 democracies that comprise its membership. As mentioned above, this problem regarding Internet censorship is not a unique one for the EU. Finding wording that all 28 governments can fully agree to has proven difficult. Moreover, member-states often bristle at the idea that they need to be monitored and influenced to the same extent as states found elsewhere around the world. As a result, we see a lack of progress within the EU on cohesive Internet censorship policies and, in fact, see states attempting to implement their own policies that can be interpreted as restrictions on Internet freedom. The most obvious case is the United Kingdom, where the government passed a law in 2013 aimed at curbing access to online pornography. The law would make the censorship of pornography the default position of all customers of Internet providers in the country. Those inter-ested in accessing pornography would need to contact the pro-vider, identify themselves, and then request to opt in. Violent sexual imagery would be banned entirely. The law also requires the development of a list of search terms that major engines would need to use to block sites dedicated to the exploitation of children (http://news.yahoo.com/british-porn-ban-way-125 958868.html). While certain religious and child-protection groups have lauded the law, others have argued that it goes too far in limiting legal content and acting as a nanny-state in censoring material that is produced by and for adults.

While Britain has gone the farthest most recently in passing these types of restrictive laws, it is not alone in the EU in exam-ining ways to limit access to the Internet. In 2010, Poland almost passed a law that would have banned online gaming sites. Only large-scale public backlash made the lawmakers reconsider. In 2011, Hungary did pass a law in the face of public outrage that severely restricted the rights of journalists both online and in print. It created a censorship authority within the government that had intrusive powers that could unilaterally judge if material online was offensive or vaguely inappropriate and demand for it to be removed. Even more troubling is the fact that Hungary passed this law when it held the EU presidency—a time when states have the opportunity to push their particular agendas forward to the EU as a whole (http://www.edri.org/edrigram/number9.1/media-law-hungary-blocks-internet).

Also in 2011, Poland, along with other EU states such as Finland, Ireland, Italy, Greece, and Portugal, signed on to the Anti-Counterfeiting Trade Agreement, which is claimed by its advocates to prevent the infringement of intellectual property rights but anti-censorship activists argue is one of the greatest threats to a free Internet. This is by no means an exhaustive list of restrictions to Internet freedom by EU member-states, but they serve to illustrate the double standard that exists inside and outside the EU's borders.

This brief analysis illustrated the double-edged sword the EU and its lawmakers always face. On the one hand, the EU continues to strengthen its resolve to prevent dictatorships from denying their citizens access to the Internet and using the Web as a tool of repression. On the other, the member-states appear willing to go their own way and enact many laws similar to those they would criticize in others. Do we commend the EU for working to try ensure that people around the world are able to access information freely online and will not be monitored online by their government? Or do we condemn the member-states for often failing to live up to the very standards they collectively have introduced? Unfortunately, as with many issues in the EU on Internet censorship, we likely have to do both.

Dr. Michael Johns is vice-dean of humanities and social sciences and chair of the Political Science Department of Laurentian University in Barrie and Sudbury, Ontario, Canada.

30 YEARS AFTER ORWELL'S *NINETEEN EIGHTY-FOUR*: PSEUDO-PRIVACY ONLINE

Michael Bachmann

1949: Influenced by the Zeitgeist during the beginning of the Cold War between superpowers that collided over ideologies, George Orwell publishes the epic novel *Nineteen Eighty-Four*, in which he envisions a dystopian future 35 years later that is shaped by perpetual war, omnipresent government domination, and public mind control. This society is one in which *Big Brother*, a totalitarian prevention and surveillance state, subjugates all citizens and even prosecutes all individual thoughts as *thoughtcrimes*.

Fast-forward 35 years to 1984: Orwell's vision hardly became a reality. Mikhail Gorbachev and his *perestroika* are bringing the Cold War to a slow end, while the young start-up company Apple advertises the Macintosh as breaking the existing conformity in personal computing. Novelist William Gibson coins the term *cyberspace* in his first cypherpunk novel *Neuromancer*, and Steven Levy publishes the landmark study "Hackers: Heroes of the Computer Revolution." In it, Levy portrays as the original hackers all early contributors to the advancement and expansion of computer technology, including innovators who developed new computer-based solutions to a multitude of human quandaries, entrepreneurs who pioneered and advanced the computer revolution, and individuals who paved the way for today's Internet Superhighway. Levy accurately depicts the original computing community as a subculture shaped by the ideals and moral concepts of the hippie movement.

The early computing community was characterized by a fundamental distrust of governmental and military monopolies, power, and authority, as were many other subculture and counterculture movements at the time. Early computer tinkerers and hackers defied corporate domination of culture and rejected traditional and conservative values, norms, and lifestyles. Instead, they applied the Enlightenment ideals of human emancipation and self-fulfillment through rational thought to the new world of micro technology. Many of the early developers of Internet technology were idealists who envisioned the use of computer technology for achieving the higher goals of intellectual discovery, for creating art and beauty, and for improving the overall quality of life. They conceived the Internet as a new means to proliferate freedom of information, knowledge, and intellectual thought, and to realize the fundamentally democratic idea that information and knowledge should be accessible for everyone without restrictions. The hope was that the expansion of Internet technologies would bring with it better-informed citizens and a freer, more egalitarian and democratic grassroots-driven society.

Fast-forward another 30 years to today: Unfortunately, the vision of the Internet as the great decentralized leveler and the entity that facilitates the collapse of power hierarchies by empowering individuals through unlimited access to information has proved to be as much an idealized fantasy as Orwell's despairing vision was. The penetration of every aspect of life by new technologies has brought society closer to the dystopian future Orwell had envisioned. No *thought police*, but *thought tracking* through cookies and browser user agents; no centralized Big Brother, but an unprecedented level of surveillance and infringements on personal privacies through an omnipresent recording, digitization, and increasing centralization of almost every facet of our lives. The biggest difference between the surveillance Orwell had envisioned and the technical reality we live in today is that the erosion of privacy is facilitated not through an oppressive Big Brother but through the users of technology themselves. We, the consumers, buy the surveillance technology ourselves and our biggest fear when broadcasting the most private aspects of our personal lives online is that nobody may be watching or listening.

The tremendous technological advancements during the last 30 years have seen the Internet transform from a medium to share ideas and disseminate knowledge into a mission-critical marketplace for almost all corporations. It has become

commercialized mainstream. Attempts such as the one under-
taken by Aaron Swartz, a hacker in the original sense of the
word, to use the Internet for the free distribution of knowledge
have become increasingly futile. In a sense, the Internet revolution has swallowed its children. Landline household telephones
have morphed into omnipresent cell phone tracking bugs in
our pockets. A vast array of technological innovations has fundamentally changed our lives, interactions, and expectations.

The mass of consumers has no need or desire to understand
the sometimes dangerous potential of their shiny new toys but
demands new convenience features and wider-reaching integra-
tion in ever faster release cycles that make it impossible for security to keep pace. The few remaining citizens still concerned
with protecting and maintaining their old-fashioned personal
privacy find it virtually impossible to do so. In today's world,
all of us are, by default, permanently leaking all sorts of personal information from our smart phones and RFID-enabled
credit cards, government-issued IDs, and even clothing.
New leaks emerge at an increasing speed, and the privacy-
concerned individual cannot thwart all of them.

Our biometric information, among them facial features, fingerprints, and even iris patterns, together with our medical histories, are stored in a multiplying number of governmental and
privately owned massive databases. Our past and present locations are broadcast by an array of technologies involving cell
phones, WLAN and IP locations, public surveillance cameras
that are increasingly outfitted with facial recognition software,
and automated license plate scanners. Triangulation of data
gathered from these technologies permits not merely the inces-
sant tracking of an individual's present and past whereabouts
but also the creation of location, movement, and behavioral
profiles that enable accurate inferential predictions of where a
person will be, who that person may be with, and what that
person might be doing at any given time.

Of particular concern are the three Vs of big data: volume,
velocity, and variety. Together, they describe the current trend

to integrate and centralize databases and the flood of personal information they contain, the goal of which is to include every facet of life into the most complete digital representation of the individual consumer. When mined with ever more complex algorithms, this accumulation of data can have unanticipated consequences, as was the case when the retail chain Target inadvertently informed an oblivious father about his teenage daughter's pregnancy through a congratulatory card that was sent on the basis of her purchasing records. We consumers willingly feed the algorithms with massive amounts of private data, be it so we can save a few dollars at the store or simply for added convenience. Such convenience is offered when users are willing to share their data, for example when users of social networks allow companies such as Facebook to search through their email and phone contacts to analyze their social relationships and to automatically discover who they may know.

User recommendations written for products purchased online are now used by Google+ for targeted advertisement to other members of that user's circles. New information of all sorts, including personal pictures, notes, documents, videos, and purchases are uploaded and shared in commercial "cloud" services. By doing so, users of such services inadvertently also share their private information with the "free" service hosts, many of whom sell this information for profit.

Most users are oblivious to the fact that large Internet corporations are increasingly connecting data provided by the users with other information the users themselves did not provide or consent to provide. Many users also seem unconcerned about the fact that data across massive and combined databases can be analytically de-anonymized. Data mining is big business, and Internet users should have no illusion that the services they use "free of cost" are not really free: all of them are paid for in personal information, the Internet's second currency after Bitcoin. When confronted with evidence that their personal information is part of a multibillion-dollar data mining industry, the question many consumers ask is, "Okay, so we allow corporations unprecedented insights into our personal lives, but where is the harm?"

Thanks to highly successful strategic marketing campaigns and user-friendly interfaces, most of us are under the impression that Google does no evil, as its informal corporate slogan suggests. Corporations such as Google and Facebook are popularly seen, not as corporate Big Brothers who know you inside and out, but as the "good guys" who greatly improve our lives and our social relationships in exchange for the intimate insights about ourselves we grant them. Personal attitudes on commercial exploitation of intimate consumer details for targeted advertising purposes aside, this view is extremely naïve, especially in the light of everything we now know from credible whistle-blowers such as Edward Snowden.

Corporate consumer information is either willingly sold in bulk to government agencies, as is the case in annual multimillion dollar deals struck between AT&T and the CIA, or simply intercepted by the NSA and other agencies through programs such as Prism, Tempora, Quantum, or Bullrun. Today, undeniable proof exists that an armada of clandestine government agencies and intelligence services across the globe intercept, record, and mine all the personal information we disseminate online. The colossal amount of information that is intercepted by unwarranted wiretapping from the NSA alone necessitated the agency to recently build an additional two billion dollar data center facility in Utah capable of storing exabytes of data. In principle, the dragnet fishing techniques employed by these agencies are the same as the data mining operations of private marketing corporations. The inputs, algorithms, and machine learning techniques are the same; solely the search terms differ.

Ultimately, the issue of privacy today comes down to the question of trust. From a consumer standpoint, this issue entails the question of *what personal data can you entrust to whom?* From a citizen's perspective, the question arises whether you can or should trust secretive intelligence agencies that conduct far-reaching domestic and international mass surveillance with only tangential oversight by secret courts. Barely supervised intelligence agencies with the capability to read all our data are but one step away from rewriting and altering this data. History books are filled with examples, such as the Stasi, that show that centralized information is power that is highly susceptible to corruption when left unchecked. The simple answer that "I needn't be concerned about who's watching because I have nothing to hide" no longer applies in today's digitally interconnected world.

We all have something to hide, chiefly our private digital lives. We should be particularly concerned about the fact that the circle of persons with access to all this information is widening. It is not just the NSA who is infringing on our constitutional rights; much of our digitized personal information can be subpoenaed without a warrant, enabling a range of persons and professions, from private investigators to divorce attorneys, to access our information and potentially reveal damaging insights into our most private activities. Moreover, governmental data mining aside, one cannot discount the impact of the many breaches of data security that wash all of this personal information into the welcoming hands of cyber criminals and fraudsters.

It is easy to become defeatist when confronted with so many mounting privacy concerns, but that does not mean one should simply abandon the idea of privacy. To the contrary, it requires users to become aware of the implications of digitized and centralized personal information, and it calls for personal action to minimize unwanted dissemination. We have to reclaim ownership of our personal information. Encryption of transmitted files and efforts to keep one's online footprint small are just the beginning. Granted, it is an uphill battle, and we still have a long way to go. We will likely have to sacrifice some convenience and ease of accessibility, but that is a small price to pay to prevent a sliding into a twenty-first-century version of an Orwellian surveillance society.

Dr. Michael Bachmann is a professor of criminal justice at Texas Christian University. His research focuses on the social dimensions behind technology-driven crimes.

CYBERSECURITY IS NOT CENSORSHIP[1]
Dorothy E. Denning

Many cybersecurity mechanisms block access to and the flow of information. Firewalls, for example, stop the flow of selected packets to and from a network. Intrusion prevention systems and anti-virus tools block packets and software that match the signatures or behavior of malicious ones. Access controls, user authentication, and cryptography prevent unfettered access to systems and information. Flow controls prevent information from flowing from objects at one classification level to those at a lower level.

Because the mechanisms used for censorship also block access to and the flow of information, cybersecurity might be seen as just a form of censorship. In this section, I argue that it differs from our common understanding of censorship in three important ways.

First, cybersecurity is more about the execution of code than information in a passive or inert sense. The reason that firewalls and intrusion prevention systems block certain packets entering a network is that the packets could trigger the automatic execution of code whose effects would be harmful. In particular, the packets might contain malicious software (malware) that would be executed upon arrival or malicious input data to programs that process the incoming packets. Similarly, anti-virus tools stop viruses and other forms of malware from running on the systems they reach. It isn't that the virus code is dangerous to look at;

---

[1]Approved for public release; distribution is unlimited. The views expressed in this document are those of the authors and do not reflect the official policy or position of the Department of Defense or the U.S. Government.

rather, the danger comes from its execution. Access controls and user authentication mechanisms do more than just keep users away from certain data—they keep users from running code against the data in order to exfiltrate or download the data, or to modify or delete it. Even security mechanisms that prevent outgoing flows of data are as much about code as data. For example, a firewall rule that blocks packets whose destination IP address matches that of the "drop server" used by malicious exfiltration code would not be needed if other security mechanisms could keep the malicious code off the network. Denial of service (DoS) and distributed DoS (DDoS) attacks are also about code. Although the immediate concern may be resource capacity, owing to the sheer volume of traffic, these attacks would not be a threat were it not for the code that drives them (e.g., to command a botnet to send out gigabits of traffic per second) and is often exploited by them (e.g., to amplify effects through DNS reflection).

By contrast, censorship is about blocking information from human eyes and ears on the grounds that people receiving the information might be harmed in some way or use the information in a way that is harmful to the censor's objectives. Here, the concern is not with the execution of software, but rather with what humans might do with the information. This distinction is apparent when one considers that computer crime laws generally allow the publication and distribution of malicious software for human viewing, but not for the purpose of triggering computer infections. For example, it is permissible to post virus or exploit code on a research Web site, but not to launch the virus or use the exploit to gain access to a system without authorization.

The second way that cybersecurity differs from censorship is that the former is concerned with the volume of data as well as its content. This is particularly true in the case of DoS and DDoS attacks. Whereas a single Web page request (i.e., HTTP GET packet) to a public-facing server usually poses no cybersecurity threat, a flood of billions of such requests does, and so might trigger controls to block the packets. Attacks that employ network scanning to find open and vulnerable access points can also trigger security controls that respond to the volume of traffic. By contrast, censorship controls are generally not concerned with volume; if they would allow a single request for a Web page, they would allow a billion.

The third way cybersecurity differs from censorship is that security controls serve to protect systems and their data from cyberattacks, whereas censorship serves to protect populations from exposure to material deemed harmful, say, because it is believed to threaten social norms or stability, national security, or political power. Further, the owners of cyber resources choose which security controls to deploy on the basis of their expected needs and risks from cyberattacks. Certain industries may be required by law to install particular security controls (e.g., to protect financial or health records), but these mandates are generally consistent with industry objectives to protect their information and that of their customers and clients.

By contrast, censorship is more about third party, particularly government, mandates and controls that have little if anything to do with preventing cyberattacks and may or may not be desired by those subject to the controls. Under censorship, an information flow from one person to another may be blocked not because either party wants that to happen, but because the state has forbidden it. The state may implement some of the controls, say, by installing packet-filtering mechanisms in backbone routers that are owned and operated by the state. The state may also direct private sector entities such as Web-hosting companies, private ISPs, search engine providers, and cyber cafes to implement the controls.

Censorship meets cybersecurity when the same blocking technologies are used for both. For example, a network owner might filter out some packets because of censorship rules from the state and others because they are known to be associated with DDoS or other types of cyberattacks that are affecting the network or its customers. Censorship meets cybersecurity also when security controls intended to block cyber threats have the side effect of also stopping non-threatening flows. For example, a company might block employee access to certain Web sites on the grounds that malware was found on the sites, but in the process effectively censor other content hosted on the sites. Still, even though blocking technologies play this dual role, cybersecurity and censorship have different objectives and concerns. Cybersecurity aims to defend against cyberattacks and is concerned with executable code and traffic volume as well as information content; censorship aims to defend against more general harm and is concerned almost exclusively with content and its impact on human populations.

Dorothy E. Denning is distinguished professor of defense analysis at the Naval Postgraduate School. She has been widely recognized for her contributions to cybersecurity and cyber conflict, and is a member of the inaugural class of the National Cyber Security Hall of Fame.

BETWEEN LIBERTY AND HARMONY: PHILOSOPHICAL PERSPECTIVES ON CENSORSHIP IN THE AGE OF THE INTERNET
Alanda D. Theriault

The topic of censorship is undoubtedly one of the more durable preoccupations within the history of Western philosophical inquiry. Indeed, the ethical richness of the question of whether suppressing certain forms of expression can ever be justified endures because it is the sort of inquiry that cuts a broadly discursive swath through a diverse forest of theory and fact that stretches through psychology, sociology, linguistics, politics, and statecraft. From Plato's Socratic dialogues to Milton (1644), Hobbes (1651), Locke (1689), de Tocqueville (1835), J. S. Mill (1859), Stalin (1922), Mao Tse-Tung (1964–1976), Rawls (1971), and Nozick (1974), the tension between what can be said and who is responsible for patrolling the limits of appropriate speech and representation cuts across culture, place, and time, thus granting the topic an indelible place in many intellectual traditions.

Contemporarily, the question of whether some information and expression requires censoring has been turned afresh toward a frontier that expands and challenges traditional modes of expression. The rise of the Internet and the de-territorialization of information access by the Internet's creators, regulators, and content generators allows for the conditions of abundant expression whether it is through the printed word, visual art and video technologies, or dissenting political opinion exchanged in open comment forums on blogs and Web sites. Having Internet access means that words and images are transmitted farther and more instantaneously than in the past, which yields considerably unique implications for state and regional politics, social cohesion, national security, and access to productivity tools for Web content generation. While philosophical arguments that traditionally define and shape the modes of argumentation about censorship remain as they primarily always have—depicting a spectrum between promoting societal harmony and defending individual liberty—the context, scope, and reach of the Internet challenges these basic tenets in unprecedented ways. The central problem for identifying the many pragmatic consequences explored elsewhere in this book on Internet censorship is, then, one that rests on making a conceptual distinction between the classical philosophical arguments about censorship and the more recent broadening scope of the Internet. In what follows I shall briefly describe this enduring spectrum of debate about censorship and argue that, in order to make sense of the practical concerns of the implementation of Internet censorship, we must distinguish the traditional audience of censorship from the new.

Between Harmony and Liberty: A Spectrum of Philosophical Arguments about Censorship

Throughout the Western philosophical tradition, the concepts of harmony and liberty have broadly guided our thoughts about the nature of, and need to, censor certain ideas. Indeed, both harmony and liberty represent opposing conceptual end stones of a broad spectrum of beliefs that captures a range of profoundly influential thoughts about the appropriate role and reach of government, the acceptability of expressing criticism, the inherent rights and freedoms of individual citizens to determine their desires and life goals, as well as the deep philosophical concern with how to attain social goods such as a peaceful social order, in addition to more abstract concerns such as attaining and understanding *The Good*. Both harmony and liberty, then, serve as the opposing ends of the debate about censorship by acting as guiding principles that express some of our highest values and hopes for a just, peaceful, and progressive society.

Those who are in support of censorship tend to use the concept of harmony as their guiding principle with the aim of developing and maintaining a peaceful social order. The notion of harmony, understood philosophically, has an extensive history of use stretching back to pre-Socratic times and is still used primarily as a political metaphor representing a well-ordered, rightfully governed, and ideally perfected state. Indeed, this notion of harmony remains a central theme in the current discourse about censorship in China and especially the state-regulated view that the primary role of journalists and news media is to "uphold correct guidance of public opinion" wherein the press must "arm the people with scientific principles, guide the people with correct public opinion, mold the people with a noble spirit, and invigorate the people with excellent works" (Zhao Ziyang, "Major Events" in *China Comment*, an internally published magazine in the Propaganda Bureau). More interestingly, in a 2007 speech to journalism students, Yuan Zhifa, an educator and former editor of *Guangming Daily*, uses the term *cadence* (韵律) euphemistically to describe the ideological importance of harmony as a social good and the role of news reporters in inculcating this virtue in its audience:

> As a form of ideology, news must have its own cadence. Cadence is an expression of the basic attributes of things. I've learned that only by grasping the cadence of news can we effectively unite the value orientations of news

with its inherent rules and in this way step into the harmonious realm of news propaganda (Yuan Zhifa, 2007).

For Yuan, the heart of his philosophical notion of cadence upholds the Propaganda Bureau's emphasis on the correct guidance of public opinion. In fact, in the same speech Yuan continues:

> Guidance of public opinion is the lifeblood of news propaganda. Correct guidance of public opinion means the prosperity of the party and the people, while incorrect guidance spells disaster for both. The question of correct and incorrect guidance concerns the fate of the party and the country.

The justification of the promotion of self-censorship among journalists and the necessity to approach news analysis using the philosophical concept of social harmony indeed echoes many similar themes used to support censorship in other sociocultural contexts. Both Stalin and Lenin held that the main use of books in the Soviet Union was to embed "cultural products into the collective memory" of the people (Plamper, 2001). The purging of libraries in the Soviet Union between 1920 and 1940 was aimed to ensure consistency of socialist and communist party ideals among its citizens and to uphold the ideological concern with the promotion of social and civil harmony.

Such concern with social harmony as the primary justification of censorship has its historical roots in perhaps the most elaborate explanation of the necessity of the state to control information consumed by citizens—that is, *The Republic*, by Plato. In what is considered to be perhaps the most important and richly complicated of the Platonic dialogues, *The Republic* casts censorship as a significant aspect in the cultivation of happy and reasoned citizens. In describing and promoting his ideal state, the main character Socrates elucidates how justice is not only a prime value of both individual and civic life, but has been largely misunderstood by the commoners and elites alike. The dialogue roams through a tremendous variety of subjects that touch on rival views of justice, differing views of human happiness, the role of education, the nature and importance of philosophy, the structure of reality, knowledge, the Forms, the virtues of good and bad souls, the nature of political regimes in addition to the role of the family, women, and community in individual moral and political development. It is, however, Plato's reasoning for the censoring of fictional representations that allows us to best understand how the harmony of the whole society is argued to outweigh individual liberty.

In reliable Platonic fashion, Socrates strategically builds his argument from the particular to the general where he relies on making a case for the betterment and harmony of the whole community by situating the need for restriction and control upon the human soul. In Books II and IV of *The Republic*, Socrates urges his friends to accept that the exercise of moderation is required in order to find happiness and harmony within the soul. The conflicting tensions between reason, the appetites, and the soul require the discipline and experience found in the education of our non-rational parts of the soul—that is, our emotions—as they are most affected by fictional representations found in poetry, painting, and music. Censorship, according to Socrates, is necessary as it allows for the proper cultivation of reason that is free from emotive affectations not grounded in reality and Truth.

Socrates's argument for censorship finds its most robust articulation in Book X (605b), when he makes the case that fictional representation blurs the distinction between appearance in reality in such a way that, hermeneutically at least, the non-rational part of the soul (emotion) cannot tell the difference between fiction and reality and thus cannot serve to regulate our action by reason.[2] Socrates holds that without censoring the fictive accounts of the world individuals will be prone to

---

[2]This problem of not acting by reason alone is known as *akrasia*—a weakness of will.

mistake their role models for those characters who are flawed and damaged as well as allowing for our attitudes to be misguided as we are prone to be emotionally aroused by tales of moral ambiguity, scandal, and generally poor or disgraceful behaviour. Socrates argues that, by censoring out the stories, allusions, metaphors, and representations of themes that do not ennoble the spirit of citizens, greater harmony, peace, and order can be more easily maintained as it is consistent with the good of the whole rather than merely the individual. Justice is a good in itself for Socrates, and this virtue requires that society be viewed as greater than an art wherein the principles of harmony, reason, and Truth must necessarily prevail.

At the other end of the philosophical spectrum of censorship are arguments that edify individual freedom of expression and discussion above the need for social harmony. While its value is not absolute, the freedom of speech and expression are taken as the triumphant markers of a liberal society wherein truth is not something that is objective and infallible, but rather something that is far more pragmatic and corrigible through free discussion and debate.[3] Unlike those arguments that seek to defend the need for censorship on the grounds that it imbues individual citizens with appropriate values and a unifying principle that encourages social harmony, arguments against

---

[3]There are in fact many restrictions on speech, expression, and representation. The standard example that expression is not a legal absolute stems from a 1919 U.S. Supreme Court case (*Schenck v. United States, Baer v. Same*), where it was affirmed that should a speech act be used in circumstances to create a "clear and present danger that they will bring about the substantive evils which Congress has a right to prevent" (http://www.law.cornell.edu/supremecourt/text/249/47). The legal discussion of this case gave rise to perhaps the most ensuring example of the government having the right to curtail an individual from playfully yelling "fire" in a crowded theater on the grounds that the speech act creates panic and danger. More modern examples of the restriction on speech and representation can be found in the current legislation in Canada against hate propaganda and pornography laws. See http://www.parl.gc.ca/Content/LOP/researchpublications/843-e.htm for more discussion.

censorship prize an individual's ability to access and know truth empirically and to act morally not merely because it provides unity to the whole society, but because it is rationally consistent with an individual's utility. The principle of utility—that is, the guiding moral principle of the nineteenth-century British social movement of *Utilitarianism* that holds that an action is morally correct when one acts proportionally to bring about the greatest good to the greatest amount of people—promotes the individualism, empiricism, and emphasis of individual happiness that influences deeply the arguments against censorship. Social harmony is too abstract and logically inconsistent a value to be considered a social good as it lacks a way to describe individual contribution to the whole. Censorship too is taken in this manner to lack the requisite utility that would allow for the maximal freedom and happiness of each individual citizen.

The roots of this utilitarian view against censorship are to be found in the writing of John Stuart Mill, the great nineteenth-century statesman, philosopher, and social reformer. For Mill, censorship stifles the ability of individuals to access and try on their own accord to know truth. In *On Liberty* (1859) he acknowledged that, because we largely must rely on our perceptions of the world through our senses (which are often inaccurate and misleading), our knowledge of the world is largely fallible and uncertain. However, because of this epistemic inaccessibility of the Truth, humans are corrigible and must seek to constantly improve our opinions about our knowledge of the world. By this reasoning, Mill maintains that state censorship prevents us from correcting our errors of thought by critical discussion and robs individuals of the ability to freely criticize the important orthodoxies of the day. Even state protection from offensive criticism is considered inappropriate for Mill since, as he argues in an 1825 paper titled "Law of Libel and Liberty of the Press," a law against offensive criticism only makes minority voices less heard and its defenders appear to be more moderate and reasonable, in addition to stretching the law inappropriately to regulate controversy. For Mill, outlawing offensive criticism against an individual or group because it is hurtful does not address the epistemic benefit of having the discussion of the criticism that he values as far greater than the need to restrict the expressive act. It is also difficult to distinguish between temperate and offensive criticism without the debate becoming arbitrary.

The Problem for Internet Censorship

With the range of philosophical arguments existing within the spectrum between harmony and liberty, providing the legal and moral groundwork for Internet censorship shall be no easy task. The range and scope of the Internet presents a unique challenge to these classic arguments, a challenge not anticipated or assumed in the philosophical cannon that operated within an understanding of a cohesive and sovereign state. The central problem posed by the Internet toward arguments about censorship, then, is largely framed by the de-territoriality of the Internet's accessibility by millions of users across the globe. State forces that in the past have at least ideologically facilitated the flow of information and power between citizen and state cannot easily legally and morally shape the audience who are the inheritors of information and services provided by Internet networks. The Internet both undermines and re-shapes traditional post-Westphalian boundaries that dominate the ostensible world in such a way that stretches the practical limitations of state laws. Philosophically speaking, the spectrum of the debate over censorship remains the provenance of ideologies and principles that work best in the contexts in a single sovereign state—that is, unchanged ideas in the *great conversation*—with only subtle relevance to the practical development and implementation of rules and restrictions over the Internet's pioneering spirit of intellectual frontier-ism. This is of course not to say that the philosophical representatives discussed in this section have no relevance to contemporary discussions about Internet censorship, but rather that we must be mindful of how our longest intellectual conversation about censorship can continue to provide the moral framework to uphold the values that we hold dear. Whether we think that censorship is helpful or harmful will depend largely on our moral and axiological standpoint. The purpose of this piece is to point out where it is that we have come from in our ideological thinking about censorship. It is hoped that an understanding of our philosophical underpinnings can guide our decisions regarding the Internet in the future.

References

"The Evolution of Pornography Laws in Canada." Prepared by: Casavant, Lyne and Robertson, James R. Law and Government Division, Web site of the Parliament of Canada. Revised 25 October 2007. http://www.parl.gc.ca/Content/LOP/researchpublications/843-e.htm.

"Guidance of Public Opinion." Media Dictionary. *China Media Project: A project of the Journalism and Media Studies Centre at the University of Hong Kong.* http://cmp.hku.hk/2013/11/05/423/

Plamper, Jan. "Abolishing Ambiguity: Soviet Censorship Practices in the 1930s." *Russian Review*, Vol. 60, no. 4(2001): 526–544.

Plato. *The Republic.* 2nd ed. Trans. Desmond Lee. New York, NY: Penguin Books, 1987.

Robson, John M and Collini, Stefan, eds. *The Collected Works of John Stuart Mill, Volume XXI: Essays on Equality, Law, and Education.* Toronto: University of Toronto Press, 1984.

Schenck v. United States. http://www.law.cornell.edu/supremecourt/text/249/47.

Yuan Zhifa, "Chinese Leaders Meditate Loudly on the Philosophy of Censorship as 17th Congress Nears." *China Media Project*. http://cmp.hku.hk/2007/08/30/584/

Alanda D. Theriault is a professor of philosophy at Georgian College in Barrie, Ontario, Canada.

2600: The Hacker Quarterly

The magazine *2600: The Hacker Quarterly* is highly regarded in the hacker community for its information and coverage of issues pertaining to the hacker underground, including freedom of information and Internet openness. The title of this publication comes from the tone used by phreaks—2600—to control telephony. First published in 1984 by Eric Corley (a.k.a. Emmanuel Goldstein) and David Ruderman, the magazine continues to be released quarterly. Its focus is on applications of hacking that extend technology to its limits. Hacking is seen as "good" if it advances the dissemination of knowledge—which should be free.

2600 is still very popular with hackers today and is considered by many to be controversial in nature—in a cognitively complex "nice" sort of way. Eric Corley remains the editor-in-chief, and Ed Cummings (a.k.a. Bernie S.) is a regular contributor and collaborator (Schell and Martin, 2006). The magazine has covered many notable issues, including free speech issues

A masked hacker, part of the Anonymous group, hacks the French presidential Elysee Palace Web site on January 20, 2012, near the eastern city of Lyon. Anonymous, which briefly knocked the FBI and Justice Department Web sites offline in retaliation for the U.S. shutdown of the file-sharing site Megaupload, is a shadowy group of international hackers with no central hierarchy. (Jean-Philippe Ksiazek/AFP/Getty Images) related to technology and Internet freedom, as well as the Digital Millennium Copyright Act (DMCA).

The DMCA copyright case involved *2600* and Universal Studios over allegations by Universal Studios that *2600* had infringed the DMCA. This intriguing case arose in November 1999 from *2600*'s publication of and linking to a computer program called DeCSS as part of its news coverage about DVD decryption software that could be used to unscramble digital video discs. Universal Studios and other members of the Motion Picture Association of America filed suit against the hacker magazine in January 2000; they sought an order that *2600* no longer publish the said contents. In particular, the complainants objected to the publication of DeCSS because, they argued, it could be used to infringe copyrights on DVD movies. The magazine, represented by Eric Corley, argued in its defense that decryption of DVD movies is necessary for a number of reasons, including to make *fair use* of movies and to play DVD movies on computers running the Linux operating system (Schell, Dodge, with Moutsatsos, 2002).

In the end, *2600* lost the legal case. Upon hearing the court's decision, the head of the Motion Picture Association of America declared that the decision "nailed down an indispensable constitutional and congressional truth. It's wrong to help others steal creative works" (Dixon, 2001, p. B22).

Subscriptions to the Internet openness–supporting magazine, back issues, and other merchandise are available from the *2600* online store; individuals may also write to *2600 Magazine*, P.O. Box 75, Middle Island, New York 11953. Nowadays, the magazine is available in paper or digital forms. The magazine's Web site is at http://www.2600.org.

American Civil Liberties Union

The U.S. founder of the American Civil Liberties Union (ACLU), Roger Baldwin, once boldly pronounced, "So long as we have enough people in this country willing to fight for their rights, we'll be called a democracy." Members of the ACLU work in courts, legislatures, and communities to defend and maintain individual rights and liberties that the U.S. Constitution and various U.S. laws guarantee citizens. The ACLU has defended the First Amendment (guaranteeing freedom of speech, association, and assembly; freedom of the press; and freedom of religion), has fought unlawful discrimination, and has argued for citizens' right to due process, should criminal charges be laid. The ACLU has also taken on the right to privacy—including freedom from unwarranted intrusion into one's private life or affairs by the government.

In June 2013, Edward Snowden released secret documents onto the Internet regarding the U.S. government's surveillance program called Prism—and then identified himself through the news media as being "the leaker." Within 24 hours of this public announcement, Dianne Feinstein of California, who heads the Senate Intelligence Committee and supports the notion of Internet surveillance, accused Edward Snowden—who actually was given a high level of security clearance—of committing an "act of treason." Feinstein argued vehemently that Snowden should be prosecuted accordingly (Jakes, 2013).

At this point, Snowden told the media that he may seek asylum in Iceland, known for its strong free-speech protections and reputation globally for providing safety for the outspoken and the outcast in democratic societies like the United States. True to form and to its commitment to fight the government's unwarranted intrusion into citizens' private lives, the ACLU immediately filed legal action to force a secret U.S. court to make a public disclosure of the justification for the scope of its surveillance, calling the programs "shockingly broad" (Jakes, 2013).

Headquartered on Broad Street in New York City, the ACLU has been active in fighting for democracy and related freedoms since 1920. Their Web site is at http://www.aclu.org/.

Anonymous

Anonymous is used to refer to the loose collective of actors who have engaged in hacking-related attacks against various targets around the world. The hacker cell's activities have been linked to the group 4 chan and other online communities where individuals share images and information in a relatively anonymous fashion. Exactly *what* Anonymous is remains somewhat of a mystery, but hackers from this clan have brought down the Vatican's Web site, taunted cabinet ministers whose policies they did not like, and inserted themselves into online national debates without being invited. But is Anonymous an agitprop activist group, or is it an international security threat? Could the group be an online cover for governments wanting to meddle in other governments' affairs, or is the group just a bunch of hacktivists whose anarchy has, literally, gone "viral" online? What IT security experts know is that Anonymous is not centralized anywhere but acts as a nebulous collection of cells and splinter groups that tend to coordinate their efforts in online chat rooms. Consistent with the hacker manifesto, Anonymous members are committed to anonymity, the free flow of information on the Internet, and transparency. Anonymous seems to embody a culture of online "creative disturbance" (Tossell, 2012).

In February 2012, Anonymous turned its virtual attention to Canada's public safety minister Vic Toews. Anonymous posted a video on YouTube calling on Toews to drop the federal government's controversial Internet surveillance Bill C-30, named the Protecting Children from Internet Predators Act—and touted as protecting children online by allowing police to access personal information about Internet users without first obtaining a search warrant. The intent, of course, was to nab online child pornographers. The YouTube video showed a headless man in a black suit under a red maple leaf, speaking in a computer-generated voice, demanding Toews's resignation (The Canadian Press, 2012). The speaker also purported to "know all about" the minister and threatened to release this information on the Internet if Bill C-30 was not dropped. The video has since been removed from YouTube. In 2011, Anonymous gained prominence after they launched cyber-attacks on PayPal and Visa. Anonymous has also had a key role in the Occupy Wall Street movement (D'Aliesio, 2012).

Opposition to the proposed Canadian Bill C-30, focusing on the federal government's "lawful access," continued to grow after the YouTube video was released, and the bill was eventually abandoned. Internet privacy advocates viewed Bill C-30 as an unnecessary intrusion into Canadians' lives. Responding to such criticisms, Toews, in trying to show that the government was justified in promoting Bill C-30 to prevent harm to Canadians, responded forcefully to such criticisms of the bill by declaring that opponents of the bill were either "with the Conservatives supporting the bill" or "with the child pornographers," an event that prompted even greater indignation (Mackrael, 2012). Toews defended his statement by adding, "If Canadians, as a nation, do not take steps" to end the proliferation of online child pornography, "this proliferation will continue. And that is simply unacceptable" (Ibbitson, 2012, p. A6).

Anonymous was part of one of the biggest online protests launched by hackers, in January 2012, as a means of stopping two pieces of controversial U.S. legislation in the U.S. House—the Stop Online Piracy Act (SOPA)—and Senate—Protect Intellectual Property Act (PIPA). As a result of this widespread online protest, some of the most popular Web sites in the world, including Wikipedia and Reddit, became difficult or impossible to access (El Akkad, 2012b).

Anonymous made media headlines worldwide in February 2012 when Interpol announced that 25 suspected members of the loose-knit hacker movement had been arrested in Europe and South America. Interpol further said that the arrests made in Argentina, Chile, Columbia, and Spain had been completed by law enforcement officers working with the support of Interpol's Latin America Working Group of Experts on Information Technology Crime. The suspects, aged 17 through 40, were held for planning coordinated cyberattacks against Columbia's defense ministry and presidential Web sites and Chile's Endesa electricity company and national library, among other targets. There was immediate Internet noise suggesting that Anonymous might launch a distributed denial-of-service (DDoS) attack against Interpol's Web site. There is little question that many of the hacktivist activities of Anonymous have increased since the global clampdown on music piracy and the international controversy caused by WikiLeaks—which Anonymous members seem to identify with (Keller, 2012).

On March 7, 2012, the media announced that Hector Xavier Monsegur, one of the purported leaders of the Lulz Security hacker group affiliated with Anonymous, had been assisting the FBI in the United States for months to help track down hackers who recorded a private conference call between the FBI and Scotland Yard. Operating under the moniker Sabu, Monsegur was well known and respected in hacking circles, but when word got out he helped the FBI snag fellow hackers, ripples of distrust among hackers surfaced. However, in an effort to quiet down the unrest, an Anonymous-affiliated group declared online: "#Anonymous Is an idea, not a group. There is no leader, there is no head. It will survive, before, during and after this time" (El Akkad, 2012b).

Julian Assange (1971–)

Julian Paul Assange is the editor-in-chief and founder of the whistle-blowing Web site WikiLeaks. During his youth in Australia, he was involved with the hacker group the International Subversives and used the handle "Mendax." Assange was caught in 1991 by police after hacking into systems of the communications company Nortel. He was also associated with hack attacks against university and U.S. government systems, and was charged with 31 counts of hacking and related offenses. In 1995, he pleaded guilty to 25 of the counts and was released with a small fine and no additional time served. The judge for this case indicated that Assange's attacks were not malicious but rather a consequence of his intelligence and curiosity. Thus, he did not merit more substantive punitive sanctions. Upon his release, Assange began working as a computer programmer and author, and he created various freeware programs designed to protect data.

In 2006, Assange founded WikiLeaks to provide "an outlet to cause regime change and open information sharing" in order to expose injustice and abuses of power. The Web site has published materials related to the Church of Scientology, Guantanamo Bay, military strikes, and classified documents around the world. The Web site is perhaps most famous for the acquisition and publication of 251,000 American diplomatic cables that range from unclassified to secret. This information was obtained by a U.S. Army soldier named Bradley Manning, who downloaded the materials while in Iraq in 2009 and 2010. He then provided the materials to WikiLeaks, who chose to release these materials over the Internet in batches over two years with the cooperation from major news outlets like *The New York Times* and *Der Spiegel* (Koring, 2012).

As noted in Chapter 1, in August, 2013, a military judge sentenced Private First Class Bradley Manning to 35 years in prison, though he will likely be eligible for parole in as few as eight years. Manning's sentence is, notably, the longest ever issued in a case involving a leak of confidential U.S. government information to the public through an online venue (Savage and Huetteman, 2013).

No wonder that Manning's sentence was so harsh; the release of these cables caused massive controversy and embarrassment for the U.S. government because of the sensitive nature of the information they contained. In fact, a DDoS was launched against the WikiLeaks Web site shortly after the first release, taking the Web site offline. Subsequently, the companies that provided funding and infrastructure for WikiLeaks, such as PayPal, pulled their support. As a consequence, the group Anonymous began DDoS attacks against the financial service providers to punish them for their actions. The controversy over these documents led some in the United States to call for the arrest of Assange, and even his execution, in some cases. Assange was wanted in 2010 in the United Kingdom on charges unrelated to WikiLeaks—rape and a sexual assault in Sweden (Harding and Quinn, 2012).

Assange has been fighting an extradition order from the Swedish government since then, and he applied for political asylum in Ecuador on June 19, 2012. Ecuador agreed to grant this request. Standing on the balcony from his Ecuadorian sanctuary, on August 20, 2012, Assange called on the United States to end its "witch hunt" or "war on whistleblowers," and he demanded, as well, that Manning be released from prison—which, it turns out, just isn't the case. Assange called Manning a hero—"an example to all of us"—which drew cheers from WikiLeaks supporters who had packed the Knightsbridge pavement below (Harding and Quinn, 2012, p. A3).

As of February 2014, Julian Assange was still in hiding in the Ecuadorian embassy in London. His publicity-generating behaviors have continued since his initial lock-up in the embassy; in September, 2013, for example, Julian set up a WikiLeaks party and released a video onto the Internet targeting his political opponents in Australia, where he decided to run for a Senate seat (Paramaribo, 2013).

Meanwhile, British officers have been stationed outside the Ecuadorian embassy ever since Assange took refuge there. Ecuador continues to grant Assange political asylum, noting that the U.K. government has failed to give assurances to Assange that he will not be extradited from Sweden to the United States to possibly face espionage-related charges. By mid-February 2013, the Scotland Yard police headquarters estimated that the costs for the 24/7 police watch had totaled £2.9 million, or $US 4.3 million. That cost amount is now worth $US 4.8 million in 2014 currency exchange. Officials at the Ecuadorian embassy have said that until they obtain these undertakings from the U.K. government, the embassy will continue to protect Julian Assange on human rights grounds enshrined in international law (ABC News, 2013).

Toward the end of the summer of 2013, a film about Julian Assange and his colleagues in WikiLeaks was released at the Toronto Film Fest. Called *The Fifth Estate*, the thriller exposed the hot-button issues of personal privacy versus public transparency with the handy use of the Internet. The film made stars of Assange (cyber Robin Hood) and Domscheit-Berg (right-hand merry man) as they set out to expose the nasty little secrets of the corrupt and the powerful in cyberspace (Lacy, 2013).

Black Hat and DefCon Hacker Conferences

The Black Hat and DefCon hacker conventions have been held each summer in Las Vegas, Nevada, since the early 1990s. The Black Hat conference is meant for legal and IT security professionals and is usually held at the Caesar's Palace Hotel. Entry into this conference has a much heftier price tag compared to that for DefCon, which is held later in the same week at a different hotel and is intended for students interested in the same topics but having little money to put toward the ticket. The visionary behind these hacker conferences is Jeff Moss ("The Dark Tangent"). Both hacker conferences have always been open to the public and the press, and the audience ranges from law enforcement agents to technophiles.

Because of its huge popularity and its broader push for freedom of information on the Internet, the Black Hat conference has changed substantially since its start as a regional hacker conference. Black Hat conferences are now also held in Europe and Abu Dhabi.

Attendees at Black Hat receive an insignia backpack, a CD, and excellent food following registration with some professional or press title; attendees at DefCon receive a bit less, and there are no meals furnished. However, DefCon attendees are happy that they receive what they came for: a convention program and a data disk containing data and files for panels, events, and other conference-related materials. An official conference identification badge is also furnished to each participant, with a different design each year. While no identifying information is required from attendees at DefCon (unlike at Black Hat), the conference identification badge must be worn at all times within the hotel in order for participants to enter panels and events. Panel presentations go on throughout the conference on a myriad of IT security issues, hardware hacking, phreaking, privacy and legal issues of concern, and abstract technical applications—all in the name of disseminating information—which should be free.

Presenters come from diverse backgrounds, and include PhDs, IT security professionals, government and FBI agents, lawyers, and hackers with specific talents. In fact, many of the speakers at Black Hat often speak without payment at DefCon as a means of educating the next-generation of tech-savvy hackers and legal wannabes.

Respected legal experts, like Jennifer Granick, currently the director of civil liberties at the Stanford Center for Internet and Society, speak on topics on Internet openness, Internet freedom, and Internet censorship. Lawyers speaking at these hacker conferences tend to focus on the controversies of the day. Granick has in recent years spoken about computer crime and IT security, electronic surveillance, consumer privacy, data protection, copyright issues, and trademarks and the DMCA.

In July 2013, Marcia Hofmann, an attorney who litigates, counsels, writes, and speaks about a broad range of technology law issues, including free expression and copyright, spoke at Black Hat. A member of the legal team appealing Andrew Auerheimer's criminal conviction on hacking charges in the United States, her talk, "What security researchers need to know about anti-hacking law," focused in part on the legal difficulties that information freedom fighter Aaron Swartz would have had in defending himself had he lived and gone to trial.

Both Black Hat and DefCon are as much a social function as an educational event, providing a wealth of unique opportunities to observe hackers, to learn more about hacking, and to network in real time with like-minded folks. More details about Black Hat and Defcon may be found at http://www.blackhat .com/usa/ and http://www.defcon.org.

The Page-Brin Google, Inc. Team

Sergey Brin, born in Russia in 1973, and Larry Page, born in the United States the same year, are two Stanford University PhD dropouts who started Google, Inc., the hugely popular Internet search engine company that has made this pair billionaires. Before Page and Brin launched Google, Inc., Internet searches often returned more useless than useful information. Users had to wade through all of the useless information to find something worthwhile—a huge waste of resources and time. The Internet's pioneers streamlined the search process to such a degree that, today, the search engine Google has taken the world by storm.

Brin's father was a Russian professor who moved to teach at the University of Maryland, and his mother worked for NASA. Page's father was also a professor employed by Michigan State University. Both Page and Brin attended Montessori schools, where, they claim, their young minds were fueled by creativity and free-thinking thoughts. Page says that when he and Brin were working on their PhDs, they really had no interest in being entrepreneurs, but when their computer science research produced a search engine faster than any other available at that time, the team abandoned academia and capitalized on their entrepreneurial spirits (Schell, 2007).

Already by 2006, Brin and Page were worth about $11 billion and were ranked the second-richest Americans under the age of 40. Like other billionaires who capitalized on creative technologies and keen marketing skills, Brin and Page were, clearly, accomplished beyond their years. But running a hugely successful global company is not easy, and challenges for the team started making media headlines. For example, in April 2011, Page announced that he would take over as CEO of the company, and at the time, he promised that he would shake up the Internet search engine giant by responding more effectively and efficiently to major corporate decisions that needed to be made to keep Google on top as a key high-tech innovator.

However, serious challenges quickly accumulated for Page. One of the challenges included a broad U.S. antitrust probe of the company's practices. Another challenge involved a protracted criminal investigation into Google's advertising business practices. A third challenge involved emerging industry forces that led him to close a deal buying mobile device maker Motorola Mobility Holdings, Inc. for $12.5 million. In August 2011, U.S. federal prosecutors informed Google that they reviewed the company's practice of allowing ads from illegal online pharmacies on its search engine since 2003; the prosecutors "singled out" Larry Page as being the top executive with the knowledge that Google was guilty of the crime but failed to prevent it. To avoid criminal charges, Google paid the prosecutors $500 million (Efrati, 2011).

For Sergey Brin, the main challenge seems to be related to his comments regarding Internet freedom and threats to the latter emerging from China, Saudi Arabia, and Iran. In 2012, Brin espoused the view that these countries are needlessly censoring and restricting the use of the Internet. In an interview with reporters, he warned that there were "very powerful forces that have lined up against the open Internet on all sides and around the world" and that the "principles of openness and universal access that underpinned the creation of the Internet three decades ago are under greater threat than ever" (Katz, 2012, p. A9).

Brin further claimed that the threat to the freedom of the Internet comes from a combination of (1) governments wanting to control access and communication by their citizens, (2) the entertainment industry's attempts to crack down on piracy, and (3) the increase in "restrictive" walled gardens like Facebook and Apple—whose executives tightly control what software can be released on their platforms—thus risk stifling innovation and balkanizing the Internet. Brin continued by saying that he and Page would not have been able to create Google if the Internet had been dominated by Facebook (Katz, 2012).

Brin also criticized restrictions placed by certain U.S. legislation. He affirmed that Google was sometimes forced to hand over personal data to the authorities and sometimes prevented by legal restrictions to notify users that they had done so. He concluded, "We push back a lot; we are able to turn down a lot of these requests. We do everything possible to protect the data. If we could wave a magic wand and not be subject to U.S. law, that would be great. If we could be in some magical jurisdiction that everyone in the world trusted, that would be great. We're doing it as well as can be done" (Katz, 2012, p. A9).

Canada's Copyright Modernization Act of 2012 (Formerly Bill C-11)

Passed June 18, 2012, Canada's Copyright Modernization Act (formerly Bill C-11) includes provisions that would lock users out of their own services and give media giants increased powers to shut down Web sites deemed to be in violation of Canada's copyright provisions. Needless to say, some Internet openness activists across Canada were hoping that the act would not become law. This was the fourth attempt over the last seven years to revamp copyright law in Canada. Some features of the act were acceptable—such as no term extension for copyright holders, a limited role for Internet service providers (ISPs), and an innovative user-created content add-on to fair dealing. However, the digital-lock provisions, in particular, were quite worrisome. The provisions of concern included the following (Winseck, 2012):

- tough rules requiring intermediaries such ISPs, search engines (like Google), social networking sites (like Facebook and Twitter), and data and Web-hosting sites (like Black Sun and other cloud-computing providers) to block access to Web sites alleged to enable copyright infringement;

- a *notice and take-down* and graduated response scheme that would allow ISPs to disconnect subscribers accused of repeated copyright infringement that would replace the less invasive *notice and notice* scheme currently practiced by the major Canadian ISPs;
- claw backs to the innovative user-generated content clause, allowing online users to make re-mixes and mash-ups for personal and noncommercial use; and
- copyright term extensions from *the lifetime of the creator plus 50 years* to *life + 70 years.*

Further, some Internet openness activists worried that if the Act were passed (which it did), there would be tough provisions, such as those found in the proposed U.S. legislation known as SOPA, which was eventually not passed after a widespread public outcry. Specifically, Bill C-11 would allow rights holders to include digital locks on their copyrighted content, which includes music, videos, e-books and software. Users could legally make copies for personal backups, but all other duplications could result in fines for the perpetrators. While the movie, music, and software industries were pleased with how quickly the Canadian Conservative government had moved to get the bill passed, other groups like librarians, educators, consumer associations, and many Canadians expressed immediate concerns about these digital locks and what the ramifications will be for the lawful distribution of content.

Cran Campbell (1949–)

Much of our discussion has centered on countries censoring content on the Internet. However, there are individuals who claim to do the same. There is a Canadian, a self-proclaimed "Craigslist crusader," who hunts down Internet openness individuals whom he believes cite offensive and racist comments on the Craigslist Web site, a classified ads Web site offering a variety of items and services. Not yet as famous as Canadian

Michael Calce ("Mafiaboy"), Cran Campbell has been flagging postings under a heading called "rants and raves" in the personals section of the company's Vancouver, British Columbia, Web site.

By calling on police, human rights tribunals, and politicians across Canada to take action, Campbell, a retired man, has asked authorities to force companies maintaining Internet servers outside the country but using the .ca domain name to comply with Canada's hate speech laws. But Campbell has a big fight ahead, for the individuals behind Web sites with .ca domains are not required to live in Canada or to operate their Internet servers there. What is even more important is the fact that the organizations managing those Web sites do not mandate what laws people must follow. Another complication is that Canada's hate speech laws are complex (Drews, 2013).

While Campbell says that he has reported his concerns to Craigslist officials through email, he has not yet received a response. However, someone else online commented that the flagger—Campbell—should be "squashed like a bug," and another online user threatened to send people after whoever wants the comments removed. The authorities say that for a message to be deemed as *hate propaganda* under Canada's Criminal Code, the message has to be made publicly and must target one of five identifiable protected groups based upon race, color, religion, ethnic origin, or sexual orientation. The authorities must also determine whether someone is attempting to cause disdain or hatred toward a protected group. Apparently, upon investigation by Canadian authorities, Campbell's complaints have repeatedly failed to meet the test (Drews, 2013).

Center for Internet and Society

The Center for Internet and Society (CIS) was founded in 2000 at Stanford Law School. It was created to be a public interest technology law and policy program that aims to bring together researchers, academics, legislators, students, and scientists to study the interaction of evolving technologies and their relationship with the changing needs of appropriate legislation. The center is particularly involved with the interaction between new technologies and the law, and how the synergy between the two can either promote or harm the public good. Topics of interest include Internet openness, free speech, Internet innovation, and Internet censorship. Founded by Lawrence Lessig, CIS continues to strive to improve both technology and law by encouraging key decision makers from relevant fields to further democratic values, whether on land or online. The Web site may be found at http://cyberlaw .stanford.edu/about-us.

Citizen Lab at the University of Toronto

The Citizen Lab, located at the University of Toronto in Ontario, Canada, is housed at the Munk School of Global Affairs. Their mission is to advance research and development aimed at the crossover between digital media, human rights, and IT security on a global basis. By utilizing experts in various fields—including political science, sociology, computer science, engineering, and graphic design—participants are motivated to collaborate together and with other research centers and organizations to monitor, analyze, and determine the impact of political power in the virtual world and promote Internet openness. The Citizen Lab's research network includes the OpenNet Initiative, OpenNet Eurasia, OpenNet Asia, and the Cyber Stewards Program. The Citizen Lab was a founding partner from 2002 through 2012 of the Information Warfare Monitor and helped create the original design for the Psiphon software to circumvent Internet censorship. The Citizen Lab is financially supported by a number of arms— including the SecDev Group; Psiphon, Inc.; the Ford Foundation; the Open Society Institute; and the Donner Canadian Foundation. Their Web site is at https://citizenlab .org/about/.

Copyright Armageddon: 3D Printers

There is a legal battle about to occur between traditional manufacturers and the Internet's capacity to deliver real-world 3D objects, given the rising popularity of 3D printers. This potential legal battle has been labeled "the copyright Armageddon." With low-end 3D printers costing only about $500, citizens could soon *print* 3D plastic items without leaving their living rooms. Think about it, with this 3D printer, one could produce musical instruments, household items, or toys for children. The possibilities for home manufacturing of all sorts of goodies are limited only by one's imagination, the possibilities for raging legal battles are high, as piracy concerns in many jurisdictions are the present-day reality—particularly in the United States. Piracy has been a popular legal issue in the United States since the passage in 1998 of the DMCA. One of the first piracy cases to make media headlines involved Shawn Fanning, the creator of the music file-sharing program known as Napster. As a result, in 2001, Napster was forced to shut down. However, concerns have remained about online theft of data (Mallough, 2013).

The big fear within the 3D printing industry is that governments will enact legislation to limit the use of this technology. In fact, in 2011, the Atlantic Council in the United States recommended a law similar to the DMCA that would allow copyright holders of various items to demand that files be removed because of copyright infringement. However, free speech activist groups like Public Knowledge and the Electronic Frontier Foundation (EFF) are recommending that companies choose to adapt to the new technology rather than spend tons of money fighting it. For example, manufacturing companies might consider selling the 3D files through an official online store, similar to how songs are sold on iTunes. However, given the history of Napster, it is probable that, like the music and film industries, the manufacturers of the 3D printers will likely decide to finish the battle in the courts rather than through some well-reasoned compromise (Mallough, 2013).

Electronic Frontier Foundation

The EFF is an organization that was rooted in the summer of 1990, primarily as a reaction to threats to free speech. The triggering event was the U.S. Secret Service's raids to track down the dissemination of a document copied illegally from a BellSouth computer. The contents included the workings of the 911 emergency system. The way the Secret Service agents saw it, if hackers knew how to access telephone lines dedicated to receiving 911 emergency phone calls, they could overload those lines, putting individuals in a real emergency at extreme risk. At the time, one of the alleged recipients of the coveted information was a systems operator employed by Steve Jackson Games. After issuing a search warrant, the Secret Service agents confiscated the computers and copies of a game book from the company's premises. The case ended with the U.S. Secret Service deciding not to charge the company of any crime, primarily because the agents could not locate any copies of the allegedly stolen 911 files on the company's computers (Schell and Martin, 2006).

However, when the game publisher received their computers back from the U.S. Secret Service, they noticed that all of the electronic mail stored on the company's bulletin board system (where users dialed in and were able to transmit personal messages to one another) was accessed and deleted. Consequently, Steve Jackson Games felt that both their rights to free speech and privacy had been violated; however, they did not know where to turn, because they felt that no civil liberties group in the United States at that time had a good enough grasp of technology to assist them in their cause. Finally, the company found people who could help them in a virtual community known as the Whole Earth 'Lectronic Link—which included some clever people like Mitch Kapor (once the president of Lotus Development Corporation), John Perry Barlow (former lyricist for the Grateful Dead musical group), and John Gilmore (of Sun Microsystems). The trio began an organization to work on civil liberties issues relevant to emerging technologies. On the day of their start-up, the group said that they were representing not only Steve Jackson Games but also some of the company's BBS users whose free speech and privacy rights had been violated. It was this event that saw the birth of the EFF (Schell and Martin, 2006).

The Steve Jackson Games legal case helped to define an appropriate legal framework for dealing with free speech and privacy infringement in the Internet world. As a result, law enforcement agents must now obtain a warrant before seizing or reading emails—a principle established in the Steve Jackson Games case. The EFF continues to defend parties whose rights are believed to be infringed in cyberspace.

Freedom House

With offices on Wall Street in New York and on Connecticut Avenue in Washington, D.C., Freedom House is a prestigious, independent private organization supporting the expansion of freedom throughout the world. Their members believe that *freedom*—be it online or on land—is possible only in democratic political systems in which governments are accountable to their own people. Moreover, the rules that prevail in that jurisdiction must be more open than closed, and freedoms of expression, association, and belief are guaranteed. Working with others around the globe who also support non-violent civic initiatives in places where freedom is at risk, Freedom House acts as a catalyst for change by analyzing the state of online information freedom or censorship on a world-wide scale. They act as an advocate to encourage American policymakers and others to adopt policies advancing human rights and democracy and take action through exchanges and technical assistance to provide training and support to human rights defenders, civil society organizations, and the media to strengthen reform efforts worldwide. Founded in 1941 by Eleanor Roosevelt, Wendel Willkie, and other Americans concerned with increased threats to peace and democracy,

Freedom House has since been a vocal proponent for democratic values and a strong opponent to dictatorships, whether they represent the Left or the Right. Their Web site is at www.freedomhouse.org.

William H. Gates (a.k.a. Bill Gates) (1955–)

Microsoft Corporation's chief software architect and chair for years is Bill Gates, who cofounded this hugely successful company with friend Steve Allen back in 1975. Apparently, Bill Gates was drawn to computers and programming at the young age of 11. He started at Harvard University in 1973, where he met Steve Ballmer, former CEO of Microsoft (Yarow and Libetti, 2013). In order to be a more effective businessman, Bill Gates chose to drop out of Harvard University in his third year of study. In 1999, Bill Gates released his book *Business @ the Speed of Thought*, which remained in *The New York Times* best-seller list for seven weeks. It is sold in more than 60 countries and has been translated into at least 25 languages (Schell, 2007).

An entrepreneur and writer, Bill Gates announced that in July 2008, he intended to step down from his daily work at the company and devote himself to more philanthropic activities. He said that he needed to join the global fight against HIV/AIDs and begin a campaign to eradicate polio and malaria. Another ambition he stated to the media was that he had to find new ways to drive innovation that will benefit the world's poorest countries. As for his views on Internet censorship, when he was speaking to students at Stanford University in February 2008, Bill Gates said, "I don't see any risk in the world at large that someone will restrict free content flow on the Internet. You cannot control the Internet." Though China has become active in censoring the Internet in recent years, Bill Gates admitted in his speech to the students that Microsoft, along with several other U.S. companies, has been involved in the crossfire. In late 2005, he said Microsoft shut down the blog of journalist Zhao Jing (a.k.a. Michael Anti) after he had blogged about a newspaper strike in China. Bill Gates concluded his speech by saying that in the long run, free speech will win out over Internet censorship because of business requirements. Restriction on free speech curtails business activities, so the reality is that commercial forces will work together to combat online censorship. "If your country wants to have a developed economy," affirmed Bill Gates, "you basically have to open up the Internet" (McMillan, 2008).

Iceland's Planned Internet Porn Ban

Though not rated by Freedom House (2012) in the *Freedom on the Net 2012* report, one has to ask the intriguing question, In the age of freedom of information and free speech, and in an era where about one-third of the population is Internet connected, can a thoroughly "wired" country like Iceland really expect to be a pornography-free zone? It appeared that in February, 2013, Icelandic authorities wanted to find out, but as of February, 2014, the small North Atlantic jurisdiction was still drafting advanced plans to ban pornographic content in print and online as a means of protecting minors. Needless to say, the proposal of interior minister Ogmundur Jonasson has met with intense public outcry around Internet censorship, in particular, on grounds that the nation's commitment to free speech is being jeopardized (Lawless and Helgason, 2013).

Advocates of the planned ban, however, feel that the positives of protecting children from serious harm far outweigh the negatives. For example, Halla Gunnarsdottir, a political advisor to the interior minister, said that an expert committee will simply be upholding existing law—which is vaguely worded—and not introduce new restrictions. Violent pornographic images are already banned in Iceland, she affirmed, and have been so for decades. Because the term *pornographic* is not clearly defined, she continued, the law is not enforced (Lawless and Helgason, 2013).

Playboy and *Penthouse* magazines are sold in stores, hard-core and violent material can be bought from so-called stag and doe shops, and adult erotica channels are part and parcel of digital-television packages that minors can easily tap into in Iceland. The authorities plan to ban porn online as a means to differentiate online erotica from pornography, the latter defined as material with violent or degrading content. The authorities have considered some measures for implementing the ban, such as making it illegal to pay to view pornographic content using an Icelandic credit card and introducing a national Internet filter to block a list of "offensive" Web site addresses. But critics have argued that such filters are flawed in that they capture innocent Web sites as well in their wide-casting net and that other adverse effects include slowing down the Internet and opening up a Pandora's box to a series of human rights, access to information, and freedom of expression issues. Other critics concerned about Iceland's economy have argued with fervor that with Iceland's current reputation as being one of the best-connected jurisdictions worldwide with one of the highest levels of Internet use by its citizens, the implementation of such a ban would hinder the country's economic growth, as the nation would then be viewed by the outside world as anything but a center for media, technology, and Internet freedoms (Lawless and Helgason, 2013).

Steve Jobs (1955–2011) and Steve Wozniak ("The Woz") (1950–)

Along with American Steve Wozniak—an information freedom fighter and founder of the famous EFF, Steve Jobs as a young adult started the well-known company Apple Computer, Inc. Of the pair, Jobs is probably best known for his entrepreneurial gifts, while Wozniak became known for his activism related to Internet freedom.

After studying physics, literature, and poetry at Reed College in Portland, Oregon, Steve Jobs sold his VW minibus in 1976 so that he could have start-up money to begin his computer company. The business was so successful that, four years later, Jobs and Wozniak were able to take their company public, at $22 a share. By 1984, the creative and entrepreneurial pair re-invented the personal computer, when they launched the Macintosh. Jobs left Apple during the period from 1986 through 1997, during which time he founded and ran another company called NeXT Software, Inc. The latter created hardware to exploit the full potential of object-oriented technologies. Jobs sold NeXT to Apple in 1997, when he re-associated himself with Apple (Schell and Martin, 2006).

Forever the entrepreneur and visionary, Jobs discovered and bought an animation company called Pixar Animation Studios in 1986. This company became the creator and producer of such top-grossing animated films as *A Bug's Life*; *Monsters, Inc.*; *Toy Story*; and *Toy Story 2*. After 1997, Steve Jobs helped Apple to produce and bring to market such innovative products as the iMac, the iBook, the iMovie, the iPod, iPhone, and the iPad. Perhaps less well known is the fact that Jobs was part of the *brain team* that positioned Apple to venture onto the Internet (Schell and Martin, 2006).

Around January 2011, the media started writing articles about the difficulties Steve Jobs was having with his health; at the end of August 2011, feeling that he was unable to continue as CEO of Apple because of his deteriorating health, Jobs resigned. The world felt that his resignation closed the book on one of the most successful and iconic technology leadership stints in U.S. corporate history. The 56-year-old cofounder of today's second-most valuable company in the world left his post with these closing words: "I have always said if there ever came a day when I could no longer meet my duties and expectations as Apple's CEO, I would be the first to let you know. Unfortunately, that day has come" (El Akkad, 2011, p. A1).

The positive creative vision that Steve Jobs had for Apple included the move into the mobile phone market with the iPad and iPhone—still the second best-selling and hugely profit-making devices in this highly competitive mobile market, despite dozens of competing products released by Microsoft, Samsung, and Hewlett-Packard since 2010. At the time of his departure from Apple as CEO, Steve recommended that Tim Cook be named as his successor, for much of Apple's success, note business gurus, is a result of the company's ability to keep costs low. And, affirmed Steve Jobs, much of that financial discipline resulted from the recommendations and sharp mind of Cook (El Akkad, 2011).

After Steve Jobs's death in 2011, Walter Isaacson produced a stimulating biography on Jobs with a motivation to have readers consider what insightful messages they could draw to enhance their leadership and entrepreneurial potential. Like his founding partner Steve Wozniak, Steve Jobs believed in the freedom of information and the positive and highly creative ongoing evolution of the Internet. Though Steve Jobs returned to Apple in 1997 and stayed with the company until his death, entrepreneurial Steve Wozniak went on his own separate path. He founded the EFF advocacy group, the Tech Museum, and the Children's Discovery Museum in San Jose (Schell, 2007).

Liu Xiabo (1955–) and Liu Xia (1959–)

In December 2010, Nobel laureate and professor Xiabo Liu, a prominent Chinese democracy activist since the 1989 demonstrations at Tiananmen Square, was sent to prison for 11 years on the grounds that he had "incited subversion" in China, a charge stemming from a pro-democracy manifesto known as Charter 08 that Liu helped to write and disseminate. At the government's command, police were deployed around Liu's and his wife's apartment building in west Beijing just hours before Liu's Nobel win was formally announced in December 2010 (MacKinnon, 2012).

The Charter 08 manifesto appealed in all media for freedom of expression—including freedom on the Internet, democratic elections in China, and human rights. In court, Liu was allowed to make a public statement. That speech, entitled "I have no enemies," was perhaps the finest articulation of the struggle for information and free speech freedom in modern China, illustrating why Liu is so deserving of the 2010 Nobel Peace Prize. In place of an acceptance speech in Oslo, Liu's "I have no enemies" was read by Norwegian film artist Liv Ullman (Halvorssen, 2012).

While Liu spends his years in a Chinese prison, his wife Xia Liu has been cut off by the Chinese authorities from the world outside of her apartment. She is not allowed guests, she cannot make telephone calls, and she cannot use the Internet to communicate with others. Though she has been charged with no crime, she is being punished for being the wife of China's most famous political dissident. Xia Liu told the Associated Press in December 2012: "I felt I was a person emotionally prepared to respond to the consequences of Liu Xiabo winning the prize. But after he won the prize, I really never imagined that after he won, I would not be able to leave my home. This is too absurd. I think Kafka could not have written anything more absurd and unbelievable than this" (MacKinnon, 2012, p. A20).

During the time of this interview, Chinese author Mo Yan headed to Stockholm to collect his Nobel Prize for literature— the first Chinese national not in jail or in exile who was allowed to win and collect a Nobel prize. And while news of Liu's Nobel Prize was effectively squelched by the Chinese authorities to the point that most Chinese citizens never even heard about this good news story, Mo, a writer with strong ties to the Communist Party, has been touted as a hero by the country's state-controlled media (MacKinnon, 2012).

Bradley Manning (a.k.a. Chelsea 1988–)

The case of U.S. soldier Bradley Manning illustrates clearly the fine line drawn between national security during a war and the role of the Internet and hackers in overriding established rules of information disclosure to the public. On day one of the court-martial, Private Manning confessed to being the source of the huge number of archives of secret military and diplomatic documents released to the public over the Internet by WikiLeaks. At this early stage of the trial, Manning's defense lawyer told the judge that his client tried to ensure that the hundreds of thousands documents that he turned over to WikiLeaks would not cause harm; he was, after all, selective about the information that he shared with WikiLeaks. According to the lawyer, Manning's motive was to make the world a better and more informed place (Savage, 2013).

On the second day of trial, however, the prosecution called to the witness stand a hacker named Adrian Lamo, who had at first befriended Manning, giving him guidance on encrypted chat lines and then turned him over to authorities. Going by the way the prosecution framed it, Manning knew that he could potentially cause harm by showing the American public the ugly reality of war in Afghanistan and Iraq. Thus, just in the first two days of the trial the disparate views at both ends of the continuum of the freedom fighter and the need for censorship came to light. The trial dragged on for months, and Manning faced eight counts of espionage as well as a federal computer fraud charge (Simpson, 2013).

By mid-August, when Private Manning took the stand, he apologized to the American people for hurting people with his actions as well as the United States. In his defense, an Army psychologist noted that while he was in the midst of a gender identification issue, Manning was on duty in a hostile workplace that would not have tolerated this reality very well. Thus, this condition, his personality and idealism, coupled with a lack of friends while stationed in Iraq, caused Manning to "reasonably conclude" that he could somehow change the world for the better by leaking classified information over the Internet (Dishneau and Jelinek, 2013).

In the end, Private Manning was sentenced to 35 years in prison for providing WikiLeaks with its biggest mainstream success: the disclosure of secret documents and a stash of about a quarter million U.S. diplomatic cables with a 40-year history. In his U.S. prison cell, Private Manning now uses the name Chelsea instead of Bradley (Lacy, 2013).

On February 19, 2014, former U.S. security contractor Edward Snowden presented an Oxford University Sam Adams award for integrity and intelligence to Chelsea Manning via YouTube from his place of hiding .in Russia. In the video, Edward Snowden warned of the dangers of government "over-classification," a term he said well describes the U.S. government's use of state secrecy privileges to keep information from the public that is actually not related to national security (Agence France-Press, 2014a).

OpenNet Initiative

The goal of the OpenNet Initiative (ONI) is to provide information to the world about how countries either allow or deny access to information to their citizens. Their mission is to identify and document Internet filtering and surveillance and provide a global forum for opening discussion on these issues. The ONI has just announced the availability of their summarized global Internet filtering data—ready for download under a Creative Commons license. This initiative involves a number of prestigious universities around the world, including Harvard Law School in the United States, the University of Toronto in Canada, and Oxford University and the University of Cambridge in England. On their Web site, found at http://opennet.net/, is an interactive map indicating the countries censoring the Internet.

Besides the affiliated universities listed above outlined above, there are other groups offering advice on how to disable or circumvent censorware. Some of these groups advocate use of proxy sites—Web pages allowing users to browse the Web without using an Internet protocol (IP) address. Once one visits the proxy site, which includes a form into which one types the URL of the restricted Web site one wants to visit, the proxy site retrieves the Web page and displays it. Outsiders, such as authorities, can only see that one has visited the proxy site and not the actual Web sites pulled up (Strickland, 2013).

And, of course, there are loose cells of hackers like Anonymous who claim that they are fighting Internet censorship by hacking into targeted Web sites and displaying prime content on the Internet for others to see.

Psiphon Software

Thanks to an ingenious piece of Canadian software called Psiphon that allows users to bypass Internet censors, citizens in censored nations can view Internet content that is deemed "inappropriate" by the authorities; the software has also sometimes been put into use by government authorities. In fact, it is estimated that about 25,000 to 40,000 Syrians currently bypass the country's sensors daily using this software. Moreover, in Iran, it is estimated that about 150,000 Internet users are able to access online services like Facebook, Twitter, and Skype with the use of this software (Braga, 2012). According to Psiphon's Web site, the primary purpose of the software is to do just that: enable online users to access Internet content that is otherwise censored and to preserve security, privacy, and access. The company's Web site is available at http://psiphon.ca/.

Researchers from the University of Toronto's Citizen Lab and the SecDev Group—both committed to exploring privacy and censorship issues within oppressive regimes around the globe—first devised the software in 2004 and then brought it to the market in 2008. The software is distributed worldwide through email, online games, and actual mail addresses that people in censorious nations tend to pass along or whisper among each other. Logistically, once an online user installs Psiphon on his or her computer, all Internet traffic is encrypted and securely funneled through a server outside of the censoring country. The server then acts as a relay, bouncing censored sites back to rebels and dissidents (Braga, 2012).

The developers of the software have nicely labeled it "a complex act of digital sleight of hand"—one that censorious authorities are daily trying to figure out. Actually, the software seems to act like a well-designed botnet, but its motivations are positive, not negative. Put another way, Psiphon's programmers seem to fully understand the persistent nature of nefarious malware but have harnessed its potential for the power of good by making the servers and software difficult for oppressive regimes to identify and then conquer. But given that Psiphon is not designed for anonymity, it is possible for governments to detect the software's presence on a country's network at this point in time—but not how it is being used. So, is there is risk associated with using this software in an Internet-censorious country? Absolutely, says the CEO of the company. "If you choose to use an anti-censorship technology, one that breaks whatever laws of your own country, that's the same as going out on the streets during a demonstration. It's not something that's inconsequential" (Braga, 2012, p. A13).

Public Knowledge

The mission of Public Knowledge is to promote the following: openness of the Internet and the public's access to knowledge, and creativity through *balanced copyright* (i.e., maintaining and protecting the rights of online consumers as they use innovative technology in a legal fashion). There is little doubt that Public Knowledge seems to work at the intersection of copyright, telecommunications, and Internet law. What is more, these fields seem to be converging. Thus, the agency's experience in all these areas seems to place it in the perfect position to lobby for policies serving the public interest. So what does Public Knowledge actually do?

According to their Web site, Public Knowledge (2013a)

- ensures universal access to affordable and so-called open networks;

- advances the transparency of government and the public's access to knowledge;
- opposes policies slowing technology, impeding innovation, or downsizing the *fair use* policies;
- educates the media and the public using lay language, through white papers and blogs;
- produces forum events for policymakers, the public, industry, and the media to exchange ideas about Public Knowledge's main mission and their established priorities.

Reporters Without Borders

While it concerns itself with the concept of Internet censorship, Reporters Without Borders's (RWB) scope and mission extend far beyond Internet practices. While RWB does keep a list of "Internet enemies"—defined by them as countries creating and maintaining the most censorious policies and restrictions on the Internet worldwide, the association also maintains a record of the journalists and netizens who have been killed as well as imprisoned (often without a fair trial). Reporters Without Borders was started in France in 1985 by four journalists: Robert Ménard, Rémy Loury, Jacques Molénat and Émilien Jubineau. This association, registered as a nonprofit organization in France since 1995, immediately took on an international dimension and has remained that way ever since. Their Web site is at http://en.rsf.org/who-we-are-12-09-2012, 32617.html.

Neda Salehi (1983–2009)

It was June 22, 2009. The place was Iran. It was hot in the car, so the young, educated woman named Neda Salehi and her singing instructor got out of their car for some fresh air on a quiet side street not far from the Iranian antigovernment protests the pair had set out to attend. Soon, a gunshot rang out, and Neda Salehi (a.k.a. Ms. Agha-Soltan) fell to the ground.

"It burned me," she said before she died. The YouTube video of her death, taken by an onlooker at the scene, circulated in Iran and around the world via the Internet (see http://www .youtube.com/verify_age?&next_url=/watch%3Fv%3DOjQxq 5N—Kc). It, literally, "went viral," making Neda Salehi, a 26-year-old who relatives said was not all that political before then, an instant symbol of the censorious antigovernment movement (Fathi, 2009).

Within 24 hours of the incident, the 40-second video of her death was transmitted around the world via the Internet. What is so very interesting is that the video avoided an intense cat-and-mouse game by Iran's Internet censors, and the man who shot the video knew that the Iranian government was blocking Web sites like YouTube and Facebook. Thus, he knew that if the authorities discovered that he had sent the video to those Web sites, he and his family members would have been at severe risk. So, instead, the man emailed the 2-megabyte video to a friend, who forwarded it to the Voice of America, *The Guardian* in London, and five online friends in Europe with this message, "Please let the world know." One of those friends, an Iranian expatriate living in The Netherlands, posted the video on Facebook. Copies of the video quickly appeared on CNN, and, despite a prolonged attempt by Iran's government to keep a media "lid" on the violent protests erupting in the streets of Iran, Neda Salehi was, through happenstance, transformed on the Internet from being a nameless victim to becoming an icon against Internet censorship (Stelter and Stone, 2009).

Yekaterina Samutsevich (1983–)

Individual heroes fighting for information freedom, freedom of expression, and political freedoms do not always choose the same venue for their activism. Some choose to do so online and are known as hacktivists, while others choose to do so on land. Pussy Riot, a punk rock group, launched a protest in Russia in February 2012, that, since then, has sparked rights discussions all over the globe. Band member Yekaterina Samutsevich and her three band mates were sentenced to two years in prison for hooliganism and acts of blasphemy against the Russian Orthodox Church. What did these women do in February 2012 that was such a crime? According to freepussyriot.org, the two-minute song that they sang in the Russian Orthodox Church had an opening lyric that, when translated, simply means "occupy the city with a kitchen frying pan." The band's "Putin Lights Up the Fires" was a single recorded by the non-imprisoned band members of Pussy Riot and released after their fellow band members were sent to prison for singing their song (Morris, 2012).

A year after her arrest in February 2013, Yekaterina Samutsevich, freed from prison, gave an interview to reporters outside of Christ the Saviour Church, where the band had staged its original freedom of information and political freedom protest against Putin's censorious government on February 21, 2012. The legal defense for her release was that the guards grabbed her before she could join in the band's "punk prayer." Though free while her friends remained in prison, Yekaterina told reporters that she still feels defeated that the band's protest song did not stop Vladimir Putin from winning a presidential election the next month—a result that upheld the leader's unhealthy and dangerous relationship with the church and the lack of genuine political freedoms for Russian citizens, she affirmed. When they got to church, maintained Yekaterina, the band members wanted to make a video clip and release it to the world, likely through the Internet. Yekaterina said, "We wanted to start a discussion in society, show our negative view of the merging of the church and state ... The problem was raised internationally, the problem of human rights was put sharply into focus ... I don't regret the performance. I only regret that they [the courts] put us in prison" (Heritage, 2013, p. A12).

On February, 2014 during the Sochi games, Nadezhda Tolokonnikova and Maria Alyokhina, two of the Pussy Riot band members, were detained by police along with other protestors for allegedly attempting to steal a woman's purse, but they were released within hours. The two women said that they went to Sochi to record a new protest song. The pair said that they were taken under arrest by police when they were innocently walking down the street (Walker, 2014).

Edward Snowden (1984–)

In mid-June 2013, politicians in the United States started asking for some real answers from the Obama administration about allegations from a till-then-unknown American computer analyst named Edward Snowden, who had proclaimed through the media that a U.S. secret surveillance program called Prism was responsible for "hacking into" Hong Kong computer systems to dig out some private and confidential information without the authorities knowing about it.

Edward Snowden, it seems, became an overnight media sensation, when he appeared to be a protagonist in some thriller film. It was early in the early summer of 2013 that 29-year-old Snowden fled to Hong King with a trove of classified material allegedly stolen from the National Security Agency (NSA), where he had been a consultant with considerable security clearance. It was there that Snowden revealed to the news media the details of an NSA program that sweeps up information on telephone calls and emails in the United States as a means of identifying patterns of possible information exchanges between terrorists. When the news broke, Hong Kong legislators, as well, took notice. Hong Kong administrator James To, for example, was quoted as saying to the press, "I am interested to know how vulnerable our cybersystems are, and I want to ask Mr. Snowden questions and verify his claims" (Coleman, 2013, p. 6A).

Snowden affirmed to *The Washington Post* and *The Guardian* that he had leaked news of this surveillance program to show the American public that President Obama had failed to follow through on his earlier pledges of transparency. Later, while taking refuge in Hong Kong, Snowden announced that he would seek asylum from any country that—like him—believed in free speech and was opposed to interfering with the online privacy of citizens (Blake, Gellman, and Miller, 2013).

After his open declarations about the U.S. surveillance programs and those of the British—who were equally as guilty, he said—Snowden was on the run for the rest of the summer. It was Julian Assange and WikiLeaks that helped Snowden make his way to his eventual asylum in Russia, over loud cries from politicians in the United States who continued to argue throughout the summer that Snowden needed to be returned to the United States to face charges over his "acts of treason" (Lacy, 2013).

On August 13, 2013, Edward Snowden thanked Russia after being granted temporary asylum for one year. He was told that he could work in Russia during this period, and at least for a year, the self-declared freedom fighter is safely out of the reach of U.S. prosecutors (Myers and Kramer, 2013).

Aaron Swartz (1987–2013)

A hacktivist born in the United States, Aaron Swartz was the founder of the Demand Progress movement—which launched a strong and successful campaign against the U.S. Internet censorship bills SOPA and PIPA. Demand Progress, an anti-Internet censorship group, now has a membership with over a million members. Aaron was also a contributing editor to *The Baffler*, a journal of art and criticism edited by John Summers with Thomas Frank and Chris Lehmann and published in print and in digital formats by MIT Press. Aaron was a frequent commentator on television, and he enjoyed writing articles on a variety of topics, from the corruption of big money in institutions to politics and public opinion. From 2010 to 2011, Aaron was a fellow at the Harvard Ethics Center Lab on Institutional Corruption, and he served on the board of Change Congress, a *good government* nonprofit organization.

His brilliant analysis of Wikipedia has been widely cited in the literature, and by working with Web inventor Tim Berners-Lee at MIT, Aaron helped develop and popularize standards for sharing data on the Web. Aaron also coauthored the RSS 1.0 specification, currently widely use for publishing news stories. In 2007, Aaron led the development of the nonprofit Open Library, a hugely ambitious project, where he set out to collect data on every book ever published. All of this information is available on Aaron Swartz's Web site http://www.aaronsw.com.

Sadly, Aaron allegedly took his own life at age 26 in January 2013 in his apartment in New York—just months before he was to face trial on hacking-related charges said to be in contravention of the Computer Fraud and Abuse Act (CFAA). His death sparked grief and angered online-rights advocates around the world as well as his family members—many of whom questioned whether Aaron's death was actually a suicide.

Peter Eckersley of the California-based activist group EFF said, "Aaron did more than anyone to make the Internet a thriving ecosystem for open knowledge and to keep it that way" (Agence France-Presse, 2013, p. A9). David Moon, a member of Aaron's Demand Progress, remarked that this hacktivist "refined advocacy for the progressive and open-information movement" (Agence France-Presse, 2013, p. A9).

Aaron's "crime" was that he broke into a closet at MIT to plug into the computer network to download millions of academic journal articles from a subscription-only service known as JSTOR. (Aaron, like many hackers, was a strong believer in free information.) Aaron Swartz pleaded not guilty to charges of computer fraud, wire fraud, and other cybercrimes all carrying a prison sentence of at least 35 years and a $1 million fine if convicted. Prominent blogger and friend Cory Doctorow said that Swartz "could have revolutionized American [and worldwide] politics. His legacy may still yet do so" (Agence France-Presse, 2013, p. A9).

In January, 2013, Jennifer Granick of the Center for Internet and Society said online that the CFAA is extremely broad, covering tons of online conduct that should not merit prison time. She continued with her line of reasoning. Though Aaron's defense under the CFAA would not be an easy task, one cannot say that he was guilty of the crime for which he was charged, for he was authorized to access JSTOR just by being on MIT's campus. Further, though the CFAA may protect "the box" from unauthorized access, it does not regulate the means or the speed of access. A critical point is that Aaron was allowed to download from JSTOR. Because the CFAA arguably applies to Aaron's alleged actions, it is time, Granick said, that this piece of legislation is amended. It is also a good reason why prosecutors must be extremely careful when bringing such cases to court. That said, many knowledgeable people feel that Aaron's prosecution was disproportionate to the offense, if any, committed (Granick, 2013).

Granick continued with her argument online as follows. The U.S. government authorities filed multiple, duplicative charges—forcing Aaron to initially see 35 years and then 50 years behind prison bars, if convicted. This is not an uncommon tactic, for case after case, the government tends to overcharge, and for the first-time defendant, the prospects can be terrifying. In this atmosphere of terror, it is quite common for the prosecutor to offer a deal—usually before dispositive motions are heard or before trial. When the facts are unclear or the case arises under a vague and an overly broad law like the CFAA, defendants like Aaron unjustly face the same tactics used against first-time offenders every day in court, especially in a computer crime context (Granick, 2013).

Jennifer Granick concluded her online statement by saying (Granick, 2013):

My hope is that this community will productively cross-pollinate with criminal justice advocates and that together we are strong enough not only to change the CFAA but also the normalization of disproportionately harsh prosecutorial tactics.

In the next few days, I'll post a short reading list and seek out compatriots at the ACLU, NACDL, and Federal Defender bar and talk to friends and colleagues about what's next.

To Aaron's friends and family: I'm sorry. In the aftermath of this great loss, all I know how to do is make a To Do list. I am going to try to make changes that will reduce the chances that something like this happens again. It will not bring our Aaron back.

Clarence Page (2013) remarked in Aaron's honor that the world will never know whether this restless Internet wizard and proponent of Internet openness would have avoided a conviction, but he clearly is a man who was ahead of his time and could not wait for Congress to catch up to his foresight.

And as David Segal, executive director of Demand Progress, stated it (Page, 2013), Aaron's indictment was "like trying to put someone in jail for allegedly checking too many books out of the library. Granted, we're talking about a lot of 'books.'" Swartz's lawyer and other legal allies insist that Aaron did nothing wrong, for MIT ran an open computer network, and JSTOR said in a statement that it settled civil claims with Swartz a month before his prosecution began in 2011. After Aaron's death, both JSTOR and MIT expressed condolences on their Web sites, and JSTOR announced that it would open its archives of more than 1,200 journals free of cost for reading by the public on a limited basis (Page, 2013).

The Censorware Project

This project, formed in 1997, has a mission of educating people about Web-filtering software and practices. On the Web site are a series of investigative reports on the major filter programs and commercial applications available on the market (such as Cyber Patrol, X-Stop, SmartFilter, WebSENSE, and Bess). As well, there are timely essays and news reports regarding Internet censorship worldwide. Though similar to another Web site Peacefire.org, whose mission it is to protect free speech on the Internet for young people, in particular, The Censorware Project was formed by a group of writers and activists who define censorware as "software which is designed to prevent another person from sending or receiving information (usually on the Web)." Their Web site is at http://sethf .com/freespeech/censorware/essays/censorwareorg.php.

Trans-Pacific Partnership Agreement

In recent years, the "big media" lobbyists have been pushing for trade agreements with copyright measures that are far more restrictive than those currently required by existing treaties or legislation in the United States and Canada; but in 2012, the big media lobbyists went international. The Open Internet activists saw the Trans-Pacific Partnership (TPP) agreement as the most threatening of these developments.

The overriding fear was that the TPP sought, among other provisions, (1) the rewriting of the global rules on intellectual property enforcement, giving the big media companies new powers to lock online users out of content and services; (2) providing new liabilities forcing ISPs to police online activities; and (3) giving the big media companies stronger powers to shut down Web sites and remove content deemed "offensive."

The Open Internet activists also fear the TPP's proposed encouragement of ISPs to block accused infringers' access to the Internet and the possibility that ISPs will give online users' private information to big media conglomerates without appropriate privacy safeguards. In other words, Open Internet activists have argued that given the number of restrictions in the proposed TPP agreement, all Internet users could become suspected copyright criminals, and it appears to criminalize content sharing, in general. It is further believed by the activists that the pro-TPP lobbyists had been paid for by U.S. megacorporations. Though these behind-door negotiations seem to have been going on since 2008, it appears that there was actually a gathering in Chile recently with discussions of more restrictive online copyright enforcement, and according to the U.S. Trade Representative's Office, negotiators were hoping to finalize the TPP agreement by July 2012. Open Internet activists have further argued that the approach that is being used to advance the TPP is undemocratic, because there has been a woeful lack of proper online citizen and stakeholder consultation. Furthermore, there has been no open access to TPP documents, and, sadly, there appear to have been no checks or balances in place to ensure the well-being of online global citizens. In short, there needs to be an adequate means of protecting content owners' needs balanced with the rights of Internet users—and this just doesn't seem to be the case (Bailey, 2012).

The 11 nations negotiating the TPP in 2013 included the United States, Canada, Australia, Peru, Malaysia, Vietnam, New Zealand, Chile, Singapore, Mexico, and Brunei Darussalam. The EFF obtained a leaked document of a February 2011 TPP draft—never officially released by the TPP—which can be found at http://keionline.org/sites/default/files/tpp-10feb2011-us-text-ipr-chapter.pdf (EFF, 2013). In 2014, Japan joined in negotiating the TPP, bringing the total number of nations involved to 12.

Furthermore, according to the EFF, TPP negotiators are trying to adopt copyright measures far more restrictive than currently required by international treaties, including the controversial Anti-Counterfeiting Trade Agreement. Moreover, all countries signing on would be required to have their domestic laws and policies comply with the provisions in the agreement—meaning that a recently leaked U.S.-proposed intellectual property chapter would include provisions exceeding current U.S. law, including the controversial aspects of the DMCA. In February, 2013, the EFF Web site said that the EFF joined 24 U.S. civil society groups to demand a baseline of transparency in TPP negotiations, and a letter was sent to Barbara Weisel, the lead negotiator for the TPP, calling for more baseline needs for transparency and increased civil involvement in the secret backdoor meetings (Sutton, 2013).

On February, 23, 2014, the 12 nations involved in the Trans-Pacific Partnership free trade negotiations continued efforts to try to clinch a deal at a ministerial meeting in Singapore, with each country engaging in bilateral talks. Japan intended to hold bilateral meetings with Canada, Mexico and New Zealand during this gathering, but Japanese negotiators were less optimistic that the bilateral meetings with the U.S. would go smoothly, as the U.S. has distinctly different views from Japan over tariff removal and automotive issues (Kyoto News International, 2014).

Finally, Public Knowledge expressed concerns in 2013 about the TPP because there has been a history of rounds of secretive negotiations, several leaks of the proposed text, and close-to-zero involvement of the public. Very worrisome is the fact that everything known about the TPP is known because of leaks; the negotiators have not even once willingly given the public or public interest organizations like the EFF and Public Knowledge any key information voluntarily. Furthermore, the schedule for negotiation seems to have become accelerated in recent months to bring a close to the process. Quite alarming, however, is that the process has become more and more closed; stakeholder forums, common at the start of the process, have been replaced by stakeholder tables (tables staffed by interested stakeholders to which negotiators may go or not go). And, disappointingly, the negotiators seem to be engaging in off-the-record "inter-session" meetings between scheduled official meetings (Public Knowledge, 2013b).

WikiLeaks

Besides the loose hacker cells collectively known as Anonymous—that advocate for Open Internet—another well-known hacker group is WikiLeaks, founded in 2006 by Julian Assange. At start-up, WikiLeaks actually touted an open contribution policy similar to that of the online encyclopedia

Wikipedia. Now, WikiLeaks publishes documents obtained from so-called reputable sources and contributors on multiple servers and domain names. Thus, this protocol makes the information easier to procure but harder to block. From a controversy standpoint, WikiLeaks became most famously known worldwide after Private Manning leaked important government documents to WikiLeaks during the Iraq War. WikiLeaks also got the media's attention after they put on the Internet some controversial details about the relationship between the governments of the United States, Venezuela, and Paraguay (Ruth and Stone, 2012).

Julian Assange was linked to the controversial Internet freedom fighter court martial case of Private Manning, who put on the Internet, with Assange's assistance, controversial cables thought to result in harm to soldiers fighting in Iraq in 2009 and 2010. The case also brought some interesting legal debates to the forefront regarding noncomplex and complex jurisdictional issues related to criminal liability (Mataconis, 2011), as detailed in Chapter 2. Private Manning will now be spending up to 35 years in a U.S. federal prison for his acts producing grievous harm to U.S. soldiers in the field (Savage and Huetteman, 2013). Wanted on charges unrelated to WikiLeaks (Paramaribo, 2013), Julian Assange remains holed up in the Ecuadorian embassy in the United Kingdom in 2014, but he continues to communicate with the world through the Internet.

Malala Yousafzai (1998–)

As noted in Chapter 2, in a democracy, freedom of expression and open access to information will likely always be perceived by citizens to be their greatest freedoms. Even in countries where limits exist regarding open access, many citizens crave these freedoms.

In 2013, a 15-year-old Pakistani schoolgirl named Malala Yousafzai was undergoing yet another operation to reconstruct her skull and restore her hearing in a British hospital after she was shot, on October 9, 2012, in Pakistan for her activism in promoting education for girls. Malala made front-page media headlines internationally after the shooting, which occurred as she was returning home on the school bus. Taliban militants in Pakistan admitted that they had targeted her because she promoted girls' education—which was clearly fueled by her inappropriate "Western kind of thinking" (Associated Press, 2013a).

A young woman who likes to speak what is on her mind, Malala had also criticized Taliban's actions once they occupied the rather scenic Swat Valley where she and her family resided. To say that Malala was not connected to the Internet would be false, for at age 11, she started writing a blog under a pseudonym for the BBC about living under the ruling Taliban. In fact, after Pakistan's military ousted the Taliban from Swat Valley in 2009, Malala was known to speak out publicly about the need for girls to be educated in Pakistan, and she often was invited to speak to the media on this topic. Considering her maturity at such a young age, Malala was rapidly making a positive name for herself and for her valiant motives; she was given one of the country's highest honors for her world-recognized bravery after the shooting Given the ugliness of the shooting of an innocent school girl, citizens in Pakistan and in countries around the world were outraged, and in an overt manifestation of her international reach as a special kind of information freedom fighter, Malala was shortlisted for *Time* magazine's Person of the Year for 2012. After her operations, Malala was definitely on the road to recovery. She was able to stand, write, and return to Swat Valley—with minimal signs of brain damage (Associated Press, 2013a).

Malala Yousafzai was invited to address the United Nations during the first third of Ramadan in mid-July 2013, a period regarded as the days of God's mercy. Her powerful speech, travelling over the Internet and heard by citizens around the world, left an indelible mark on the global citizenry. She started her speech by praising God and then masterfully wove throughout her short but eloquent discussion five important themes: inclusiveness, non-violence toward others, forgiveness for wrongs committed, the importance of education regardless of gender, and the importance of female self-reliance. She invoked the names of past freedom fighters like Nelson Mandela, Martin Luther King, and Muhammad Ali Jinnah, reminding Muslims worldwide to search beyond their own comfortable spheres and reach out into the vast expanse of universal principles embodied by the many intricate and richly woven strands of humanity (Kahn, 2013).

On July 12, 2013, the UN-designated Malala Day (on her 16th birthday), the information freedom fighter said to the U.N. Assembly: "One child, one teacher, one book, and one pen can change the world" (Hui, 2013, p. A9).

In 2014, Malala continues her outreach for freedom of information and education for women and children. In February, she urged the world to help Syrian refugee children receive a proper education, as she visited a school in northern Jordan's Zaatari refugee camp. A video of her talk was posted on the Web site of the United Nations refugee agency. The Malala Fund is currently working with the Save the Children Fund to construct a new school in Jordan and to expand one there for refugees (Agence France-Presse, 2014b).

Bassem Youssef (1975–)

A doctor in Egypt, Bassem Youssef rose quickly to fame when his video blogs mocking Egyptian politics received hundreds of thousands of hits shortly after the 2011 uprising that brought down the long-time former leader Hosni Mubarak—an 84-year-old man now being held in a military hospital for failing to prevent the killing of almost 900 protestors during the 2011 uprising (Associated Press, 2013b).

The Egyptian prosecutors launched an investigation on New Year's Day 2013 against the popular part-time television and video blog satirist Youssef for allegedly insulting his country and its leaders. The case of Youssef, a believer in free speech, came at a time when the opposition media and independent journalists had grown worried about press freedoms under a new constitution widely supported by an extremist Islamic government. Bassem Youssef's crime appears to be that he insulted then-president Mohammed Morsi and his Islamist allies by "putting the Islamist leader's image on a pillow and parodying his speeches" (Batrawy, 2013).

Aged 38, Youssef has his own television show modeled after Jon Stewart's *The Daily Show*, on which he has appeared as a guest. One of Egypt's most popular television presenters, with 1.4 million fans on Facebook and nearly 850,000 followers on Twitter, Youssef has been cited as a freedom of information hero. Egyptian citizens maintain that Youssef tells them things that they never knew because of his belief in freedom of information and Internet openness. At the time of this incident, Youssef had nearly as many followers on Facebook and Twitter as Egypt's president (Batrawy, 2013).

References

ABC News. "Assange stand-off costing London police $4.3 million." 2013, http://www.abc.net.au/news/2013-02-17/assange-stand-off-costing-london-police-4-million-dollars/4523300 (accessed February 16).

Agence France-Presse. "Advocates angered by death of 26-year-old hacktivist." *The Globe and Mail*, January 14, 2013, p. A9.

Agence France-Presse. "Privacy: Snowden presents award via YouTube." *The Globe and Mail*, February 20, 2014a, p. A14.

Agence France-Presse. "Education: Malala fights for rights of Syrian children." *The Globe and Mail*, February 20, 2014b, p. A14.

Associated Press. "Pakistani girl shot in head by Taliban in stable condition after 2 successful surgeries at U.K. hospital." 2013a, http://news.nationalpost.com/2013/02/03/pakistani-girl-shot-in-head-by-taliban-in-stable-condition-after-2-successful-surgeries-at-u-k-hospital/ (accessed February 3).

Associated Press. "Retrial for Mubarak could make political stability more elusive." *The Globe and Mail*, January 14, 2013b, p. A9.

Bailey, A. "TPP: The secretive agreement that could criminalize your Internet use." 2012, http://openmedia.ca/blog/tpp-secretive-agreement-could-criminalize-your-internet-use (accessed May 14).

Batrawy, A. "Egypt's answer to Jon Steward comes under state scrutiny." *The Globe and Mail*, January 2, 2013, p. A14.

Blake, A., B. Gellman, and G. Miller. "NSA secrets leaker revealed." *Las Vegas Review-Journal*, June 10, 2013, pp. 1A, 4A.

Braga, M. "Canadian software beating Syrian censors." *The Globe and Mail*, July 16, 2012, p. A13.

Canadian Press. "Toews under 'direct threat' by online collective Anonymous." *The Globe and Mail*, March 7, 2012, p. A3.

The Center for Internet and Society. "Jennifer Granick." 2013, http://cyberlaw.stanford.edu/about/people/jennifer-granick (accessed February 16).

Coleman, Z. "Snowden's claims intrigue Hong Kong." *USA Today*, June 14, 2013, p. 6A.

D'Aliesio, R. "Anonymous wants transparency, hides behind name." *The Globe and Mail*, February 20, 2012, p. A4.

Dishneau, D., and P. Jelinkek. "WikiLeaker sorry 'actions hurt people.'" *The Globe and Mail*, August 15, 2013, p. A14.

Dixon, G. "Hackers under attack over copyrights." *The Globe and Mail*, August 2, 2001, p. B22.

Drews, K. "Craigslist crusader hunts Internet haters." *The Globe and Mail*, February 19, 2013, p. A8.

EFF. "Trans Pacific Partnership Agreement." 2013, https://www.eff.org/issues/tpp (accessed February 5).

Efrati, A. "'Honeymoon over' for Google's CEO." *The Globe and Mail*, August 20, 2011, p. 12.

El Akkad, O. "Unable to continue, Apple's Jobs steps down." *The Globe and Mail*, August 25, 2011, pp. A1, A12.

El Akkad, O. "Hacker crackdown." *The Globe and Mail*, March 7, 2012a, p. A3.

El Akkad, O. "Online protest prompts retreat on privacy bills." *The Globe and Mail*, January 19, 2012b, p. A12.

El Akkad, O. "Why Facebook paid $1-billion for Instagram." *The Globe and Mail*, April 10, 2012c, p. B3.

Fathi, N. "In a death seen around the world, a symbol of Iranian protests." 2009, http://www.nytimes.com/2009/06/23/world/middleeast/23neda.html (accessed June 22).

Granick, J. "Towards learning from losing Aaron Swartz: Part 2." 2013, http://cyberlaw.stanford.edu/blog/2013/01/towards-learning-losing-aaron-swartz-part-2 (accessed January 15).

Halvorssen, T. "Nobel laureate Liu Xiaobo's imprisonment a painful reminder of China's dictatorship." 2012, http://www.huffingtonpost.com/thor-halvorssen/nobel-laureate-liu-xiaobo_b_1166012.html (accessed December 10).

Harding, L., and B. Quinn. "From his Ecuadorean sanctuary, Assange calls on U.S. to end 'witch hunt.'" *The Globe and Mail*, August 20, 2012, p. A3.

Heritage, T. "Pussy Riot protest sparked rights' discussions." *The Globe and Mail*, February 22, 2013, p. A12.

Hui, A. "One pen can change the world." *The Globe and Mail*, July 13, 2013, p. A9.

Ibbitson, J. "Cybercrime bill sparks backlash." *The Globe and Mail*, February 15, 2012, p. A6.

Jakes, L. "U.S. spying raises fresh anger." *Las Vegas Review-Journal*, June 11, 2013, pp. 1A, 6A.

Kahn, S. "Malala spoke. Muslims, listen." *The Globe and Mail*, July 17, 2013, p. A15.

Katz, I. "Web freedom is seriously threatened, says Google co-founder." *The Globe and Mail*, April 17, 2012, p. A9.

Keller, G. "Police sweep nets 25 alleged Anonymous hackers." *The Globe and Mail*, February 29, 2012, p. A14.

Koring, P. "Bradley Manning testifies at pretrial." *The Globe and Mail*, December 6, 2012, p. A16.

Kyoto News International. "TPP countries continue talks to clinch deal in Singapore. 2014," http://www.globalpost.com/dispatch/news/kyodo-news-international/140223/tpp-countries-continue-talks-clinch-deal-singapore-0 (accessed February 26).

Lacy, L. "TIFF'13: Vantage Point." *The Globe and Mail*, August 31, 2013, pp. R1, R7.

Lawless, J., and G. Helgason. "Porn ban plan sparks free speech uproar." *The Globe and Mail*, February 26, 2013, p. A16.

MacKinnon, M. "Nobel laureate's wife a prisoner in her home." *The Globe and Mail*, December 7, 2012, p. A20.

Mackrael, K. "Toews faces personal threats over Internet bill." *The Globe and Mail*, February 20, 2012, p. A4.

Mallough, R. "The new age of piracy." *Maclean's, 126* (4) (2013): 42.

Mataconis, D. "Direct link between Bradley Manning and Julian Assange discovered?" 2011, http://www.outsidethebeltway.com/direct-link-between-bradley-manning-and-julian-assange-discovered/ (accessed December 20).

McMillan, R. "Bill Gates: Internet censorship won't work." 2008, http://www.nytimes.com/idg/IDG_002570DE00740E18882573F50010C487.html?x=1361336400&en=dd5f1577b37941cd&ei=5088&partner=rssnyt&emc=rss (accessed February 20).

Morris, D. "Pussy Riot, a critical assessment." *The Globe and Mail*, August 20, 2012, p. R2.

Myers, S., and A. Kramer. "Snowden thanks Russia after being granted temporary asylum for a year." *The Globe and Mail*, August 2, 2013, p. A3.

Page, C. "Sad farewell to Aaron Swartz, Internet Freedom Fighter." 2013, http://www.newsday.com/opinion/oped/page-sad-farewell-to-aaron-swartz-internet-freedom-fighter-1.4452273 (accessed January 18).

Paramaribo, S. "Ecuador rebukes Assange for mocking Australian politicians in video." *The Globe and Mail*, August 31, 2013, p. A20.

Public Knowledge. "About our work." 2013a, http://publicknowledge.org/about (accessed February 24).

Public Knowledge. "The Trans-Pacific Partnership Agreement." 2013b, http://tppinfo.org/ (accessed February 24).

Ruth, S., and S. Stone. "Hactivism–A legislator's dilemma." *IEEE Internet Computing 16* (6): 78–81, 2012.

Savage, C. "Leaker portrayed as 'good-intentioned' and a traitor." *The Globe and Mail*, June 4, 2013, p. A3.

Savage, C., and E. Huetteman. "Manning's 35-year sentence 'the longest in a leak case.'" *The Globe and Mail*, August 22, 2013, p. A3.

Schell, B. *Contemporary World Issues: The Internet and Society.* Santa Barbara, CA: ABC-CLIO, 2007.

Schell, B., J. Dodge, with S. Moutsatsos. *The Hacking of America: Who's Doing It, Why, and How.* Westport, CT: Quorum Books, 2002.

Schell, B., and C. Martin. *Webster's New World Hacker Dictionary.* Indiana: Wiley, 2006.

Simpson, I. "Witness at Manning trial focuses on motives." *The Globe and Mail*, June 5, 2013, p. A11.

Stelter, B., and B. Stone. "Web pries lid of Iranian censorship." 2009, http://www.nytimes.com/2009/06/23/world/middleeast/23censor.html?ef=middleeast (accessed June 23).

Strickland, J. "How censorship works." 2013, http://computer.howstuffworks.com/internet-censorship3.htm (accessed March 3).

Sutton, M. "EFF joins 24 US civil society groups in demanding a baseline of transparency in TPP negotiations." 2013, https://www.eff.org/deeplinks/2013/02/eff-joins-24-us-civil-society-groups-demanding-baseline-transparency-tpp (accessed February 5).

Tossell, I. "The ABCs of cybersecurity." *The Globe and Mail Report on Business, 28* (10): 55–60, May 2012.

Walker, S. "Pussy Riot members among group of activists arrested in Sochi." 2014, http://www.theguardian.com/music/2014/feb/18/pussy-riot-members-arrested-sochi-winter-olympics (accessed February 26).

Winseck, D. "Debunking Bill C-11: Why Canadians should be concerned." 2012, http://openmedia.ca/blog/debunking-bill-c-11-why-Canadians-should-be-concerned (accessed March 10).

Yarow, J., and R. Libetti. "How Steve Ballmer became Microsoft's CEO and what he has to do to keep his job." 2013, http://www.businessinsider.com/steve-ballmer-bio-video-2013-2 (accessed February 25).

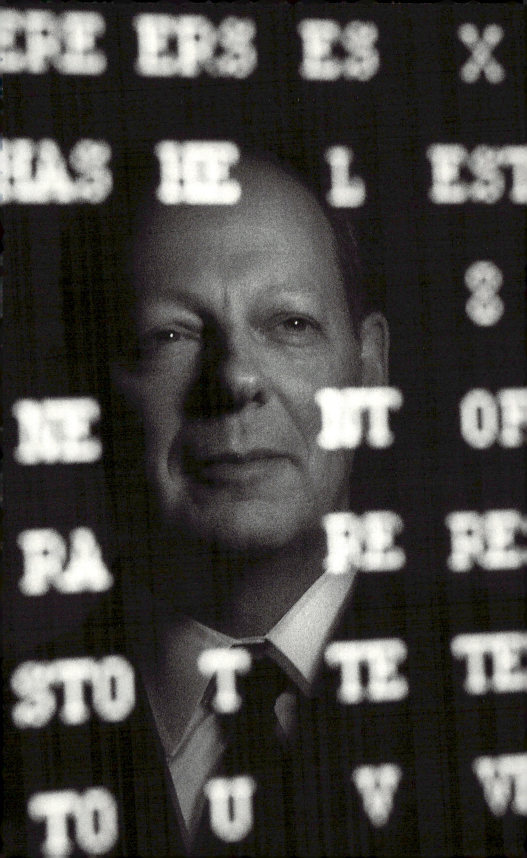

In some cases, the world is applying digital technologies faster than our ability to understand the security implications and mitigate potential risks.
　　　　—James Clapper, U.S. Director of National Intelligence
　　　　　　　　　　　(Mazzetti and Shane, 2013, p. A15)

This chapter presents some statistics on Internet usage worldwide and Internet penetration by region. The discussion then turns to some findings from the *Freedom on the Net 2012* report, with a particular emphasis on differentiating the countries designated as "free" by the editors of this report relative to the countries designated as "not free." We then look more closely at the tactics used by the highly censoring countries, particularly over the period 2011–2012. The remainder of the chapter looks at the kinds of legislation and other guidelines that nations have for controlling the Internet in their particular jurisdictions—with a discussion of recent controversial pieces of legislation that have been attempted by various countries to further control Internet behaviors and activities, beginning with the United States.

Navy Rear Admiral William E. Leigher, one of the nation's top military experts on cybersecurity, is reflected in a computer screen displaying a numerical code on November 7, 2013. (AP Photo/Robert F. Bukaty)

Statistics on Internet Usage Worldwide

According to the Internet World Stats (2013), as of June 30, 2012, there were 2,405,518,376 known Internet users worldwide, a phenomenal 566.4 percent growth rate in Internet usage since 2000 (see Table 5.1).

However, when one looks at the Internet penetration rates (defined as the percentage of the total population of a given country or region that uses the Internet) on the basis of the world's population (7,017,846,922) relative to the estimated Internet users as of June 30, 2012 (2,405,518,376), the world Internet penetration rates by geographic regions show a drastically different picture, as illustrated in Table 5.2 (Internet World Stats, 2013). Considering these world Internet penetration rates, the world's average is estimated by the Internet World Stats (2013) to be about 34.3 percent. Countries with penetration rates above 50%—such as the U.S., Canada, and Norway—are considered to have sound Internet penetration rates. Countries having penetration rates below 50% are indicative of areas that could be improved. Looking at Table 5.2, both Asia and Africa have penetration rates below the world average.

A Closer Look at the *Freedom on the Net 2012* Findings

Are the geographic locations that have above-average Internet penetration rates more apt to provide their citizens

Table 5.1   Internet Usage Worldwide

Region	Internet Usage (%)
Asia	45
Europe	21
North America	11
Latin America and the Caribbean	11
Africa	7
Middle East	4
Australia	1

Source: Internet World Stats (2013).

Table 5.2   Internet Penetration Rates

Region	Internet Penetration Rates (%)
Asia	27.5
Europe	63.2
North America	78.6
Latin America and the Caribbean	42.9
Africa	15.6
Middle East	40.2
Australia/Oceania	67.6

Source: Internet World Stats (2013).

freer and open Internet access? On the basis of the *Freedom on the Net 2012* report (Kelly, Cook, and Truong, 2012), the answer appears to be "yes." Table 5.3 shows the two extremes as determined by the authors of the report: (1) the countries deemed to be "free" (i.e., whose penetration rates are placed well above the mean) and (2) those deemed to be "not free" (i.e., whose penetration rates are placed very near or below the mean). Regarding metrics pertaining to the freedom on the net total score, obstacles to Internet access, limits on Web site content, and violations of user rights for "inappropriate" online content, the lower the score, the better, meaning that users should be experiencing a fair degree of Internet openness and freedom of speech. Entries in bold refer to countries for which the metrics for the freedom on the net total score had slight or significant negative trajectories over the period 2011–2012—meaning that things got worse rather than better. These countries (in bold) are also those *Freedom on the Net 2012* has labeled as "blockers," meaning that their governments have chosen to block a large number of politically relevant Web sites, often placing tight blocks on certain social media platforms. As well, these blocker governments seem to invest a huge amount of resources in technical capacity and staffing to identify "inappropriate" online content.

In the censoring countries shown in bold in Table 5.3, authorities use a number of tactics to maintain or increase control over

Table 5.3   "Free" and "Not Free" Internet Geographical Locations

Country	Freedom on the net status	Freedom on the net total (0–100)*	Obstacles to access (0–25)*	Limits on content (0–35)*	Violations of user rights (0–40)*
Estonia	Free	10	2	3	5
United States	Free	12	4	1	7
Germany	Free	15	4	3	8
Australia	Free	18	2	6	10
Hungary	Free	19	5	6	8
Italy	Free	23	4	7	12
Philippines	Free	23	10	5	8
United Kingdom	Free	25	1	8	16
Argentina	Free	26	9	9	8
South Africa	Free	26	8	8	10
Brazil	Free	27	7	6	14
Ukraine	Free	27	7	8	12
Kenya	Free	29	10	7	12
Georgia	Free	30	9	10	11
Thailand	Not free	61	11	21	29
Pakistan	Not free	63	19	18	26
Belarus	Not free	69	16	23	30
Bahrain	Not free	71	12	25	34
Saudi Arabia*	Not free	71	14	26	31
Vietnam	Not free	73	16	26	31
Burma	Not free	75	22	23	30
Ethiopia	Not free	75	22	27	26
Uzbekistan	Not free	77	19	28	30
Syria	Not free	83	23	25	35
China	Not free	85	18	29	38
Cuba	Not free	86	24	29	33
Iran	Not Free	90	21	32	37

*Lower numbers indicate greater Internet openness.
Source: Kelly, Cook, and Truong (2012).

the Internet—including blocking Web 2.0, exhibiting notable political blocking, having localized or nationwide Information Communication Technology (ICT) shutdowns, hiring pro-government commentators to manipulate online discussions, passing new laws or guidelines to increase censorship or punishment, passing new laws to increase online surveillance or restrict anonymity, arresting bloggers and ICT users for their political or social writings, and physically attacking or killing bloggers and ICT users for "inappropriate" online content. Table 5.4 shows the tactics used by each one of these highly censoring countries over the period 2011–2012 (Kelly, Cook, and Truong, 2012).

Internet Legislation in the United States Related to Privacy, Security, Trust, and Censorship

Newsworthy Internet crimes prosecuted in the United States, as described in Chapters 1 and 2, have generally fallen under the computer crimes statute 18 U.S.C. Section 1030. In this jurisdiction, the Computer Fraud and Abuse Act (CFAA) has been the primary federal statute criminalizing Internet abuses regarding privacy, security, trust, and censorship. To strengthen its powers, it was modified in 1994 and again in 1996 by the National Information Infrastructure Protection Act and codified at U.S.C. subsection 1030, Fraud and Related Activity in Connection with Computers. Following the 9/11 terrorist attacks on the World Trade Center and the Pentagon, the U.S. government passed a number of laws to curb Internet crimes and cope with potential terrorist and cyber terrorist activities. We now discuss more details pertaining to Internet legislation in the United States (Schell, 2007).

18 U.S.C.

As noted, statute 18 U.S.C., Section 1030, is the primary federal statute criminalizing Internet abuses in the United States; thus, it is aptly named the Computer Fraud and Abuse Act. Enacted in 1986, it was amended in 1994, 1996, and

Table 5.4 Tactics Used by Highly Censoring Countries

Censoring country	Web 2.0 blocked	Notable political blocking	Localized or nationwide ICT shutdowns	Pro-government commentators manipulate online discussions	New laws passed to increase censorship, punishment, surveillance or to restrict anonymity	Bloggers and ICT users arrested for posting "offensive" political or social content	Bloggers and ICT users physically attacked or killed for posting "offensive" political or social content
Pakistan		X	X		X	X	X
Bahrain	X	X	X	X		X	X
Saudi Arabia		X		X	X	X	X
Ethiopia	X	X		X		X	
China	X	X	X	X	X	X	X
Iran	X	X		X	X	X	X

again in 2001 by the USA PATRIOT Act, following the 9/11 attacks. Section 1030, in particular, deals with fraud and associated activity aimed at or using computers. At its inception, the CFAA applied only to government computers, but today it applies to a broad group of protected computers, including those used in interstate commerce. Drafted with the future in mind, the CFAA provides the principal basis for criminal prosecution of the various kinds of cybercrime occurring within the jurisdiction of the United States. Broad in its application, the CFAA has been modified to address emerging changes in technology and tech-savvy criminal techniques used to commit exploits. A conviction for violating most of the provisions of the CFAA can be up to five years in prison for each count and up to a $500,000 fine for a second offense. The CFAA also permits any target suffering damage or loss by reason of a violation of the CFAA to bring civil action against the perpetrator for damages (Schell and Martin, 2006).

The following statutes pertain to specific kinds of Internet crime under 18 U.S.C. (Schell, 2007):

- Section 1020: Fraud and related activity regarding access devices
- Section 1030: Fraud and related activity regarding computers
- Section 1362: Communication lines, stations, or systems
- Section 2510: Wire and electronic communications interception as well as the interception of oral communications
- Section 2512: The manufacture, distribution, possession, and advertising of wire, oral, or electronic communication intercepting devices prohibited
- Section 2517: Authorization for disclosure and use of intercepted wire, oral, or electronic communications
- Section 2520: Recovery of civil damages authorized
- Section 2701: Unlawful access to stored communications

- Section 2702: Voluntary disclosure of customers' communications or records
- Section 2703: Required disclosure of customers' communications or records
- Section 3121: Recording of dialing, routing, addressing, and signaling information
- Section 3125: Emergency pen register and trap and trace device installation

A high-profile case of a hacker charged under the CFAA was that of Aaron Swartz, a student at MIT. His alleged crime was that he broke into a closet at the university he attended to plug into the computer network to download millions of academic journal articles from a subscription-only service known as JSTOR. Fuller details on this fascinating case are given in Chapter 4 under his name (Agence France-Presse, 2013).

For More Information: 18 U.S.C. 1030. United States Code, 2006 Edition, Supplement 4, Title 18—Crimes and Criminal Procedure. Available at http://www.gpo.gov/fdsys/granule/USCODE-2010-title18/USCODE-2010-title18-partI-chap47-sec1030/content-detail.html

Health Insurance Portability and Accountability Act of 1996

The Health Insurance Portability and Accountability Act (HIPAA) of 1996 focuses on health protection for U.S. employees in a number of ways, with the Centers for Medicare and Medicaid Services having the responsibility to implement various unrelated provisions of HIPAA. Title I of the Act maintains that health insurance coverage for individuals and their families continues when they transfer or lose employment, and Title II requires the Department of Health and Human Services to develop and maintain national standards for electronic transactions regarding health care in the United States. As well, Title II speaks to the security and privacy of online health data—that which can be sent through the Internet. The developers of HIPAA felt that such standards would improve the efficiency and effectiveness of the U.S. health care system by demanding secure and private handling of electronic data. From an IT security angle, HIPAA requires a double-entry or double-check of data entered by staff. All U.S. healthcare organizations had to be compliant with the HIPAA Security Rule by April 21, 2005—which meant taking extra measures to secure online citizens' health information (Schell and Martin, 2006).

In 2009, the U.S. Department of Health and Human Services Office for Civil Rights announced a final rule that implemented a number of provisions of the Health Information Technology for Economic and Clinical Health Act—enacted as part of the American Recovery and Reinvestment Act of 2009—to increase the privacy and security provisions for health information set out in HIPAA. The latter rule was designed to strike a balance between permitting important uses of health information for patients while protecting their privacy rights. Given the diversity of the health care market in the United States, the rule was designed to be flexible and comprehensive in order to effectively cover the variety of uses and disclosures needing to be addressed. HIPAA-covered health plans are now required to use standardized HIPAA electronic transactions (U.S. Department of Health and Human Services, 2013).

In January 2012, an interesting *California Watch* media story focused on possible questionable Medicare billing practices at the Prime Healthcare Services hospital chain in the United States. The FBI was apparently investigating the hospital chain after some questionable information had surfaced. Over an 18-month period beginning in July 2010, three California congressmen asked Medicare to investigate the Prime Healthcare Services chain for a type of Medicare fraud known as *up-coding*, whereby a health care provider files false claims via computerized billing codes in order to receive enhanced reimbursements. The hospital chain has former employees who claimed that the chain's owner, Dr. Prem Reddy, encouraged physicians and coders to log conditions paying a premium when treating elderly Medicare patients. The hospital chain denied any wrongdoing, saying its Medicare billings are legal and proper (Williams, 2012).

In 2013, the controversy around Prime Healthcare Services continued to grow. In an effort to rebut the *California Watch* story, the hospital chain apparently shared a certain patient's medical files with local newspapers and hundreds of employees. This outcome caused California regulators to fine the hospital chain $95,000 for violating state confidentiality laws as well as the HIPAA federal law. The lawyer representing the hospital chain insisted that the company was not guilty of any wrongdoing. The company said that they would likely sue *California Watch* for defamation, because of the report that the company was under investigation by the FBI (Cocchi, 2013). However, the allegations around the misdeeds continued to mount.

For More Information: Summary of the HIPAA Privacy Rule. Available at http://www.hhs.gov/ocr/privacy/hipaa/understanding/summary/

Digital Millennium Copyright Act of 1998

The protection of intellectual property rights (IPR) from attack by criminals using the Internet is for many corporations today a hugely important concern. The Digital Millennium Copyright Act (DMCA) of 1998 implements certain worldwide copyright laws to cope with emerging technologies by providing protections against the disabling of or bypassing of technical measures designed to protect copyright. Thus, the DMCA sanctions apply to anyone attempting to impair or disable an encryption device (Schell and Martin, 2006).

In 2009, U.S. news headlines carried an interesting story about a would-be satellite television "pirate" who was arrested after allegedly offering a $250,000 reward for secret code for a satellite television smartcard, according to a federal grand jury indictment. Apparently Jung Kwak, the owner of a company importing receiver boxes that pick up satellite television signals, had made a deal with two other people to hire a tech-savvy person to crack the latest encryption scheme used by Echostar Corporation's Dish Network.

Known as Nagra 3, the encryption scheme was implemented by the Echostar Dish Network in 2007 to ward off pirates who had cracked earlier versions of their encryption to obtain programs illegally. Practically speaking, the encryption scheme required subscribers to use special smartcards (made by Nagrastar) in their receiver boxes to unscramble the network's legitimately paid-for proprietary content. In a nutshell, Kwak's company Viewtech typically imported and sold Viewsat receiver boxes to capture supposedly *only free* satellite television programs capturing a small niche market, for example, for religious programs (Zetter, 2009).

To increase his market share, Kwak and his two pals went to a cracker and allegedly reimbursed that person $8,500 to buy a specialized and costly microscope used for reverse-engineering the smartcards. Kwak apparently also agreed to pay the cracker $250,000 if he was able to secure Nagra cards' erasable programmable read-only memory, the gist of the chip needed to reverse-engineer Dish Network's encryption scheme. Jung Kwak, Phillip Allison ("the broken"), and Robert Ward ("thedssguy") were charged with one count of conspiring to violate the DMCA (Zetter, 2009).

On a related note, on January 26, 2013, a new law went into effect in the United States making it illegal for cell phone users to unlock their cell phones in order to switch carriers. Anyone who infringes this law, given recent changes made to the DMCA can be fined between $2,500 and $500,000, and, in some cases, spend time behind prison bars. In essence, the lock feature on mobile devices gives carriers a means of preventing customers from switching to a new plan with another company. So, without a carrier's permission to unlock a cell phone, unlocking it becomes a crime in this jurisdiction (Clarke, 2013).

A digital rights analyst with the Electronic Frontier Foundation (EFF) commented that this amended law was not good one, because cell phone users should be able to unlock their phones to do what they want to do with the device that they legally purchased. The original law was meant to combat copyright infringement, not to stop people from doing what they want with a purchased cell phone, the analyst affirmed (Clarke, 2013).

For More Information: Digital Millennium Copyright Act. Available at http://www.gpo.gov/fdsys/pkg/PLAW-105publ304/pdf/PLAW-105publ304.pdf

Gramm-Leach Bliley Act of 1999 (Financial Services Modernization Act)

Personal information that many online citizens would consider to be private—such as bank account numbers and bank account balances—is routinely exchanged for a price by banks and credit card companies. The Gramm-Leach-Bliley Act (GLBA), also known as the Financial Services Modernization Act of 1999, brought in some privacy protections against the sale of citizens' private information, particularly that of a financial nature. Moreover, the GLBA codified protections against *pre-texting*, defined as the act of getting someone's personal information by a false means.

Before the GLBA's passage, an insurance company having citizens' health records would be deemed to be distinct from a banking institution having personal information on a client wanting a house mortgage; thus, insurance companies and banks, upon a merger, could share information on their clients (Schell, 2007).

With the passage of the GLBA, a number of privacy risks became evident; therefore, the GLBA included three requirements to protect the online personal data and privacy of individuals (Schell, 2007):

1. Information had to be securely stored;
2. The merged institutions had to advise clients about their policy of sharing personal financial information with others; and
3. The institutions had to give consumers the right to *opt out* of the information-sharing schemes, if they so desired.

Because of the awkwardness of the opt out clauses, however, on July 26, 2001, EPIC and Public Citizen, along with other organizations concerned with privacy protection issues, submitted a petition to the GLBA authorities stating their concerns. They argued that the notices distributed by financial institutions used dense, misleading statements that confused consumers about how to go about opting-out. So, these privacy concerns groups requested an amendment to the GLBA to ensure that consumers are provided with better notice and a more convenient way to opt out of the information-sharing scheme (EPIC, 2013).

It is not well known that a Victoria's Secret lingerie catalog—distributed to consumers online and in print—was one of the key reasons that U.S. Congress included privacy protections for financial information when passing the GLBA. The debate started in Congress when Joe Barton talked about his concerns that his credit union had sold his address to the lingerie company, after which he started getting the catalogs at his home. He claimed that he became stressed when they arrived in his mailbox, because he did not want his wife to think that he was entertaining himself with the lingerie-clad attractive women featured in the catalogs. He emphasized that neither he nor his wife had ever purchased anything from the store—online, in person, or from a catalog. Barton also claimed that since he spent so little money in Washington, he knew that his credit union was the only business having his home address. He concluded by saying that since he believed he should be able to stop financial institutions from selling personal information to third parties, he was supporting the passage of the GLBA. Following passage of the act, individuals have the right, of course, to direct financial institutions *not* to sell personal information to third parties (Schell, 2007).

Finally, other Congress representatives were concerned that, given physical access to a computer network could be obtained, where such personal data on clients were stored, gaining illegal access could cause harm to clients' privacy rights or even result in identity theft. Company owners and employees are personally liable for up to $10,000 per violation of the GLBA. Severe civil and criminal penalties for fraud and negligence exist for violations of the GLBA, including huge fines and imprisonment (Innovarus, 2012).

Unfortunately, in recent years, hackers have gotten access to critical personal information of insurance company clients. For example, in October, 2012, the Nationwide Mutual Insurance Company announced that a cracking exploit targeting their network had exposed over 1 million people to identity fraud. The network was also used by Alliance Insurance; data stolen from the insurers included names, Social Security numbers, drivers' license numbers, and clients' birth dates. Nationwide notified authorities shortly after discovering the breach and then started notifying the victims. Because more than 5,000 of the victims were from California, the California Department of Insurance also began reviewing the security measures that the Nationwide and allied group of insurance companies had in place to see if they adequately protected the consumers. Immediately after the breach and during the review (whose results have not been made public), the Nationwide insurance company offered clients a free credit-monitoring and identity theft protection product for a year through their partnership with Equafax, though there was not any evidence at the time of the breach to indicate that the stolen data was being misused by the hackers. The company also said that it would provide clients with a notification of any adverse change in their credit rating, and that it would cover up to $1 million related to identity theft expense coverage. In recent years,

U.S. courts have broadened their definition of the damages that consumers can suffer from such breaches, making companies now liable for actual and future damages, given that identity theft fraud can occur considerably after the network breaches are discovered (Gonsalves, 2012).

For more information: Gramm-Leach-Bliley Act. Available at http://www.gpo.gov/fdsys/pkg/PLAW-106publ102/pdf/PLAW -106publ102.pdf

Trademark Law, Patent Law, and the U.S. Anti-cybersquatting Consumer Protection Act of 1999

Trademark law governs disputes between businesses over the names, logos, and other means used to identify their products and services in the market and online. If someone owns a trademark or a service mark (federally registered or not), there could be, for example, some domain names on the Internet infringing on that trademark. Although individuals may not realize this fact, under U.S. trademark law, trademark owners have a duty to police their trademarks and to notify authorities of perceived infringements (Schell, 2007).

What should you do to protect yourself if someone alleges that you have violated, say, the U.S. Anti-cybersquatting Consumer Protection Act (ACPA)? Let's say that you have received a trademark infringement and cyber squatting threat letter from a trademark owner claiming that you have engaged in *bad faith* cyber squatting. Domain name disputes typically occur between trademark owners and domain name registrants over allegations of cyber squatting, or between the trademark owners and Web site developers or business partners over domain name theft (or hijacking). Let's assume that in the threat letter, the trademark owner says that he has had a registered trademark filed with the U.S. Patent and Trademark Office since 2002, but that you had registered your domain name with the same trademark in 2006. The letter goes on to say that you are in violation of the ACPA, and that the owner of the trademark is thinking about filing an ACPA lawsuit, naming you as a defendant and claiming $100,000 in damages plus attorney's fees (Schaefer, 2012).

So, what should you now do? According to U.S. cyber squatting law attorney Enrico Schaefer, you should take the threat letter seriously. If you are thinking of turning over the domain name, be careful how you verbalize that in your response letter, because often your incorrectly written letter will in court prove that you have been, in fact, cyber squatting. Schaefer's bottom line is this: get a good attorney to defend you early on in the game to obtain a settlement and release. Once in court, the damages can sky-rocket well above the $100,000 mark—as numerous cases fought in U.S. courts in recent years have shown (Schaefer, 2012).

For more information: Anti-cybersquatting Consumer Protection Act. Available at http://www.gpo.gov/fdsys/pkg/BILLS -106s1255is/pdf/BILLS-106s1255is.pdf

USA PATRIOT Act of 2001 and PATRIOT Act II

In October 2001, following the 9/11 terrorist attacks, the Uniting and Strengthening America by Providing Appropriate Tools Required to Intercept and Obstruct Terrorism—the USA PATRIOT Act of 2001—was hastily enacted into law. In fact, Congressman Ron Paul told *The Washington Times* that no one in Congress was allowed to read in full the text of PATRIOT I. When eventually shown to the public, that remark seemed to upset civil libertarians as well as constitutional scholars. William Safire, in writing for *The New York Times*, remarked that in passing the act so quickly, President Bush was, in effect, seizing dictatorial control.

Then, in early February 2003, the Center for Public Integrity, a public interest think tank in Washington, D.C., disclosed the entire text of the highly controversial Domestic Security Enhancement Act of 2003—better known as PATRIOT Act II. This proposed piece of legislation was never brought to Congress in its entirety. Some of the controversy surrounding this proposed piece was caused by provisions that would give the executive power the ability to, say, revoke American citizenship from a citizen suspected of terrorism, allow the CIA and FBI to partake in domestic spying, mandate the collection of DNA samples from "persons of interest," and revoke certain aspects of the Freedom of Information Act—including the right to obtain information about detained family members who may themselves be terrorists. All of these provisions would adversely impact civil liberties, the public interest tanks argued, thus killing the eventual passage of the PATRIOT Act II (Schell, 2007).

For more information: USA PATRIOT Act. Available at http://www.gpo.gov/fdsys/pkg/BILLS-107hr3162enr/pdf/BILLS-107hr3162enr.pdf. Center for Public Integrity, "Justice Dept. drafts sweeping expansion of anti-terrorism act." Available at http://www.publicintegrity.org/2003/02/07/3159/justice-dept-drafts-sweeping-expansion-anti-terrorism-act

Cybersecurity Enhancement Act of 2002 or Homeland Security Act of 2002

In 2002, the U.S. Senate proposed the Cybersecurity Enhancement Act, or Homeland Security Act, on November 25, establishing the Department of Homeland Security. The act was clearly meant to keep the networked critical infrastructure safe from attack or to have a readiness response if they were attacked. The nine subsections of the Homeland Security Act are as follows (Schell, 2007):

1. Title I: The Department of Homeland Security (DHS) and its missions and functions
2. Title II: Information analysis and infrastructure protection
3. Title III: Chemical, biological, radiological, and nuclear countermeasures
4. Title IV: Border and transportation security

5. Title V: Emergency preparedness and response
6. Title VI: Internal management of the DHS
7. Title VII: General provisions and coordination with nonfederal entities, the inspector general, and the U.S. Secret Service
8. Title VIII: Transitional items
9. Title IX: Conforming and other technical amendments

It is important to note that civil liberties groups objected strongly to the Homeland Security Act right from the beginning, arguing that it is characterized by three trends that can adversely impact citizens: reduced privacy, increased government secrecy, and increased government power to protect their own special interests. In fact, Allen Weinstein, the president of the Center for Democracy in Washington, D.C., labeled it "a law of unintended consequences" (9-11 Research, 2012).

For more information: Cybersecurity Enhancement Act of 2002. Available at http://www.gpo.gov/fdsys/pkg/BILLS-107hr 3482rfs/pdf/BILLS-107hr3482rfs.pdf. Homeland Security Act of 2002. Available at http://www.dhs.gov/xlibrary/assets/hr_5005 _enr.pdf

PROTECT Act of 2003, COPPA of 1998, and CIPA of 2000

An important piece of U.S. legislation is the PROTECT Act—or the Prosecutorial Remedies and Other Tools to End the Exploitation of Children Today Act of 2003. It was passed by the U.S. Senate in February 2003, with an extraordinary vote of 84 senators in favor and none opposed. The purpose of this piece was to assist law enforcement in their attempts to protect children from criminal exploitation by adults, particularly relating to the production and distribution of child pornography over the Internet.

The PROTECT Act also attempted to extend prosecutorial powers beyond U.S. jurisdictions; thus, the national AMBER alert system was enhanced. For example, within the PROTECT Act, the AMBER alert sections provide a means for improved national coordination of established state programs, such that an official from the U.S. Department of Justice is assigned as the national AMBER alert coordinator, who establishes a set of minimum standards to apply when deciding to issue an alert across U.S. states. These standards, which most U.S. states employ, include the following: (1) a law enforcement agency confirms an abduction has taken place of a child aged 17 or younger; (2) the law enforcement agency believes the child abducted is in danger of bodily harm or death; and (3) there is enough descriptive information about the child and the abductor, or the abductor's vehicle, that if made available to the public, could help find and save the child.

An AMBER alert, however, can be activated by law enforcement only in the most serious of cases. These alerts can be transmitted over the radio and television (often on a "crawl" information strip at the bottom of the screen), through the Internet, and on electronic traffic information signs on highways. The AMBER alert system was put into place after 9-year-old Amber Hagerman was kidnapped as she was riding her bike outside of her home in Arlington, Texas, in broad daylight and in view of witnesses. Her body was found four days later at the bottom of a creek. The cause of death was a slit throat, and her murderer was not found (U.S. Government Printing Office Access, 2013).

The PROTECT Act also redefined child pornography to include not only images of real children engaging in sexually explicit conduct with adults but of computer-generated depictions indistinguishable from real children engaging in such acts. *Indistinguishable* was further defined as that which an ordinary person viewing the image would conclude is a real child engaging in sexually explicit acts. However, cartoons, drawings, paintings, and sculptures depicting minors or adults engaging in sexually explicit acts, as well as depictions of actual adults that look like minors engaging in sexually explicit acts, were excluded from the definition (Schell, 2007).

Furthermore, the Children's Online Privacy Protection Act (COPPA) of 1998, which actually became effective in 2000, applied to the online collection of personal information from children under age 13. COPPA details what a Web site operator must include in their privacy policy, when and how to seek verifiable consent from parents or guardians, and what actions an operator must take to protect children's privacy and online safety. These Internet safety policies require the use of filters to protect users against access to visual depictions considered as obscene or harmful to minors. By definition, a filter is a device for suppressing or minimizing waves or oscillations of certain frequencies. As a result, filtering software blocks access to blacklisted Web sites (Schell, 2007).

Finally, the Children's Internet Protection Act (CIPA) of 2000 requires that U.S. libraries receiving electronic-rate discounts or grants for Internet access enforce stipulated policies using technological protection measures—primarily filters—to keep minors safe from harmful Web site viewing. What is deemed harmful is child pornography, content that is obscene, and information that is generally considered to be harmful to minors. This law does not require filters to block other text-based material (Schell, 2007).

For more information:

PROTECT Act of 2003. Available at http://www.gpo.gov/fdsys/pkg/BILLS-108s151enr/pdf/BILLS-108s151enr.pdf

Children's Online Privacy Protection Rule. Available at http://www.ftc.gov/enforcement/rules/rulemaking-regulatory-reform-proceedings/childrens-online-privacy-protection-rule

Children's Internet Protection Act. Available at http://ifea.net/cipa.pdf

CAN-SPAM Act of 2003

Known officially as the Controlling the Assault of Non-solicited Pornography and Marketing Act of 2003, the act was passed by the U.S. Senate on November 25, 2003, to regulate interstate commerce by imposing penalties on online users transmitting unsolicited email through the Internet—spam.

President George W. Bush signed it into law on December 16, 2003, and it took effect on January 1, 2004. Penalties included fines as high as $1 million or jail terms up to five years, or both. There were critics to the act, such as Steve Linford, the director of the Spamhaus Project, who argued that with the passage of such a law, the U.S. government seems not to understand the extent and danger of the spam problem. Linford compared the legislation to that passed in the United Kingdom, which he said had more teeth because it made spam illegal. Linford further argued that the CAN-SPAM Act simply attempts to regulate spam rather than ban it. Moreover, he said that because the act requires online citizens to read and react to every spam opt out clause, millions of email users will inadvertently find their email addresses sold on the Internet. Linford argued that ultimately there would have to be a new U.S. federal law passed that would properly ban spam (Schell and Martin, 2006).

Offenders of the CAN-SPAM Act of 2003 are considered to be individuals who knowingly (Schell, 2007)

- gain access to a protected computer without authorization and intentionally initiate the sending of multiple commercial email messages from or through that computer and a connection to the Internet;
- use a protected computer to relay or retransmit multiple commercial email messages to intentionally either deceive or mislead receivers or any Internet access service as to the origin of such email messages;
- intentionally falsify header information in multiple commercial email messages and intentionally initiate the sending of such messages;
- register using information falsifying the identity of the actual registrant for five or more email accounts, or online user accounts of two or more domain names, and intentionally initiate the sending of multiple commercial email messages from any combination of these accounts or domain names;

- intentionally falsely represent oneself as a legitimate registrant of five or more Internet protocol (IP) addresses, and then intentionally initiate the sending of many commercial email messages from such addresses.

Jurisdictions besides the United States have in recent years passed similar pieces of legislation to curb spammers. For example, the European Union (EU) has a number of pieces of legislation, including the E-Privacy Directive, the E-Commerce Directive, and the Data Protection Directive. Canada's online anti-intrusion legislation involving section 342.1 of the Canadian Criminal Code is aimed at several potential harms to property and persons, including stealing computer services, invading online individuals' privacy rights, and trading in computer passwords or cracking encryption systems. Charges for breaches of this nature are typically made with regard to applicable sections of the Canadian Criminal Code, such as theft, fraud, computer abuse, information abuse, and the interception of communications (Schell, 2007).

Some interesting spammer court cases have made media headlines in recent years. In 2009, a U.S. man who bragged about being "the godfather of spam" was sentenced to 51 months in a federal prison by a judge in Detroit, Maryland, for his role as the protagonist in an email stock scam scheme. Alan Ralsky, then aged 64, faced five years of probation after fulfilling his prison term and had to hand over $250,000 seized by the U.S. government agents in 2007. Ralsky's son-in-law Scott Bradley, then aged 48, received 40 months in prison and 5 years of probation after his release from prison. The pair were charged with committing wire and mail fraud, money laundering, and violation of the CAN-SPAM Act of 2003. In the end, they pleaded guilty to the charges (Yousuf, 2009).

For more information: Controlling the Assault of Non-Solicited Pornography and Marketing Act of 2003. Available at http://www.gpo.gov/fdsys/pkg/PLAW-108publ187/pdf/PLAW-108publ187.pdf

Cybersecurity Enhancement Act of 2005/2002

Though the Cybersecurity Enhancement Act of 2001 was introduced and sent to the House Judiciary by Lamar Smith in December 2001, and later sent to the U.S. Senate in 2002, it wasn't until April 20, 2005, that the House Committee on Homeland Security, Subcommittee on Cybersecurity, Infrastructure Protection, and Security Technologies passed HR 285—known as the Cybersecurity Enhancement Act. This act stated that the assistant secretary for cybersecurity would be head of the Directorate's Office of Cybersecurity and Communications within the National Protection and Programs. The head of the Directorate was responsible for enhancing the security, resilience, and reliability of the United States' cyber and communications infrastructure and creating an effective cyberattack warning system for the nation (Schell, 2007).

In March 2013, additional changes were proposed to the Cybersecurity Enhancement Act. Under HR 756, as ordered by the House Committee on Science, Space, and Technology, the Act would reauthorize a number of programs under the National Science Foundation to enhance cybersecurity by better protecting networks from breaches, it would require the National Institute of Standards and Technology (NIST) to carry on with its cybersecurity awareness program and with the development of standards for better managing personal information being stored on computers, and establish a task force for recommending appropriate actions to Congress for upgrading R & D activities to improve cybersecurity. *For More Information:* Cybersecurity Enhancement Act of 2005. Available at https://www.govtrack.us/congress/bills/109/hr285/text

Recent Internet Laws *Not* Passed in the United States Related to Privacy, Security, Trust, and Censorship: CISPA, SOPA, and PIPA—and Why

What is probably noteworthy is the demand of U.S. online citizens that their government provide adequate protections through effective and evolving legislation—making it unlawful for another online user to intrude into their personal data or attack critical infrastructure binding the United States and holding the economy together. As well, there are high-profile pressure groups like the EFF and hacktivist cells like Anonymous that forcefully allege that some pieces of proposed legislation aimed at safeguarding online citizens represent serious threats to Internet freedom, privacy, and openness. Clearly, then, one of the major challenges met in passing Internet-related legislation in the United States (or in any jurisdiction, for that matter) is to balance such competing interests. Often, the balancing of competing interests can mean delays in getting legislation passed, or total roadblocks.

In fact, there are sometimes rather interesting real-life events that expose the truly complex relationships existing between the government's information technology policy interests and society, in general. For example, a practical real-world question that has arisen over the past 15 years or so is this: should the U.S. and other governments openly pursue the unique talents of hackers in order to help keep the nation's networks safe from cyber invasions? And in some jurisdictions like the United States and China, the answer appears to be "yes."

As a case in point, in July 2012, a U.S. four star general, Keith Alexander, the director of the U.S. National Security Agency, dressed in jeans and a T-shirt, told thousands of male and female Black Hat and DefCon hacker attendees in Las Vegas that the NSA needs great talent; though they do not pay as much as other competitors, the NSA is fun to be around.

That said, other events have shown that with the activities of hacker cells like Anonymous and WikiLeaks, governments around the world seem to be thinking twice about hiring talented individuals lurking in the Computer Underground in order to safeguard networks. It is one thing, say onlookers, that Anonymous hacker cells took on the Church of Scientology in 2008, when hackers within their fold tried removing online access to interviews with actor Tom Cruise, a strong supporter of that church. It is quite another thing that hacker cells like Anonymous and WikiLeaks have moved on to attacking government networks and exposing critical information on the Internet to allegedly protect the openness of the Internet.

As a case in point, in April 2012, Anonymous disabled several U.K. government Web sites through distributed denial-of-service attacks as a response to existing British legislation or new proposals aimed at authorizing the surveillance of citizens' Internet activities.

As hacking exploits, online piracy, and online theft increased dramatically worldwide in 2012, legislators in various jurisdictions were in a constant debate about which laws to pass to stop Internet-based security threats—and how, so as to protect online citizens' freedoms. For example, in April 2012, the U.S. House of Representatives passed a pretty stringent Cyber Intelligence Sharing and Protection Act (CISPA), but because of such concerns and public outcry, the Senate modified the act considerably. The result was that the revised law, known as the Cybersecurity Act of 2012, was significantly less restrictive than its original version but, unlike the earlier version, it had President Obama's support. What the president liked about the revision was that it helped companies—with reasonable liability protection—to share data with government officials when their networks had been attacked to help them recover from this kind of costly disaster (Ruth and Stone, 2012).

A major reason that the CISPA bill was revised was that lobbying groups like the EFF argued for less restrictive language. Also, the EFF pushed for voluntary compliance from businesses and a voluntary self-certification process that would be overseen by a new National Cybersecurity Council, with members from the private and public sectors as well as government. The EFF was also opposed to excessive surveillance measures that the U.S. government wanted to implement with this piece of legislation. After many discussions on a number of fronts, on August 3, 2012, just prior to the month-long recess of

Congress, the revised CISPA bill was defeated. What's more, no active U.S. cybersecurity legislation was pending. The sponsors of CISPA, therefore, vowed to revive their discussions through 2013, in the hopes of eventually getting the bill passed (Ruth and Stone, 2012). The bill was passed by the House and amended April 18, 2013.

For more information: Cyber Intelligence Sharing and Protection Act. Available at http://intelligence.house.gov/sites/ intelligence.house.gov/files/documents/CISPAPassedApril 2013.pdf

SOPA and PIPA

In January 2012, digital rights activists, online citizens, and a number of high-profile technology companies collaborated on an Internet blackout to protest against two U.S. Congressional bills: the Stop Online Piracy Act (SOPA) and the PROTECT IP Act (PIPA). The high-tech companies included the popular news-sharing Web site reddit, the browser pioneer Mozilla, Google, and the photo-sharing Web site Twitpic. All expressed solidarity with the protest by putting anti-SOPA material on their home pages. Furthermore, these online protests were accompanied by on-land protests, in New York City, where thousands of the city's technology industry participants demonstrated outside the offices of U.S. senators Chuck Schumer (D-NY) and Kristen Gillibrand (D-NY) (Carter and Grimm, 2012).

Both of these bills had the objective of combating piracy on non-U.S. Web sites hosting content allegedly infringing on U.S. copyrights. If passed, they would have allowed the U.S. attorney general to order that ISPs had to block any Web site that contained so-called infringing material. However, both bills were withdrawn after the online blackout and public outrage.

Following the failure of SOPA to pass as law, the U.S. government authorities decided to use other means to bring down groups that they believe are dissident and a menace to society. For example, the micro-blogging Web site Twitter received a number of subpoenas from the U.S. government asking for information on so-called anti-secrecy organizations like WikiLeaks (the hacker group founded in 2006 and known worldwide after they claimed to have leaked online several confidential files regarding the violence in Syria) and the Occupy Wall Street movement (a leaderless hactivist movement whose Web site says that members are opposed to the greed and corruption "of the 1%" and will use tactics of the revolutionary Arab Spring to achieve their ends). However, rather than giving the U.S. government the information being subpoenaed, Twitter challenged these requests in court, and was successful (Freedom House, 2012; Ruth and Stone, 2012).

For more information:

Stop Online Piracy Act. Available at http://www.gpo.gov/fdsys/pkg/BILLS-112hr3261ih/pdf/BILLS-112hr3261ih.pdf

PROTECT IP Act of 2011. Available at http://www.leahy.senate.gov/imo/media/doc/BillText-PROTECTIPAct.pdf

Internet Legislation Attempts Globally Related to Privacy, Security, Trust, and Censorship: The Budapest Convention on Cybercrime

In 2001, group action on an international front was being taken to combat Internet crime. On November 8, 2001, at the 109th Session of the Council of Europe, the Committee of Ministers of the council adopted a Convention on Cybercrime and its explanatory report and then opened it for signature in Budapest on November 23, 2001. Known as the Budapest Convention on Cybercrime, it came into force on July 1, 2004. This convention was the first global legislative attempt to set standards on Internet-related crime and develop policies and procedures to govern international cooperation in order to combat it. The treaty was to enter into force when at least five states, three of which were members of the Council of Europe, had ratified it (Schell, 2007).

On November 17, 2003, President Bush transmitted the convention to the U.S. Senate for ratification. The convention requires countries ratifying it to adopt similar criminal laws on cracking, infringements of IPR, Internet-related fraud, and Internet-disseminated child pornography. It also contains provisions on investigative powers and procedures, including the search of computer networks and the interception of communications. In particular, the convention requires cooperation between cross-border law enforcement agencies in searches, seizures, and extradition. After the outset, it was amended by an additional protocol making any online publication of racist propaganda a criminal offense (Schell, 2007).

As of October 28, 2010, 30 states had signed, ratified, and acceded to the Budapest Convention, whereas a further 16 states had signed but not ratified it. Moreover, on July 2, 2013, in Brussels, the high representative of the European Union for Foreign Affairs and Security Policy issued a joint communication to the European Parliament, The Council, The European Economic and Social Committee, and the Committee of the Regions. Titled, "Cybersecurity Strategy of the European Union: An Open, Safe and Secure Cyberspace," this report was a rather comprehensive cybersecurity strategy proposal for the EU. It outlined the EU's vision and actions for strongly protecting and promoting citizens' online rights and making EU's online environment one of the safest in the world. Accepting that this vision could be realized only through a true partnership between many actors, the proposal called for member states that have not yet ratified the Budapest Convention to ratify it and implement its provisions as early as possible (High Representative of the European Union for Foreign Affairs and Security Policy, 2013). As of January, 2014, 41 states had ratified.

For more information: Budapest Convention on Cybercrime. Available at http://conventions.coe.int/Treaty/en/Treaties/Html/185.htm

Anti-Counterfeiting Trade Agreement

Besides SOPA and PIPA, the U.S. government advocated an online copyright protection and antipiracy measure, known as the Anti-Counterfeiting Trade Agreement (ACTA). ACTA had a number of provisions like SOPA and PIPA; plus it had support from the U.S., Mexican, and Moroccan governments, to mention just a few. However, once WikiLeaks in 2008 disclosed some online details of the "secret" international negotiations and alleged that ACTA would authorize signatory nations to "peer inside your iPod" at border crossings, ACTA's progress and usefulness were immediately questioned outside of the United States and Japan (Ruth and Stone, 2012).

Organizations representing non-governmental interests argued that ACTA could infringe citizens' fundamental rights, including freedom of expression and privacy. Doctors Without Borders maintained that the passage of ACTA would jeopardize access to medicines in developing nations, and the Electronic Frontier Foundation argued that because of the secret nature of the negotiations, key parties were missing— such as civil society groups and developing nations.

The final blow to ACTA came in July 2012, when the 27-member-state European Parliament loudly and collaboratively defeated it, saying that it was an anti-Internet and pro-censorship bill. In short, apart from a few tries to legislate tiny parts of the former SOPA law—like requiring U.S. embassies to move foreign copyright experts from State Department supervision to U.S. Patent and Trademark Office supervision—the United States is unlikely to pass any kind of major antipiracy legislation being passed any time soon (Ruth and Stone, 2012).

For more information: Anti-Counterfeiting Trade Agreement. Available at http://www.ipo.gov.uk/pro-crime-acta

Trans-Pacific Partnership Agreement

In recent years, the "big media" lobbyists have been pushing for trade agreements with copyright measures that are far more restrictive than those currently required by existing treaties or legislation in the United States; but in 2012, the big media lobbyists went international. The Open Internet activists saw the Trans-Pacific Partnership (TPP) agreement as the most threatening of these developments.

The overriding fear is that the TPP seeks, among other provisions, (1) the rewriting of the global rules on intellectual property enforcement, giving the big media new powers to lock online users out of content and services, (2) providing new liabilities forcing ISPs to police online activities, and (3) giving the big media companies stronger powers to shut down Web sites and to remove content deemed to be "offensive."

The Open Internet activists also fear the TPP's proposed encouragement of ISPs to block accused infringers' access to the Internet and the possibility that ISPs could give online users' private information to big media conglomerates without appropriate privacy safeguards. In other words, the Open Internet activists argue that given the number of restrictions in the proposed TPP, all Internet users could become suspected copyright criminals, and it appears to criminalize content sharing, in general. It is further believed by the activists that the pro-TPP lobbyists have been paid for by U.S. mega-corporations.

These behind-closed-door negotiations seem to have been going on since 2008, and according to the U.S. Trade Representative's Office, negotiators were hoping to finalize the TPP by July 2012. However, as of December 2012, the negotiations seem to be continuing, with a sixteenth round of TPP negotiations scheduled to take place in Singapore from March 4 to 13, 2013 (Office of the United States Trade Representative, 2013).

The Open Internet activists have vehemently argued that the approach being used to advance the TPP is undemocratic, because there has been a woeful lack of proper online citizen and stakeholder consultation. Furthermore, there has been no open access to TPP documents, and, sadly, they argue, there appear to have been no checks or balances put in place to ensure the well-being of online global citizens. In short, there has to be an adequate means of protecting content owners' needs, balanced with the rights of Internet users—and this just doesn't seem to be the case with the TPP (Bailey, 2012).

The 11 nations currently negotiating the TPP are the United States, Canada, Australia, Peru, Malaysia, Vietnam, New Zealand, Chile, Singapore, Mexico, and Brunei Darussalam. The EFF obtained a leaked document of a February 2011 TPP draft—never officially released by the TPP—which can be found at http://keionline.org/sites/default/files/tpp-10feb2011 -us-text-ipr-chapter.pdf (EFF, 2013).

Furthermore, according to the EFF, U.S. negotiators are trying to adopt copyright measures far more restrictive than those currently required by international treaties, including the controversial ACTA. Moreover, all countries signing on would be required to conform their domestic laws and policies to the provisions in the Agreement—meaning that a recently leaked U.S.-proposed intellectual property chapter would include provisions exceeding current U.S. law, including the controversial aspects of the Digital Millennium Copyright Act, or DMCA. On February 5, 2013, the EFF Web site said that the EFF joined 24 U.S. civil society groups to demand a baseline of transparency in TPP negotiations, and a letter was sent to Barbara Weisel, the lead negotiator for the TPP, calling for more needs for transparency and an increased civil involvement instead of the secret backdoor meetings (Sutton, 2013).

Finally, the Public Knowledge Web site has expressed similar concerns about the TPP. As of mid-2012, they affirm, there have been about thirteen rounds of secretive negotiations, five leaks of the proposed text, and close to zero involvement by the public. Very worrisome is the fact that everything known about the TPP is known because of leaks through the Internet, and the negotiators have not even once willingly given the public or public interest organizations like the EFF and Public Knowledge any key information voluntarily. Furthermore, the schedule for negotiation seems to have become accelerated in recent months in order to bring a "close" to the process (Public Knowledge, 2013).

For more information: Trans-Pacific Partnership. Available at http://www.ustr.gov/tpp

The United Nations: Unprecedented Power over Web Content and Infrastructure?

The International Telecommunications Union (ITU) convened the World Conference on International Telecommunications in Dubai, United Arab Emirates, from December 3 to 14, 2012. This landmark conference had as its priority a review of the International Telecommunication Regulations, which acts as the binding global treaty to facilitate international interconnection and interoperability of information by ensuring global usefulness and open access to the Internet (ITU, 2013).

However, several nations hoped to use this conference to push for more stringent Internet controls by pressing to tactically take away control of the Internet's technical specifications control and the domain name system from U.S. bodies and to give them to an international organization similar to—if not to—the United Nations. Advocates for this change included Russia and China, along with other nations that wanted the "less biased" international organization to have unprecedented power over Web content and infrastructure.

Some Open Internet activists and high-tech companies like Google saw such a proposed move as increasing the censorship of the Internet and going against the basic principle of Internet freedom and openness. In fact, a Google spokesperson voiced concerns that only governments had a voice at the ITU conference—and not high-tech companies or others that have a stake in the Internet's development and ongoing evolution (Emmanuel, 2012).

In an attempt to ensure that Internet regulation continues to be as free and open as possible (and considering that many of the Internet-regulating organizations reside in the United

States), in August 2012, the U.S. House rushed to pass a unanimous resolution against any increase in the United Nations', or some similar body's, control over the Internet The resolution stated that the US would continue to work on a policy to promote a global Internet free from government control (Ashford, 2012).

Despite Russia's above proposal advocating a more open Internet, the Russian Duma, following a day's protest blackout of Russian-language content on the Wikipedia Web site—along with claims of online censorship—passed by a vote of 441 to 9 a bill aimed at blacklisting over 400 "harmful Internet sites"; the bill took effect in November 2012 (Ruth and Stone, 2012).

A similar paradox exists in China. Although China is home to the world's largest population of Internet users—many of whom have manifested increasing creativity in fighting online censorship (such as imprisoned Nobel laureate Liu Xiabo), China remains one of the world's most restrictive online environments. One academic study reviewed censorship across almost 1,400 blog-hosting and bulletin board platforms in China and found that about 13 percent of the posts were deleted, many within a 24-hour period after being deemed by government authorities as "sensitive" or espousing an "inappropriate" message regarding the Chinese Communist Party (Freedom House, 2012).

What's more, China has been known to act in other aggressive, censoring ways, such as imprisoning what is estimated to be at least 190,000 online users whose behavior was deemed by government agents to be "in need of reform." These online users are placed in one of the country's network of 350 work camps, typically without the bother of any charges, lawyers, trials, or appeals. These work camps were penal systems designed by Mao Zedong to deal quickly with Chinese government political opponents (MacKinnon, 2013).

Nowadays, Chinese citizens can be sentenced to up to four years of "re-education through labour." Ren Jianyu, having served his time in such a work camp, is now free. Ren believes that he was sent to one outside of Chongqing, because he posted something online that offended Bo Xilai, the ex-boss of the local communist party (MacKinnon, 2013).

Actually, Ren's imprisonment struck a chord nationwide, because he was not a political or religious activist; he was just somebody who had posted his thoughts on the Internet. Another famous person who spent three years in a work camp was Liu Xiabo, the alleged dissident and Nobel laureate who questioned the Communist Party's right to rule. Besides doing menial labor in the camps, which human rights activists have negatively called "the re-education archipelago," prisoners undergo an educational portion of the rehabilitation program, including hearing constant and numerous tales of Communist Party heroes. China has recently thrown its support behind the United Nations' having tighter control over the Internet. Zhou Litai, a prominent Chongqing lawyer, said on Ren's release (MacKinnon, 2013, p. A9): "Factually, [the labor-camp system] has become a tool that local governments used to get revenge on ordinary people. [It] is the opposite of what China's current social and legal system requires."

For more information: International Telecommunication Regulations. Available at http://www.itu.int/en/wcit-12/Pages/itrs.aspx

Conclusion

Over the past 20 years, the Internet has had a tremendous and very positive impact on all parts of society—citizens' daily lives, their fundamental rights, their social interactions, and their nations' economies. This chapter opened with a look at Internet usage worldwide and Internet penetration. Some countries were viewed as being strong advocates of the Open Internet—such as the United States and Estonia, while other countries like China and Iran were viewed as being strong advocates for Internet censorship, particularly around politically sensitive issues.

Legal experts have argued that, for cyberspace to remain open and free, the same norms, principles, freedoms, and values that are upheld on land should be upheld online. An open and free cyberspace has promoted political and social inclusion worldwide, taken down barriers between countries and its citizens, allowed for the interaction and sharing of information globally, provided a forum for freedom of expression and fundamental rights, and empowered online citizens in nondemocratic governments to continue pushing for democratic and more just societies—as demonstrated recently by the Arab Spring (Ruth and Stone, 2012).

But, as the balance of this chapter has discussed, in order for the Internet to remain open and free, fundamental rights, democracy, and rule of law all need to be protected. So, exactly where have passed or not-passed legislation or data collection guidelines leave governments trying to curb cybercrime and online censorship? The answer plainly is, "It varies widely."

On March 13, 2013, for example, the Canadian federal government, concerned that we live in an information age where data mining can invade online citizens' privacy rights, announced that it has changed its own restrictions regarding data gathering when Canadians visit government Web sites. Among other things, the new rules prohibit the government from profiling individuals' online activities by tracking their computer's IP address. Furthermore, any use of the IP address to measure Web site traffic must also ensure that the address is rendered anonymous. However, these rules do not cover the data available to the government via social media Web sites created by individual departments, which clearly operate beyond the bounds of Canadian federal policy (Canadian Press, 2013).

Also on March 13, 2013, according to the U.S. Intelligence chief James Clapper (whose quote appears at the start of this chapter), the present-day reality is that a devastating cyberattack could cripple America's infrastructure and economy. Clapper warned Congress that such cyberattacks pose the most dangerous immediate threat to the United States—more pressing than, say, a land attack by global terrorist networks. Clapper's testimony took note of the negative consequences of the Arab Spring, saying that while "some countries have made progress toward democratic rule, most are experiencing uncertainty, violence and political backsliding," including ethnic violence and on-land terrorist attacks. As a result of the Arab Spring backlash, he said that the United States needs to worry about impending, devastating cyberattacks, because of three main issues: (1) the possibility that political chaos will produce "ungoverned spaces" from which extremists could plot against the United States, (2) the fact that high unemployment rates and severe economic distress found in these spaces could exacerbate the destabilization here, and (3) the likelihood that anti-American sentiments on the part of new, populist governments in these volatile regions could cause heated flare-ups (Mazzetti and Shane, 2013, p. A15).

So what immediate remedies would legal and cybersecurity experts suggest to cope more effectively with these concerns? Some legal experts have argued that the various laws currently available in the United States and elsewhere, plus more voluntary actions by major ISPs, could help to keep such cyberattacks at bay. Other more conservative factions have argued that more restrictive laws like SOPA and PIPA need to be enacted in the United States or elsewhere. And when certain pieces of more restrictive legislation like SOPA, PIPA, and CISPA are defeated in the United States or elsewhere—usually as a result of activist groups' loud outcries that Internet censorship is harmful to online citizens' rights—government officials, as a means of providing stopgap measures, seem to start drafting executive orders not requiring formal approval by bodies like the U.S. Congress.

In the meantime, affirm the bulk of cybersecurity experts, the potential dangers of tech-savvy cyber criminals continue to grow day by day—bringing with them the real possibility for cyberattacks on targeted nations' networks responsible for water, power, fuel, transportation, and finance. Clearly, some more effective solutions need to be found.

References

9-11 Research. "The Homeland Security Act." 2012, http://911research.wtc7.net/post911/legislation/hsa.html (accessed December 21).

Agence France-Presse. "Advocates angered by death of 26-year-old hacktivist." *The Globe and Mail,* January 14, 2013, p. A9.

Ashford, W. "US passes resolution to block UN control of the Internet." 2012, http://www.computerweekly.com/news/2240160979/US-passes-resolution-to-block-UN-control-of-the-internet (accessed August 6).

Bailey, A. "TPP: The secretive agreement that could criminalize your Internet use." 2012, http://openmedia.ca/blog/tpp-secretive-agreement-could-criminalize-your-internet-use (accessed May 14).

Canadian Press. "Privacy: Tories restrict online data mining, but not for social media." *The Globe and Mail,* March 13, 2013, p. A8.

Carter, Z., and R. Grimm. "SOPA blackout aims to block Internet censorship bill." 2012, http://www.huffingtonpost.com/2012/01/18/sopa-blackout-internet-censorship_n_1211905.html?iew=print&comm_ref=false (accessed January 20).

Clarke, J. "Jailbreaking cell phones to become ILLEGAL at midnight: Law makes 'unlocking' devices to switch carriers punishable by fines and even prison." 2013, http://www.dailymail.co.uk/news/article-2268743/New-law-makes-unlocking-cell-phones-switch-carriers-punishable-fines-prison.html (accessed January 26).

Cocchi, R. "Hospital chain faces two federal investigations." 2013, http://healthexecnews.com/hospital-chain-faces-federal-investigations (accessed February 8).

EFF. "Trans Pacific Partnership Agreement." 2013, https://www.eff.org/issues/tpp (accessed February 5).

Emmanuel, O. "Google steps up pressure on UN's Internet treaty conference." 2012, http://premiumtimesng.com/news/109644-google-steps-up-pressure-on-uns-internet-treaty-conference.html (accessed December 3).

EPIC. "The Gramm-Leach Bliley Act." 2013, http://epic.org/privacy/glba/ (accessed March 6).

Gonsalves, A. "Nationwide/Allied security breach highlights litigation fears." 2012, http://www.cso.com.au/article/444079/nationwide_allied_security_breach_highlights_litigation_fears/ (accessed December 7).

High Representative of the European Union for Foreign Affairs and Security Policy. "Joint Communication to the European Parliament, The Council, The European Economic and Social Committee and The Committee of the Regions 'Cybersecurity Strategy of the European Union: An Open, Safe and Secure Cyberspace.' " 2013, http://ec.europa.eu/digital-agenda/en/news/eu-cybersecurity-plan-protect-open-internet-and-online-freedom-and-opportunity-cyber-security (accessed and downloaded from a related link February 7).

Innovarus. "Gramm-Leach Bliley Act." 2012, http://innovarus.com/glba.htm (accessed March 2).

Internet World Stats. "World Internet Users Statistics: Usage and World Population Stats." 2013, http://www.internetworldstats.com/stats.htm (accessed February 17).

ITU. "World Conference on International Telecommunications (WCIT-12)." 2013, http://www.itu.int/en/wcit-12/Pages/default.aspx (accessed March 12).

Kelly, S., S. Cook, and M. Truong. *Freedom on the Net 2012: A Global Assessment of Internet and Digital Media.* New York: Freedom House, 2012, http://www.freedomhouse.org/sites/default/files/FOTN%202012%20FINAL.pdf (accessed December 30).

MacKinnon, M. "One man's crusade against China's re-education camps." *The Globe and Mail*, March 11, 2013, pp. A1, A9.

Mazzetti, M., and S. Shane. "Cyberattacks top threat to US, intelligence chief says." *The Globe and Mail*, March 13, 2013, p. A15.

Office of the United States Trade Representative. "Trans-Pacific Partnership (TPP): 16th round of TPP negotiations set for Singapore—March 4–13, 2013." 2013, http://www.ustr.gov/tpp (accessed March 12).

Public Knowledge. "The Trans-Pacific Partnership Agreement." 2013, http://tppinfo.org/ (accessed February 24).

Ruth, S., and S. Stone. "A legislator's dilemma," *IEEE Internet Computing* 16 (6): 78–81, Nov–Dec, 2012.

Schaefer, E. "How to defend against a claim of cybersquatting: Litigation stories from the jury box." 2012, http://tcattorney.typepad.com/domainnamedispute/2012/07/how-to-defend-against-a-claim-of-cybersquatting-litigation-stories-from-the-jury-box.html#more (accessed July 19).

Schell, B. *Contemporary World Issues: The Internet and Society.* Santa Barbara, CA: ABC-CLIO, 2007.

Schell, B., and C. Martin. *Webster's New World Hacker Dictionary.* Indiana: Wiley, 2006.

Sutton, M. "EFF joins 24 US civil society groups in demanding a baseline of transparency in TPP negotiations." 2013, https://www.eff.org/deeplinks/2013/02/eff-joins-24-us-civil-society-groups-demanding-baseline-transparency-tpp (accessed February 5).

U.S. Department of Health and Human Services. "Omnibus HIPAA Rulemaking." 2013, http://www.hhs.gov/ocr/privacy/hipaa/administrative/omnibus/index.html (accessed March 6).

U.S. Government Printing Office Access. "The Protect Act of 2003." 2013, http://www.gpoaccess.gov/index.html (accessed March 8).

Williams, L. "Local Prime patient visited by Feds." 2012, http://www.redding.com/news/2012/jan/10/local-prime -patient-visited-by-feds/ (accessed January 10).

Yousuf, H. " 'Godfather of Spam' going to prison." 2009, http://money.cnn.com/2009/11/24/technology/King_of _spam_lawsuit_fraud_Ralsky/index.htm# (accessed November 30).

Zetter, K. "Feds: Would-be satellite TV pirate offered $250,000 reward to smartcard cracker." 2009, http://www .wired.com/threatlevel/2009/07/satellite/ (accessed July 15).

This chapter focuses on print and nonprint resources on Internet censorship and related Internet topics like hacking and cyber-crime. In the print section are Internet censorship and hacking-related books, magazines, and Web sites having downloadable news stories and white papers on a wide range of relevant topics. In the nonprint section are the Web sites for the following: organizations advocating for Internet freedom, Internet censorship videos, and companies offering software classified as anti-virus, firewall, content filtering, and filtering bypass. Finally, key U.S. government agencies and independent organizations concerned about Internet abuses are delineated.

The U.S. Department of Justice's Computer Crime and Intellectual Property Section (CCIPS) has an email service that gives updates on various forms of Internet-related crimes. To receive updates and to be added to the list, readers can send a message to http://www.justice.gov/govdelivery/subscribe.html?code=USDOJ.

Furthermore, the CCIPS Web site www.usdoj.gov/criminal/cybercrime/index.html has links to the following:

- Press releases from 1999 to the present (including the September 17, 2012, press release entitled "Two Romanian

Nationals Plead Guilty to Participating in Multimillion Dollar Scheme to Remotely Hack Into and Steal Payment Card Data from Hundreds of US Merchants' Companies")

- Manuals and reports on Internet-related crimes (including *Prosecuting Computer Crimes, Searching and Seizing Computers and Obtaining Electronic Evidence in Criminal Investigations* manual, *Prosecuting Intellectual Property Crimes*, and *Digital Forensic Analysis Methodology Flowchart*) as well as reports regarding intellectual property (IP) protection
- A summary of important criminal cases involving the Internet at http://www.justice.gov/publications/case-highlights.html
- How to report Internet-related crime, including network cracking and the breaching of IP

Print: Books

Abbott, J. P. *The Political Economy of the Internet in Asia and the Pacific: Digital Divides, Economic Competitiveness, and Security Challenges.* Westport, CT: Praeger (Greenwood), 2004.

> Though many people think that the Internet can level the playing field in jurisdictions where freedom of speech is controlled by the government, the essays in this book show that despite the opportunities the Internet provides, there are countries, like China, where censorship remains.

Alford, L. *The Great Firewall of China: An Evaluation of Internet Censorship in China.* Saarbruken, Germany: VDM Verlag Dr. Müller, 2010.

> This book is actually a set of study results that takes an innovative approach to viewing Internet censorship in China, because it looks at the many forces in this jurisdiction that are opposing censorship by the government authorities.

Ammori, M. *On Internet Freedom.* Washington, DC: Elkat Books, 2013.

An Internet freedom advocate, lawyer, and scholar focusing on the First Amendment, Marvin Ammori comprehensively discusses why freedom of the Internet is under constant threat—because of power struggles by corporations, governments, and hacker cells. A fascinating and powerful book on this important topic.

Arguilla, J., and D. F. Ronfeldt. *Networks and Netwars: The Future of Terror, Crime, and Militancy.* Santa Monica, CA: Rand, 2001.

This interesting book describes emerging forms of cyber conflict using the Internet. Among other topics, the book discusses netwars (conflicts involving terrorists, criminals, gangs, and ethic extremists) and various ways of coping with them.

Barbour, S. *Censorship: Opposing Viewpoints.* Farmington Hills, MI: Greenhaven Press, 2010.

This book gives some interesting and very countering views about censorship and what it means for society.

Beaver, K. *Hacking for Dummies*, 3rd Edition. New York: Wiley, 2010.

This book is a good foundational one for understanding malicious hacking. Preventive measures are outlined with easy-to-understand descriptions. This book also explains ethical hacking and why it is useful in today's virtual world. The book includes a lot of useful details on Web application hacking, mobile hacking, and VoIP hacking.

Berkowitz, B. D. *The New Face of War: How War Will Be Fought in the 21st Century.* New York: Simon & Schuster, 2003.

This book discusses the emerging types of information wars, details on how they have revolutionized combat using the Internet, and how a war against cyber terrorists could be waged.

Blunden, B. *The Rootkit Arsenal: Escape and Evasion in the Dark Corners of the System*, 2nd Edition. Burlington, MA: Jones & Bartlett Learning, 2012.

This book presents a comprehensive and up-to-date coverage of forensic countermeasures for network exploits. Topics include designing and deploying covert channels and ways of discovering new hack attacks.

Boyden, C. M. *Internet Censorship and Freedom in China: Policies and Concerns.* Hauppauge, NY: Nova Science Publication, Inc., 2013.

This book gives a fascinating look at the kinds of tactics that are used inside of China to maintain control over the Internet. It looks at why the United States and other nations are, therefore, concerned about human rights abuses, trade and investment issues, and cybersecurity threats commencing in this country.

Buyya, R., J. Broberg, and A. Goscinski. *Cloud Computing: Principles and Paradigms.* New York: Wiley, 2011.

This book is meant to be used by professionals and IT and business graduate students interested in having a solid grasp of the principles underlying cloud computing. The book also cites research topics that relate to cloud computing.

Casey, E. *Digital Evidence and Computer Crimes.* San Diego, CA: Academic, 2000.

This book details the law as it applies to computer networks. It also describes how evidence stored on or transmitted by computers can play a role in a wide range of crimes—including homicide, child abuse, stalking and harassment, fraud, theft, and terrorism.

Castells, M. *Networks of Outrage and Hope: Social Movements in the Internet Age.* Cambridge, UK: Polity, 2012.

The author looks at new forms of social movements and protests worldwide, particularly their unique ways of organizing and using the Internet as an effective means of communicating with others around the globe. Movements like the Arab Spring and the Occupy Wall Street in the United States were created by the autonomous communication networks available through the Internet and wireless communication.

Chirillo, J. *Hack Attacks Encyclopedia: A Complete History of Hacks, Cracks, Phreaks, and Spies over Time*. New York: Wiley, 2001.

Written by a security expert, this book covers historical texts, program files, code snippets, hacking and security tools, and a series of more advanced topics on password programs, sniffers, spoofers, and flooders.

Clarke, R. A., and R. Knake. *Cyber War: The Next Threat to National Security and What to Do about It*. New York: Ecco, 2012.

The authors, one an international security expert who worked for the U.S. government and the other a cyber expert, talk about the role of the Internet in cyber wars—hostile attempts by one nation to penetrate the networks of another nation for critical information. Recent past and present-day cyber wars are detailed in this very interesting and well-written book.

Clifford, R. D. *Cybercrime: The Investigation, Prosecution, and Defense of a Computer-Related Crime*. Durham, NC: Carolina Academic, 2001.

Intended primarily for a legal audience, this book covers topics such as what conduct is considered to be a cybercrime, how to investigate kinds of cyber conduct such as malicious hacking, how to try a cybercrime case as a prosecuting or defending attorney, and how to handle the international aspects of cybercrimes.

Cohen, N. *You Can't Read This Book: Censorship in an Age of Freedom*. New York: HarperCollins, 2012.

This intriguing book talks about censorship in countries that purport to be active on the Internet and supporters of an age of freedom. The author explores the present-day Internet reality in Iran, China, and elsewhere. The Great Firewall of China is discussed, along with the importance of religion, power, and dictatorships in keeping censorship alive and well in some key jurisdictions connected to the Internet.

Congressional Executive Commission on China. *China's Censorship of the Internet and Social Media: The Human Toll and Trade I*. Seattle, WA: CreateSpace, 2012.

This book presents the results of a hearing on China's predisposition to violate human rights and disregard the Internet laws and international standards that authorities say they believe in and uphold. Yet, they have not only increased censorship and control over the Internet, but they have been known to violate their citizens' human rights and dignity.

Davidoff, S., and J. Ham. *Network Forensics: Tracking Hackers through Cyberspace*. Upper Saddle River, NJ: Prentice Hall, 2012.

This book provides a nice foundation and road map for those trying to get the gist of cloud computing, advantages for businesses to move to the cloud, and concerns about IT security in the cloud. The book details the various kinds of "footprints" that hackers leave when they exploit networks.

Duthel, H. *Internet Censorship: Reports, Ratings, and Trends around the World*. Seattle, WA: CreateSpace, 2010.

The author presents a fulsome view of Internet censorship in various jurisdictions around the world. It is an interesting read because of some conspiracy theories linking Facebook, Google, and the CIA.

Duthel, H. *Freedom of the Press Report: Censorship—Internet Censorship*. Seattle, WA: CreateSpace, 2011.

Freedom of the press and Internet censorship are closely related. The author details why in this book and compares and contrasts jurisdictions where the press is most free (such as Finland, Iceland, the Netherlands, Norway, and Sweden) and where the press is least free (such as Eritrea, North Korea, Turkmenistan, Iran, and Myanmar [Burma]).

Engebretson, P. *The Basics of Hacking and Penetration Testing: Ethical Hacking and Penetration Testing Made Easy.* Rockland, MA: Syngress Publishing, 2011.

This book provides the basics for completing a penetration test for conducting ethical hacks using such available tools as Metasploit, Whois, Google, Backtrack Linux, and Nmap. Written by an experienced penetration tester, the book takes a hands-on approach for conducting penetration testing.

EPIC. *Filters and Freedom 2.0: Free Speech Perspectives on Internet Content Controls.* Washington, DC: EPIC, 2001.

This book talks at length about how Internet filtering affects online freedom of expression more severely than laws implemented in various jurisdictions for censoring Internet content. The book also discusses newer forms of legislation passed in the United States and within the European Union to create a uniform rating scheme for online material, as well as the use of filters in libraries.

Erikson, J. *Hacking: The Art of Exploitation*, 2nd Edition. San Francisco, CA: No Starch Press, 2008.

Written by a hacker who believes in the power of creative hacking, the book explains how hacking techniques work. Included are basics on C programming, Linux programming, assembly language, and shell scripts. The book's hands-on approach covers such important topics as buffer overflows, bypassing protections, cracking wireless devices, and high-jacking network communications.

Furnell, S. *Cybercrime: Vandalizing the Information Society.* Reading, MA: Addison-Wesley, 2001.

Written by a British computer security expert, this book gives a thorough overview of cracking, viral code, and electronic fraud. It covers a wide range of crimes and abuses related to IT. Unlike many other hacking books on the market, this one does not require advanced technological knowledge to understand the bulk of the material covered.

Goldsmith, J., and T. Wu. *Who Controls the Internet?* Oxford, UK: Oxford University Press, 2008.

Will the Internet bring an end to the geographic boundaries that currently exist? This book explores this question at length, as viewed through the lens of two law professors. Their main thesis is that national governments will keep their independence even with the Internet, largely because of economics. The authors argue their points with colorful illustrations from worldwide court cases involving big companies like eBay and Yahoo.

Goldstein, E. *The Best of 2600: Collector's Edition—A Hacker Odyssey.* New York: Wiley, 2009.

A top seller among hackers, this is a 912-page volume packed with real-life hacking events and exploits written by hackers. Emmanuel Goldstein (whose real-life name is Eric Corley) gives brilliant insights into the hacker culture as well as a series of controversial articles that depict IT security milestones and the evolution of technology over the past 25 years. As a bonus, a CD-ROM featuring some hit episodes of Goldstein's *Off the Hook* 2600 radio shows is also included in the collector's edition.

Goodman, S. F., and A. D. Sofaer. *The Transnational Dimension of Cybercrime and Terrorism.* Prague, Czech Republic: Hoover Institute, 2001.

Unlike maps showing the boundaries of countries around the globe, the Internet has no virtual boundaries. Thus, this interesting book, intended for a more advanced audience, covers the important topics of transnational cybercrime and cyber terrorism.

Greenberg, A. *This Machine Kills Secrets: How WikiLeakers, Cypherpunks, and Hacktivists Aim to Free the World's Information.* New York: Dutton Adult (Penguin Books), 2012.

The Guardian, and M. Belam. *Battle for the Internet: An Open Democracy or a Walled Garden?* London: Guardian Books, 2012.

The Internet can help shape democratic societies worldwide or enforce the surveillance by censorious governments of online citizens and perceived dissidents. This book details the different philosophical stances of countries utilizing the Internet to optimize their own objectives. The author looks at how the software and systems underpinning the Internet call into question not only how IP can be protected but how it can be accessed by *the enemy*.

Hadnagy, C. *Social Engineering: The Art of Human Hacking.* New York: Wiley, 2010.

This book covers a lot of interesting topics related to social engineering, such as the psychological principles used and abused by hackers, steps to complete a successful social engineering exploit, and how to capitalize on cracking cameras, GPS devices, and caller IDs for ensuring a successful hack attack.

Harper, A., S. Harris, and J. Ness. *Gray Hat Hacking: The Ethical Hackers Handbook*, 3rd Edition. New York: McGraw Hill Companies, Inc., 2011.

This book, written by experts in the field, provides useful and practical techniques for discovering and repairing security flaws. It also outlines legal disclosure methods. Penetration testing, malware, SCADA attacks, Web security, social engineering, and Metasploit usage are just a few of the important topics detailed in this book.

Herumin, W. *Censorship on the Internet: From Filters to Freedom of Speech*. Berkeley Heights, NJ: Enslow Publishing, Inc., 2004.

This book is a good one for younger children who want to get a better understanding of the relationship between free speech and the Internet. A number of laws passed in the United States are discussed, particularly as they relate to filters used to control the content on the Internet.

Himanen, P., M. Castells, and L. Torvald. *The Hacker Ethic and the Spirit of the Information Age*. New York: Random House, 2001.

This is one of a few books focusing on White Hat hacking, its values, and beliefs. The underlying theme of this book is that individuals can create great things by joining forces and using information and the Internet in imaginative ways.

Holt, T. J., and B. H. Schell. *Corporate Hacking and Technology-Driven Crime: Social Dynamics and Implications*. Hershey, PA: Information Science Reference, 2011.

This book presents a series of refereed chapters on important corporate hacking issues. Experts in the field have contributed a variety of views on control systems security and the social dynamics and the future of technology-driven crime; compared hackers and white-collar criminals; and examined the language of carders.

Holt, T. J., and B. Schell. *Contemporary World Issues: Hackers and Hacking*. Santa Barbara, CA: ABC-CLIO, 2013.

This book answers a lot of interesting questions, such as What defines the social world of hackers, and what motivates them to hack? This book traces the origins of hacking from the 1950s to today, gives readers a thought-provoking look at the ways in which hackers define themselves, details how and why they hack, and presents essays from experts in cybercrime about hackers and how they function in the unique cyber world they live and work in.

House, J. *Internet Censorship in China.* Ann Arbor, MI: ProQuest, UMI Dissertation Publishing, 2012.

This thesis is an academic focus on China's sophisticated Internet censorship schema used to help the country maintain its authoritarian government. The thesis gives an in-depth and interesting look at the history, players, and tactics used by the Chinese government to control content on the Internet.

Huff, M., K. Bendib, and Project Censored. *Censored 2013: The Top Censored Stories and Media Analysis of 2011–2012.* New York: Seven Stories Press, 2012.

Since 1976 and every year afterward into the present, Project Censored, the United States' oldest news-monitoring group, now under the leadership of the first author, has published the top 25 news stories that should have made it to the media but did not because of a combination of media bias and self-censorship. This book is a fascinating read.

International Group of Experts at the Invitation of the NATO Cooperative Cyber Defence Centre of Excellence. *Tallinn Manual on the International Law Applicable to Cyber Warfare.* Cambridge, UK: Oxford University Press, 2013.

This book was prepared by a team of 20 legal experts working with the International Committee of the Red Cross and the U.S. Cyber Command for NATO. This team of experts warns that state-sponsored cyberattacks must avoid sensitive civilian targets, like hospitals, dams, and nuclear power stations. It also says that hacktivists who participate in online attacks during a war could become *legitimate* targets even though, technically, they are civilians.

Komar, B., J. Wettern, and R. Beekelaar. *Firewalls for Dummies.* New York, NJ: Wiley, 2003.

This book presents key facts about firewalls to assist businesses and individuals wanting to protect their computer systems against hack attacks. The book is quite easy to understand, even though it is written by computer security experts.

Kulesza, J. *International Internet Law.* London: Routledge, 2012.

This important book looks at critical international legal issues and debates related to Internet governance. Topics include international copyright protection, cyber terrorism, identity theft, fake Internet Web sites, denial of service attacks, and international privacy protections. The author looks at how various jurisdictions view these issues, including China, the United States, the European Union, and Singapore.

Lankford, R. D. *Censorship (Issues That Concern You).* Farmington Hills, MI: Greenhaven Press, 2010.

This book examines a lot of important topics on censorship, including if censorship is ever acceptable, whether parents and the government should restrict content on the Internet, and the role of Internet service providers (ISPs) in censoring online content. It also looks at workplace infringements on free expression online.

Levy, S. *Hackers: Heroes of the Computer Revolution.* New York: Penguin, 2001.

A classic, this book was written for young people to inform them about the importance of MIT's Tech Model Railroad Club as a key pioneering effort in hacking history. This is where the White Hat hackers had their critical beginnings.

Littman, J. *The Fugitive Game: Online with Kevin Mitnick.*
Boston, MA: Little, Brown and Company, 1997.

> A great book to accompany the reading of *Ghost in the
> Wires* (see later in this section), this book details the online
> pranks of convicted cracker Kevin Mitnick. It is an excit-
> ing read, for it provides interviews with Kevin while he
> was on the run from the FBI. Kevin's views on the power
> of social engineering are especially insightful.

Littman, J. *The Watchman: The Twisted Life and Times of Serial
Hacker Kevin Poulsen.* Boston, MA: Little, Brown and Company,
1997.

> This book covers the interesting exploits of former hacker
> and now writer Kevin Poulsen, the first man in the United
> States accused of carrying out espionage using a computer.
> By ensuring that he was the 101st caller into radio stations
> in the United States, Poulsen accrued two Porsches and
> over $22,000 in cash. A very interesting read, indeed.

Lynch, M. *The Arab Uprising: The Unfinished Revolutions of the
New Middle East.* New York: PublicAffairs, 2013.

> A political science professor in the United States, the
> author looks at the many implications of the Arab
> Spring. In this day and age of young people being inter-
> connected to the world through the Internet, can the
> young people in the Middle East who want more
> democratic freedom overcome their leaders' capacity to
> kill their own citizens so that they can remain in
> power? This book explores the answer to this intriguing
> question.

MacKinnon, R. *Consent of the Networked: The Worldwide
Struggle for Internet Freedom.* New York: Basic Books, 2012.

> The author, a journalist and Internet policy analyst, says
> that while the Internet was meant to liberate online users,
> for every media piece talking about how empowering the

Internet is, there is a media piece talking about how companies and governments collect personal data on online citizens without their permission. This book addresses the hugely important question of how technology should be governed to uphold the rights and liberties of online users worldwide.

McChesney, R. W. *Digital Disconnect: How Capitalism Is Turning the Internet against Democracy.* New York: The New Press, 2013.

A professor of communications at the University of Illinois, the author explores the relationship between the digital world and economic powers—suggesting that capitalism is turning the Internet against democracy and the nations that practice it. The author further suggests that monopolies dominate the political economy, including Google (with 97 percent of the mobile search market) and Microsoft (whose operating system is inside over 90 percent of the world's computers). The author also says that with the marked declines in jurisdictions enforcing antitrust violations and the increase in patents on digital technologies, the Internet has become a virtual world of commercialism. This book is a fascinating read.

McClure, S., J. Scambray, and G. Kurtz. *Hacking Exposed: Network Security Secrets and Solutions*, 6th Edition. New York: McGraw-Hill, 2009.

This popular book discusses a practical approach to network security and presents an extensive catalog of the weaponry that Black Hats utilize. Detailed explanations of concepts such as war dialing and rootkits are presented. There is also a comprehensive discussion of how to use hacking software. The language and concepts are advanced and are intended for experts like system administrators. The authors also talk about how to locate and patch system vulnerabilities, wireless and radio-frequency identification (RFID) attacks, Web 2.0 vulnerabilities, and anonymous hacking tools.

Meinel, C. P. *The Happy Hacker*, 4th Edition. Tucson, AZ: American Eagle, 2001.

This book is part of a series of hacker books written by self-proclaimed female hacker Carolyn Meinel. The basic theme in all of her books is that hacking is fun but cracking is not. This book is especially useful for neophytes interested in hacking.

Miles, J. *The SOPA & PIPA Conspiracy: Taking CONTROL through Internet Censorship.* Seattle, WA: Amazon Digital Services, Inc., 2012.

This book takes an in-depth look at the controversies over recent laws proposed by the United States: SOPA and PIPA. The author gives an interesting view of what would have happened to Internet censorship in this jurisdiction if these laws had been passed, and what could happen in the future if similar laws are considered.

Mitnick, K., and W. L. Simon. *The Art of Deception: Controlling the Human Element of Security.* New York: Wiley, 2002.

This book, written by ex-convict Kevin Mitnick (whose hacking exploits put him behind prison bars a number of times) and writer William Simon, gives readers important tips about securing business computer networks and honing one's own expertise in social engineering.

Mitnick, K., and W. L. Simon. *The Art of Intrusion: The Real Stories behind the Exploits of Hackers, Intruders, and Deceivers.* New York: Wiley, 2005.

This fascinating book details some interesting hacking exploits of individuals bilking Las Vegas casinos of millions of dollars, hackers who have joined terrorist groups like

Al-Qaeda to cause harm, and a prisoner who communicates with the outside world unbeknownst to prison officials with the help of his computer. Because the book avoids technical complexities, readers unfamiliar with the workings of computers will find the contents compelling and to be an interesting read.

Mitnick, K., S. Wozniak, and W. L. Simon. *Ghost in the Wires: My Adventures as the World's Most Wanted Hacker.* Boston, MA: Little, Brown and Company, 2011.

Coauthored by a hacker who was once on the FBI's Most Wanted list and in and out of prison a number of times—Kevin Mitnick—this book details his strategies as he was on the run from the law for his hacking exploits into networks at Motorola, Sun Microsystems, and Pacific Bell. The other famous hacker coauthor (of the White Hat variety) is Steve Wozniak.

Morozov, E. *The Net Delusion: The Dark Side of Internet Freedom.* New York: PublicAffairs, 2012.

The author, a visiting scholar at Stanford University, has written for *The New York Times, The Wall Street Journal, The Financial Times,* and other high-quality publications. This book, employing a case study approach, talks about the freedoms of the Internet in some jurisdictions like the United States and the severe restrictions placed on the Internet in jurisdictions like China and Iran.

Nunziato, D. *Virtual Freedom: Net Neutrality and Free Speech in the Internet Age.* Stanford, CA: Stanford Law Books, 2009.

The author argues that communications giants, like Google and AT&T, as key providers of broadband access and Internet search engines, not only have the unique capacity to monitor and control online communications but also may be required to obstruct email messages to censoring cablecasts because of recent amendments to U.S. free speech legislation. The author maintains that the U.S. Supreme Court has failed to protect online citizens' rights to a broad range of content on the Internet. Consequently, he outlines a strategy for preserving free speech for online citizens.

Nuwere, E. *Hacker Cracker: A Journey from the Mean Streets of Brooklyn to the Frontiers of Cyberspace.* New York: William Morrow, 2002.

Written by a then-21-year-old cracker who is now a respected IT security specialist, this book provides young readers with a novel look into the Black Hat world.

Olson, P. *We Are Anonymous: Inside the Hacker World of LulzSec, Anonymous, and the Global Cyber Insurgency.* Boston, MA: Little, Brown and Company, 2012.

The author documents the interesting hacktivist attempts of the LulzSec and Anonymous hacker cells operating on the Internet. Interesting attacks on SONY, Visa, and PayPal networks in retaliation for their poor treatment of WikiLeaks are described in detail.

Pager, S. A., and A. Candeub. *Transnational Culture in the Internet Age.* Northampton, MA: Edward Elgar Publisher, 2012.

This book on cyber law addresses the legal and economic parameters of the Internet. As well, the important role of jurisdiction is discussed from various disciplines. As well, there is an examination of online threats to free speech and harms caused by identity theft.

Peterson, T. F. *Nightwork: A History of the Hacks and Pranks at MIT.* Cambridge, MA: MIT Press, 2002.

Young readers and adults will find this book interesting, as it gives insights into the history of the pioneers at MIT who were involved in the very early stages of White Hat hacking, during the 1960s and 1970s.

Poulsen, K. *Kingpin: How One Hacker Took over the Billion Dollar Cybercrime Underground.* New York: Crown Publishers, 2011.

> It is safe to say that Kevin Poulsen, who himself is a well-named hacker in hackerdom history, has watched other interesting hackers in his midst. In this book, the protagonist is a White Hat hacker who turns bad. The book is well written and reads like a thriller. The pages are filled with gripping descriptions of online fraud markets, murderous Russian criminals, phishing attacks, trojan horses, and outlandish hack attacks designed to bilk unsuspecting Americans of billions of dollars.

Raymond, E. S. *The New Hacker's Dictionary.* Cambridge, MA: MIT Press, 1996.

> This book is a classic regarding early hacking history and computer folklore. It defines the jargon used by hackers and programmers in the Computer Underground in the early days.

Ringmar, E. *A Blogger's Manifesto: Free Speech and Censorship in the Age of the Internet.* New York: Anthem Press, 2007.

> This interesting book talks about the role of bloggers as thinkers and online activists in terms of freedom of speech. The author describes the special role that the Internet plays in making this a virtual reality.

Schell, B. H. *The Internet and Society: A Reference Handbook.* Santa Barbara, CA: ABC-CLIO, 2007.

> This book summarizes the background and history of the Internet, provides biographical sketches of famous people who have contributed to the growth of the Internet, and gives details on various forms of U.S. legislation dealing with Internet security issues.

Schell, B. H., and C. Martin. *Cybercrime: A Reference Handbook.* Santa Barbara, CA: ABC-CLIO, 2004.

This book details the history and types of cybercrime; the issues, controversies, and solutions associated with computer system intrusions; a series of cybercrime legal cases; and biographical sketches of famous cyber criminals.

Schell, B. H., and C. Martin. *Webster's New World Hacker Dictionary.* New York: Wiley, 2006.

This dictionary describes almost 900 hacker terms, pieces of legislation aimed at combating malicious hack attacks, and famous hackers from the past and present.

Schell, B. H., J. L. Dodge, and S. S. Moutsatsos. *The Hacking of America: Who's Doing It, Why, and How.* New York: Quorum, 2002.

This book describes the 2000 study of hundreds of hackers who attended the DefCon and HOPE conferences. The study used numerous previously validated inventories to profile the personalities and behavioral traits of many self-admitted hackers in an attempt to answer the question, Is the vilification of hackers justified?

Shimomura, T., and J. Markoff. *Takedown: The Pursuit and Capture of Kevin Mitnick, America's Most Wanted Computer Outlaw, by the Man Who Did It.* New York: Warner, 1996.

This book describes the capture of Kevin Mitnick by the authorities with the assistance of White Hat hacker Tsutomu Shimomura. Besides giving some details on the author's personal life, the book also covers some of the technical, legal, and ethical questions surrounding the Kevin Mitnick hacking case that put Mitnick on the FBI's Most Wanted list.

Solove, D. J. *The Future of Reputation: Gossip, Rumor, and Privacy on the Internet.* New Haven, CT: Yale University Press, 2008.

A law professor, the author does an excellent job of explaining the key legal issues surrounding privacy and free speech on the Internet. Though most online users view the Internet as a friendly place to communicate with others through chat rooms, blogs, and social networking Web sites, the author maintains that there is a dark side as well—a lasting image of the Web sites that users visit. There are trails of information about us that are available to interested parties who may want to use that information in a variety of ways, some good and some bad.

Spinello, R., and H. T. Tavani. *Readings in Cyber Ethics.* Boston, MA: Jones and Bartlett, 2001.

This book is an anthology of more than 40 essays presenting conflicting points of view about new moral and ethical questions raised by Internet usage. Topics include free speech and content controls, IP protection, privacy and security protection, and professional ethics and codes of conduct regarding Internet usage.

Sterling, B. *The Hacker Crackdown: Law and Disorder on the Electronic Frontier.* New York: Bantam, 1993.

This classic book details the authority crackdowns on hackers that occurred during the early 1990s. It explains well the paranoia that hackers have been experiencing and their fear about being caught for engaging in illegal hacker exploits.

Stoll, C. *The Cuckoo's Egg: Tracking a Spy through the Maze of Computer Espionage.* New York: Gallery Books, 2005.

Originally published in 1985, this book was written by an astrophysicist who hunted down a hacker who attempted to exploit around 450 networks affiliated with U.S. national security. The hunt paid off with Stoll finding the culprit: a 25-year-old hacker from Germany named Markus Hess, allegedly also a member of a spy ring. The book reads like a thriller and is understandable to those without a strong computer background.

Szoka, B., J. Benlevi, R. MacKinnon, J. O. McGinnis, and J. Kuznicki. *Does Internet Activism Work?* Washington, DC: Cato Institute, 2012.

> The authors address the intriguing link between technology, freedom, and power. The book provides detailed discussions on how the Internet has provided an interesting screen for various scenarios incorporating power and liberty, or power and the lack of liberty.

Travis, H. *Cyberspace Law: Censorship and Regulation of the Internet.* London: Routledge, 2013.

> This book discusses in detail what the American Civil Liberties Union has labeled the "third era in cyber space," whereby filters change the Internet's architectural structure, reducing online free speech. Although the courts and other organizations insist that liberties online must be defended, the author says that large, multinational companies have produced tools and strategies enhancing Internet censorship.

U.S. Department of Justice. *21st Century Guide to Cybercrime.* Washington, DC: U.S. Department of Justice, 2003.

> This resource provides extensive coverage of the Department of Justice's work on computer crime and IP crimes and discusses the role of the National Infrastructure Protection Center (NIPC). The topics covered include searching and seizing computers in criminal investigations, legal issues in computer crime, international aspects of computer crime, cyber ethics, and sound standards for prosecuting cyber criminals.

Wang, W. *Steal This Computer Book 3.* San Francisco, CA: No Starch Press, 2003.

> This book has it all: humor, comprehensive topics on IT security, and valuable insights into the topic of personal computer security. Written for a wide-ranging audience

from young to more mature readers, this book outlines key tools and techniques utilized by hackers.

White, A. E. *Virtually Obscene: The Case for an Uncensored Internet.* Jefferson, NC: McFarland and Company, 2006.

This book looks at Internet pornography as a means of showing its importance in a broader argument about Internet regulations, community standards of tolerance, free speech debates, and its adverse impact on minors, women, and the morals of society, in general.

Yang, G. *The Power of the Internet in China: Citizen Activism Online.* New York: Columbia University Press, 2011.

The author maintains that since the mid-1990s, the Internet has aided creative expression in China, despite the willingness of the government to control the Internet's contents. The author says that Chinese online activism, like many other present-day online protest forms, is alive and well, despite the government's efforts to effect the contrary. The tradition of protest in China and a unique partnership with Internet companies has encouraged an interesting synergy between commerce and online activism in this jurisdiction.

Zalewski, M. *Silence on the Wire: A Field Guide to Passive Reconnaissance and Indirect Attacks.* San Francisco, CA: No Starch Press, 2005.

There are numerous ways that potential attackers can intercept information or learn more about the target as information passes through the Internet. The author discusses in this book the many kinds of stealth-like insidious attacks that often go unnoticed by system administrators, though intrusion detection, anti-virus software, and firewalls are available to monitor known or direct attacks. He provides a comprehensive view of passive reconnaissance and indirect attacks and how to protect networks against them.

Zuchora-Walske, C. *Internet Censorship: Protecting Citizens or Trampling Freedom? (USA Today's Debate: Voices and Perspectives).* Minneapolis, MN: Twenty-First Century Books, 2010.

> This is an excellent book looking at the topic of Internet censorship. Besides giving the history of Internet censorship, starting with the Declaration of Independence and moving into more controversial modern U.S. legislation like the PATRIOT Act, this book presents some fascinating real-life cases. It also gives readers insights into privacy issues, online child safety, intellectual property rights, and the importance to society of online privacy, security, trust, and a lack of censorship.

Print: Network Security Magazines and Hacker News Sites, Internet Freedom White Papers, and Internet-Related Downloadable Reports

Network Security Magazines and Hacker News Sites

2600: The Hacker Quarterly
http://www.2600.com/

This Web site/magazine is a favorite among hackers. The proud sponsor of the HOPE hacker conference, this often politically motivated Web site has two weekly live Net broadcasts: Off the Wall on Tuesdays and Off the Hook on Wednesdays. Emmanuel Goldstein also has a featured book for sale called *Dear Hacker*, featuring letters sent to him by colleagues in the Computer Underground.

Anon News
http://anonnews.org/

Anon News is an independent, uncensored, but monitored news platform for Anonymous, where anyone is welcome to post news. In October 2012, a popular news piece on this

Web site involved Anonymous's hacks of the Siemens and Fujitsu company Web sites.

Infosecnews
http://www.infosecnews.com

This Web site presents the latest news in the IT security world. For example, on October 12, 2012, Dan Kaplan wrote an interesting news story "Second LulzSec Member Pleads Out in Sony Pictures Attack." Also on this date appeared another story, by Danielle Walker: "Presidential Election Spurs Malware-laden CNN Spam." The Web site features interesting white papers like "Privileged Password Sharing the 'Root' of All Evil." There is also a special section for Canadian IT security news. For example, a story by Danny Bradbury running September 10, 2012, had this heading: "Canadian Energy Companies under Threat from Anonymous, Say Agencies."

LulzSec
News c/net
http://www.news.com

News c/net is all about information technology. Under the Security and Privacy tab for October 2012 were such timely articles as "Pre-emptive cyberattack possible, Panetta warns," "Anonymous turns its back on WikiLeaks after Paypal dispute," and "Mozilla rereleases Firefox 16 after fixing critical flaw." In 2014, fascinating topics include: "Colbert turns his funny gun on Snowden in RSA keynote" and "Yahoo, ICQ chats still vulnerable to government snoops."

PC World
http://www.pcworld.com

This IT magazine's Web site is anything but boring. There are group chat showdowns that featured, for example, "Which instant messenger service is best?" There are also some very interesting review features, such as "Hacker rift: Anonymous takes offense at WikiLeaks."

Security Magazine
http://www.secmag.com

This online magazine has featured stories on current IT security issues. For example, in October 2012, a feature story was "How cloud computing changes risk management"; in September 2012, there was "Making a difference in fraud detection"; and in October 2012, under the Critical Infrastructures tab, there was "Secretary of Defense says future cyberattacks could rival 9/11." In 2014, interesting stories like the following have been featured: "U.S. businesses lead the pack in cybersecurity readiness" and "Three in four Britons concerned about Internet privacy according to a new poll."

ZD Net
http://www.zdnet.com

This online high-tech magazine has news, blogs, and white papers dealing with secure transactions over the Internet. Moreover, the magazine's white paper directory is purportedly one of the largest online libraries containing free IT updates and numerous case studies on data management, IT management, networking, communications, enterprise applications, and IT privacy, security, and trust issues. There is also a special section devoted to cloud computing and data centers. Under the Security heading are interesting, timely stories like; "IT security in the Snowden era" and "Snowden's legacy and the NSA of everything."

Internet Freedom White Papers—A Sampling

ACLU. "Fahrenheit 451.2: Is cyberspace burning?" 2002, http://www.aclu.org/technology-and-liberty/fahrenheit -4512-cyberspace-burning (accessed March 17).

Eber-Schmid, N. "The effect of new media censorship on the world-NMI White Paper." 2009, http://www.newmedia. org/articles/the-effect-of-new-media-censorship-on-the -world—nmi-white-paper.html (accessed June 27).

Electronic Frontiers Australia. "Internet censorship: Law & policy around the world." 2002, https://www.efa.org.au/ Issues/Censor/cens3.html (accessed March 28).

Friedman, A. "Cybersecurity in the balance: Weighing the risks of the PROTECT IP Act and the Stop Online Piracy Act." 2013, http://www.brookings.edu/research/papers/2011/11/ 15-cybersecurity-friedman (accessed March 17).

Global Internet Freedom Consortium. "Defeat Internet censorship: Overview of advanced technologies and products." 2007, http://www.internetfreedom.org/archive/Defeat _Internet_Censorship_White_Paper.pdf (accessed November 21).

Google. "Enabling trade in the era of information technologies: Breaking down barriers to the free flow of information." 2010, http://static.googleusercontent.com/external _content/untrusted_dlcp/www.google.com/en//google blogs/pdfs/trade_free_flow_of_information.pdf (accessed November 15).

Hannemyr, G. "Cyber-censorship in Norway." 2012, http:// hannemyr.com/en/censorship01.php (accessed January 24).

Information Office of the State Council of the People's Republic of China. "The Internet in China." 2010, http:// china.org.cn/government/whitepaper/node_7093508.htm (accessed June 8).

Synthesio. "Social media and censorship in China." 2011, http://synthesio.com/corporate/en/2011/case-studies/ social-media-and-censorship-in-china/ (accessed January).

Weinstein, L. "Censorship, governments, and flagellating Google." 2011, http://lauren.vortex.com/censorship

-governments-google-white-paper-05-04-2011.html
(accessed May 4).

Key Internet-Related Downloadable Reports

Cooperative Association for Internet Data Analysis (CAIDA).
2013, http://www.caida.org/home/ (accessed March 25).
This Web site provides tools and analyses promoting the
engineering and ongoing maintenance of a sustainable, scalable
international Internet infrastructure. Two interesting 2014
papers on the Web site include: "Analysis of country-wide
Internet outages caused by censorship" and "A coordinated
view of the temporal evolution of large-scale Internet events."

Freedom House. "Freedom on the Net 2012." 2012, http://
www.freedomhouse.org/sites/default/files/FOTN%
202012%20FINAL.pdf (accessed September 24). This
downloadable report gives detailed "Free" or "Not Free"
Internet ratings for jurisdictions globally.

Internet Traffic Report. 2013, http://internettrafficreport.com/
(accessed March 25). This Internet traffic is an ongoing
"living" report that details how the Web site it monitors
flows of data through the Internet worldwide, with displays
of values between 0 and 100. Higher numbers indicate a
faster Internet with reliable connections

Mandiant. "APT1: Exposing one of China's cyber espionage
units." 2013, http://intelreport.mandiant.com/Mandiant
_APT1_Report.pdf (accessed February 19). This 60-page
report outlines the findings of the firm's tracking of China's
most sophisticated hacking groups Comment Crew and
Shanghai Group, which have allegedly stolen corporate
proprietary information from the networks of large
companies in North America and elsewhere.

Renesys. 2013, http://www.renesys.com/(accessed March 25).
Renesys, an Internet intelligence authority, provides an array

of downloadable data and observations on the global state of the Internet. Recent 2014 observations include: "Syria, Venezuela, Ukraine: Internet under fire" and "Protests lead to outage in Thailand."

Nonprint: Web Sites of Internet Openness Advocacy Groups

http://www.aclu.org/
American Civil Liberties Union (ACLU). The U.S. founder of the ACLU, Roger Baldwin, once said, "So long as we have enough people in this country willing to fight for their rights, we'll be called a democracy." ACLU members are found in courts, legislatures, and communities defending individual rights and liberties that are guaranteed by the U.S. Constitution and various U.S. laws. The ACLU defends the First Amendment (guaranteeing freedom of speech, association, and assembly; freedom of the press, and freedom of religion) and is headquartered on Broad Street in New York City. The ACLU has been active since 1920.

https://citizenlab.org/about/
The Citizen Lab. The Citizen Lab, located at the University of Toronto in Ontario, Canada, is housed at the Munk School of Global Affairs. Its mission is to advance research and development aimed at the crossover between digital media, human rights, and IT security on a global basis. By using experts in a variety of fields—political science, computer science, and engineering—the group collaborates with other researchers to monitor, analyze, and determine the impact of political powers in the virtual world and to promote Internet openness.

https://www.eff.org/
Electronic Frontier Foundation (EFF). With their main office in San Francisco, California, the EFF is an organization that was rooted in the summer of 1990, primarily as a reaction to threats against free speech. The EFF continues to defend

parties whose rights they believe have been infringed in cyber-space. For example, when Russian Dmitry Sklyrov was arrested in Las Vegas at the DefCon hacker convention, the EFF stepped in to defend his rights and freedoms.

www.freedomhouse.org
Freedom House. With offices on Wall Street in New York and on Connecticut Avenue in Washington, D.C., Freedom House is a prestigious, independent private organization supporting the expansion of freedom throughout the world. Their members believe that *freedom*—whether it be online or on land—is possible only in democratic political systems in which governments are accountable to their own people.

http://www.nacdl.org/about.aspx
National Association of Criminal Defense Lawyers (NACDL). Their Web site saying that they are "liberty's last chance," the NACDL is located in the United States and has the mission of ensuring justice and due process for individuals accused of a variety of crimes, including hacking. Founded in 1958, NACDL has about 40,000 defense lawyers, judges, public defenders, U.S. military defense lawyers, and law professors located in 28 countries—all dedicated to preserving fairness within the criminal justice system.

http://opennet.net/
The OpenNet Initiative. The goal of the OpenNet Initiative is to provide information to the world about the various ways and means that countries around the globe either allow or deny access to information to their citizens. Their mission is to identify and document Internet filtering and surveillance and provide a global forum for opening discussion on these issues.

http://publicknowledge.org/
Public Knowledge. With their office located at 1818 N Street, NW in Washington, DC, the mission of Public Knowledge is

to promote openness of the Internet and the public's access to knowledge, as well as creativity through "balanced copyright" (i.e., maintaining and protecting the rights of online consumers as they use innovative technology legally).

http://en.rsf.org/who-we-are-12-09-2012,32617.html
Reporters Without Borders (RWB). While they concern themselves with the concept of Internet censorship, RWB's scope and mission extends far beyond Internet practices. While the RWB does keep a list of Internet enemies—defined by them as countries creating and maintaining the most censorious policies and restrictions on the Internet worldwide—the association also maintains a record of the journalists and netizens who have been killed or imprisoned (often without a fair trial). Reporters Without Borders was started in France in 1985 by four journalists: Robert Ménard, Rémy Loury, Jacques Molénat, and Émilien Jubineau. This association, registered as a nonprofit organization in France since 1995, immediately took on an international dimension and has remained that way ever since.

Nonprint: Internet Censorship Videos

Biden on Internet Freedom Anti SOPA
Date: 2012
Length: 2 minutes
This short video gives Vice President Joe Biden's candid views on why the SOPA legislation is detrimental to the United States.
http://www.youtube.com/watch?v=ZXS5lIV2XNs

Hackers Strike After U.S. Internet Piracy Clampdown
Date: 2012
Length: 1 minute
This short video discusses why the loose hacker cell known as Anonymous hacked the Web sites of the U.S. Department of

Justice, the FBI, and the White House as a sign of Internet censorship following the arrest of members of MegaUpload.
http://www.youtube.com/watch?v=ruSlO_-CZMI

iFI: Internet Freedom is Love
Date: 2012
Length: 3 minutes
This video is actually a musical album dedicated to the sharing of emotion and sentiment across huge distances without censorship or infringement.
http://www.youtube.com/watch?feature=player_detailpage&v=rE
kK00ZvVrU

Internet Freedom and Authoritarianism: Author Rebecca MacKinnon
Date: 2012
Length: 9 minutes
This intriguing video talks about the worldwide struggle for Internet freedom by the author of the book *Consent of the Network*. The author was a former reporter in China in 1995, when the Internet first arrived there. Her talk also focuses on the role that authoritarian systems have played in censoring content on the Internet, and why.
http://www.youtube.com/watch?v=LuWQMeNkJBU

Internet Freedom in Danger After Court Ruling
Date: 2010
Length: 4 minutes
The video discusses the controversies around a ruling in the United States against the Federal Communications Commission (FCC) on the issue of net neutrality and why Internet freedom is in danger.
http://www.youtube.com/watch?v=RbAoRZJyoJI

Internet Regulation, Internet Freedom, Internet Activism
Date: 2011
Length: 30 minutes
This interesting video discusses some controversial political movements suggested in the United States, including taxing services on the Internet.
http://www.youtube.com/watch?v=bOYAodmVcFQ

The Internet of Tomorrow
Date: 2006
Length: 1 minute
This extremely short video is motivational in nature, in that it advocates net neutrality. It cites concerns about the future of the Internet if high-tech companies do not support the critical aspects of freedom of information worldwide.
http://www.youtube.com/watch?v=8CHzuSTowRg

Protecting Internet Freedom and Privacy
Date: 2012
Length: 6 minutes
Senator Rand Paul talks about the continual erosion of the Fourth Amendment in the United States, considering the present-day reality that considerable personal information of citizens is held by third parties. He discusses key ramifications of the PATRIOT Act.
http://www.youtube.com/watch?v=377-mueo21c

Hillary Clinton *Secretary Clinton on "Internet Rights and Wrongs: Choices and Challenges in a Networked World"*
Date: 2011
Length: 44 minutes
Secretary Clinton speaks on the George Washington University campus to an audience interested in Internet openness and Internet freedom. Secretary Clinton speaks to the importance of global events like the Egyptian and Iranian governments

shutting down citizens' access to the Internet during periods of protest and homeland disputes.
http://www.youtube.com/watch?v=Pa-8z2p0SfA

Secretary Clinton Speaks on Internet Freedom
Date: 2010
Length: 60 minutes
Secretary of State Hillary Clinton eloquently speaks about the importance of Internet freedom as a means of safeguarding a series of freedoms for nations in the networked cyber world.
http://www.youtube.com/watch?v=ccGzOJHE1rw

Secretary Clinton Speaks on U.S.-China Relations in the 21st Century
Date: 2011
Length: 40 minutes
Secretary Clinton discusses the future of U.S.-China relations, emphasizing the importance of allowing citizens in China to have open access to the Internet and to respecting citizens' human rights and dignity as they try to access this information.
http://www.youtube.com/watch?v=yv4qLYCE3XI

Sopa Pipa Acta & Hr 1981 Vs Internet Freedom
Date: 2012
Length: 5 minutes
This brief video outlines why the passage of SOPA and PIPA would have adversely impacted on Internet freedom in the United States.
http://www.viduba.com/video:
QdlTJRleONlVGJFMWtmVrRmeFdXWn1TP

Stop ACTA! 2012 Internet Freedom!
Date: 2012
Length: 2 minutes
This video discusses the negative role that the passage of ACTA (Anti-Counterfeiting Trade Agreement) would have on

Internet freedom in at least 39 countries that secretly engaged in its design and promotion—including the United States, Mexico, and Morocco. If passed, the ISPs who give citizens around the world access to the Internet would then become known as "the copyright police."
http://www.youtube.com/watch?v=fXGCoudsNAw

Nonprint: Web Sites of Companies Offering Anti-virus Software

Two kinds of virus-scanning software exist to protect computer networks. One type is used on individual computers, while the other scans traffic going to and from the Internet at a gateway—looking for potentially harmful code. Both types of software not only try to remove any attached viruses, worms, or trojans from software programs and documents but also inform users about some actions being taken.

The Web sites listed below offer a wide range of anti-virus and anti-malware products for gateway-based and local installations. These products differ primarily in their licensing and packaging schemes. These products are regularly tested by the computer security companies producing them, and the companies' Web site content is, therefore, continually updated to reflect the findings of those tests. Most of the companies listed also provide information services to their customers as well as to the public about newly released malware on the Internet. The Web site content also details known countermeasures, commonly called *patches* or *fixes*.

F-Secure
http://www.f-secure.com
The F-Secure 2013 package is part of an award-winning product line for this U.S.-based security software company. For example, the F-Secure Internet Security 2013 product line was the AV-Test Best Protection 2012 Award. The 2013 security package guards against existing and emerging threats to

computer networks—and it has gone to the cloud. The F-Secure Web site says that it will keep companies' and government networks secure using real-time cloud-based technology to guard against viruses, spyware, and other forms of malicious attacks. What's more, the company produces a user-friendly firewall to thwart hack attacks, block spam and phishing attacks, and prevent identity theft. For the home computer user, the F-secure protection package allows parents to block harmful sites from children or block children's uncontrolled surfing.

Corporate headquarters: San Jose, California, and Helsinki, Finland

Network Associates—McAfee
http://www.mcafee.com
The McAfee, Inc. Web site has this clever saying: "Safety is not a privilege. It is a right." To this end, the new McAfee anti-virus protection package is marketed as a total defense protection suite that has "best of breed" rootkit protection, quick-scan and one-step easy installation, and automatic scanning of USB drives. This company was founded in 1987 by John McAfee and continues to make technology advances annually.

Corporate headquarters: Santa Clara, California

SafeNet
http://www.safenet-inc.com/?aldn=true
SafeNet is one of the largest data security companies in the world. More than 25,000 government agencies and businesses across 100 companies rely on this company's products to help safeguard their networks—whether it be data protection, two-factor authentication, cloud security, cybersecurity, software security, or software licensing.

Corporate headquarters: Belcamp, Maryland

Sophos

The Sophos company markets their suite of products as being able to effectively protect networks, servers, data, endpoints, and mobile devices. The goal of the company is to eliminate malware, protect data on corporate and home networks, prove compliance, and protect mobile devices from hack attacks. The company claims, "We make the Internet safer and more productive." Their Web site also provides up-to-date IT security news and trends.

Corporate headquarters: Abingdon, Oxford, and Burlington, Massachusetts

Symantec

Symantec lets online users become better informed about the Norton AntiVirus protection product line to help them safeguard their networks against spyware and virus invasion. Thus, the Norton Internet Security and Norton 360 products are aimed at providing the ultimate virus protection—complete with backup and 2 GB online storage. The company Web site offers online visitors interesting videos, such as this one with the attention-getting message for enterprise IT security administrators: "Data center down! Is your business prepared to recover?"

Corporate headquarters: Mountain View, California

Trend Micro

http://www.trendmicro.com

The Trend Micro Web site opens with this attention-getting sentence: "Securing your journey to the cloud." It goes on to remark to visitors: "Relax. We make it easier to secure your digital life" and "Trend Micro Smart Protection Network unleashes big data in the fight against 'Tomorrow's Threats.'" Founded in 1988 in the United States, Steve Chang is the cofounder and chair of the corporation, and Eva Chen is the cofounder and CEO.

Corporate headquarters: Tokyo, Japan

Nonprint: Web Sites of Companies Offering Firewall, Web-Filtering, and Web-Filtering Bypass Software

Businesses and government agencies, alike, rely on firewalls as well as Web-filtering software. Thus, by using firewalls, both can literally pick and choose which Web pages or even entire domains to block. This way, companies and government agencies can avoid blocking Web sites that employees or citizens need to access legitimately. Even in countries deemed to be free, when an online user tries to access a restricted Web site, he or she will see a message that typically includes the option of petitioning the network administrator to unblock access if he or she feels that the Web site is wrongfully blocked. Afterward, the network administrator can adjust which Web sites are restricted through firewall settings.

Web Sites of Companies Offering Firewall Software

The firewall suppliers listed below have all provided well-designed products for these objectives. What is equally interesting is that these companies have created new technologies beyond firewalls to contend with emerging trends like cloud computing and RFID tracking and control.

Check Point
http://www.checkpt.com
When one goes on the Check Point Web site, the company motto appears: "Helping retailers grow profitably." The company has specific IT solutions for retailers in these market segments: apparel, food markets, warehouses, pharmacies, hardware stores, and specialty stores. Besides providing protections, the company's solutions offer retailers in-stock information on their product line inventory.

Corporate headquarters: Thorofare, New Jersey

Cisco
http://www.cisco.com
The company's products are wide ranging and include application networking services, data center automation and management, blade switches, networking software, physical security software, routers, unified computing and servers, and video conferencing software. The company's services are also wide-ranging and include borderless network services, data center and virtualization services, routing and security services, storage networking services, and WebEx collaboration services.

Corporate headquarters: San Jose, California

DellSonicWALL
http://www.sonicwall.com
In 2012, DellSonicWALL Next-Generation firewalls earned recognition for the product line from three of the industry's most influential third-party evaluators. The company's network and security products include secure remote access, anti-spam and email security solutions, backup and recovery solutions, management and reporting solutions, and endpoint security solutions. Originally founded in 1991 under the name SonicWALL, the company was acquired by Dell in 2012.

Corporate headquarters: San Jose, California

Web Sites of Companies Offering Web-Filtering Software

Most Web filters use two main techniques to block Internet content: blacklists (Web sites designated as undesirable) and keyword blocking (whereby the software scans a Web page to determine if certain keywords exist and if the Web page is deemed to be inappropriate, the users' access is blocked). The SmartFilter software originally made by the Secure Computing company in California and then bought by McAfee in 2008 is reportedly used in countries like Tunisia, Saudi Arabia, Sudan, Iran, Bahrain, the United States, and the United Kingdom. The WebSense Web filter is reportedly used in Myanmar and Yemen, and the Canadian-produced Netsweeper is reportedly used in Qatar, the United Arab Emirates, and Yemen. The company Web sites for these Web-filtering software products are given below.

Netsweeper
http://netsweeper.com/what-we-do/
The Netsweeper software filters Web content so that companies can better manage threats against their networks by controlling access to content deemed to be inappropriate. This company's solutions use a cloud-based artificial intelligence categorization engine with configuration and administrations tools allowing organizations to tailor solutions to their particular needs. Also, the Web filtering is said to be *smart*, in that it continuously learns and improves its capabilities by recognizing the usage patterns of employees and millions of other Netsweeper users worldwide.

Corporate headquarters: Guelph, Ontario, Canada

SmartFilter by McAfee
http://www.mcafee.com/us/products/smartfilter.aspx
The McAfee company, known for its anti-virus software, produces the SmartFilter software to prevent companies' employees from accessing Web sites known to expose the network to viruses, malware, and other security issues. Also, the software is said to reduce legal liability and to save bandwidth for business-related activities rather than for those activities perceived to adversely impact employees' productivity. McAfee says that the software has predefined filtering policies for over 35 million Web sites in almost 100 categories.

Corporate headquarters: Santa Clara, California

WebSense by GuardSense.com
http://www.guardsense.com/Web-Filter.asp
The WebSense Web-filtering software has been on the market
for over 15 years, making it one of the oldest products being
used to control employees' access to Web sites deemed to have
inappropriate content. There are many more current versions
of the software product that deal more effectively with today's
sophisticated network attack agents.

Corporate headquarters: Irvine, California
   The following companies offer software products to introduce filtering on Web content in order to keep children safe
from predators while they are online:

CyberSitter by Solid Oak Software
http://cybersitter.com/
Solid Oak Software, located in Santa Barbara, California,
makes CyberSitter. CyberSitter produces filtering software to
keep children safe while online. It blocks inappropriate adult-
only content, certain social networking sites and online games,
and other customized Web sites that parents feel are inappropriate for viewing by their children. This software also records
Facebook chats and posts.

Corporate headquarters: Santa Barbara California

Net Nanny
http://www.netnanny.com/
The Net Nanny software is designed to be a filtering device that
parents can use to keep their children safe while online by determining the use of words or phrases in context. If the word *breast* appears,
for example, the software is said to be able to differentiate between
when it is used in a normative sense and when it is used in a pornographic sense. If it is used inappropriately, that Web site is blocked.

Corporate headquarters: Salt Lake City, Utah

Web Site of a Company Offering Web-Filtering Bypass Software

Psiphon

http://psiphon.ca/

The Psiphon open source software, produced in Canada, has been put to use to bypass Internet censors that have been put into effect by government authorities in certain jurisdictions. In fact, it is estimated that about 25,000 to 40,000 Syrians currently bypass their country's sensors daily using this software. Also, in Iran, it is estimated that about 150,000 Internet users can access online services like Facebook, Twitter, and Skype with this software. Researchers from the University of Toronto's Citizen Lab in Ontario, Canada, and the SecDev Group devised the software in 2004 and then took it to market in 2008.

Corporate headquarters: Toronto, Ontario, Canada

Nonprint: U.S. Government Agencies and Independent Organizations Fighting Internet Abuses

The FBI, IC3, the National White Collar Crime Center (NWC3), the Department of Homeland Security, the NIPC, and the National Computer Security Center (NCSC) are involved in the fight against malicious hacking in the United States, besides the U.S. Department of Justice. An independent organization with similar motivations includes the United States Computer Emergency Readiness Team (U.S.-CERT). The locators for these U.S. government agencies and independent organizations are given below.

The Department of Homeland Security
http://www.dhs.gov/
Homeland Security Operations Center
Washington, DC
Telephone: (202) 282-8101

The creation of the Department of Homeland Security (DHS) was the most significant transformation of the U.S. government since 1947, when Harry S. Truman merged the various branches of the U.S. armed forces with the Department of Defense to better coordinate the nation's defense against military threats. The DHS represents a similar high-tech consolidation, both in style and in substance.

In the aftermath of the terrorist attacks of 9/11, President George W. Bush decided that 22 previously disparate domestic homeland security agencies needed to be coordinated into one department to better protect the nation against threats. Thus, the new department's priority objective was to protect the nation against further terrorist attacks. Component agencies assist in analyzing threats and intelligence, guarding borders and airports, protecting critical infrastructure, and coordinating the responses to future emergencies. The DHS is dedicated to protecting the rights of American citizens and enhancing public services (such as natural disaster assistance) by dedicating offices to them, besides providing a better-coordinated defense of the U.S. homeland.

Federal Bureau of Investigation

The function of the FBI is to protect American citizens of all ages from threats such as internal and external terrorists, gangs, and cyber criminals. To this end, the FBI has taken on a proactive role of fighting crime to present and emerging threats as a means of keeping US citizens safe.

http://www.fbi.gov
J. Edgar Hoover Building
935 Pennsylvania Ave. NW
Washington, DC
Telephone: (202) 324-2000

Internet Crime Complaint Center or IC3

http://www.ic3.gov

The IC3 accepts complaints about Internet crime from either the victim or a third party representing the victim. Many of the complaints this government agency deals with involve online fraud. The IC3 is a partnership between the FBI and the National White Collar Crime Center. The Web site gives Internet crime–prevention tips and outlines current reported trends (such as the Nigerian Letter scheme, also known as 419).

National White Collar Crime Center
http://www.nw3c.org
Telephone: (803) 273-NW3C
The NWC3 is a U.S.-based center that provides a support system for law enforcement and regulatory agencies in the prevention, investigation, and prosecution of high-tech crimes. This agency conducts specialized training in computer forensics, conducts research on the many facets of white collar crime, and partners with the IC3. The NWC3 was formed in 1978, when it was known as the Leviticus Project (whose mission it was to investigate crime dealing with the coal industry), but the agency's name was changed to NW3C in 1992 to reflect an expanded mandate involving high-tech crimes.

NIPC
Information Analysis Infrastructure Protection
Washington, DC
Telephone: (202) 323-3205
Founded in 1998, NIPC was initially housed in the FBI headquarters. In 2003, it was moved to the Department of Homeland Security. NIPC is the government agency charged with safeguarding the U.S. infrastructure networks from attack by hackers and malware.

The NIPC issues three levels of infrastructure warnings:

- Level one assessments provide general information about nonspecific threats.
- Level two advisories address particular dangers requiring greater preparedness or a change in posture.
- Level three alerts warn of major and specific threats.

For example, in 2002, the NIPC issued a level one assessment warning against possible hacktivism exploits connected with upcoming meetings of the International Monetary Fund and the World Bank.

NSA National Computer Security Center
NSA INFOSEC Service Center
INFOSEC Awareness, Attn: Y13
Fort George G. Meade, MD
Telephone: (800) 688-6115
Founded in 1981, the NCSC provides solutions, products, and services and conducts defense information operations to keep the critical U.S. infrastructure safe from attack. A part of the National Computer Security Agency, the NCSC provides information systems security standards and solutions.

Working in partnership with industry, academic institutions, and other U.S. government agencies, the NCSC initiates needed research and develops and publishes standards and criteria for trusted information systems. The NCSC also promotes information systems security awareness, education, and technology transfer through cooperative efforts, public seminars, and an annual National Information Systems Security conference.

U.S. Computer Emergency Readiness Team
http://www.us-cert.gov
U.S.-CERT is jointly run by the Department of Homeland Security and CERT at Carnegie-Mellon University. Their mission is to coordinate previously dispersed efforts to counter threats from all forms of cybercrime. Therefore, U.S.-CERT does the following:

- Analyzes and attempts to reduce cyber threats and vulnerabilities
- Disseminates cyber threat warning information
- Coordinates incident responses

Individuals wanting to subscribe to CERT's mailing lists and feeds in order to get the latest information on vulnerability and threat information or wanting to report a known vulnerability are encouraged to enter their Web site: http://www.kb.cert .org/vuls/html/report-a-vulnerability/

U.S. Department of Justice
10th and Constitution Ave. NW
Criminal Division
John C. Keeney Building, Suite 600
Washington, DC
Telephone: (202) 514-1026
http://www.cybercrime.gov

This chapter delineates in chronological order selected Internet development and Internet censorship events, beginning with the Internet's humble beginnings (the 1940s through the 1960s); moving to the Internet's adolescent years (the 1970s and the 1980s), where the dark side of computer hacking often stole the media headlines; and concluding with the Internet's adult years (from 1990 to the present), where we begin to understand how various governments around the world justify the need to censor Web site content as a means of keeping their online citizens safe.

The Internet's Humble Beginnings (the 1940s through the 1960s)

1947–1948   John Bardeen and Walter Brattain develop transistors.

1958–1959   Jack Kilby and Robert Noyce develop integrated circuits, aiding in the further development of computers. With the development of integrated circuits, instead of making transistors one by one, several transistors can be made at the same time and on the same piece of semiconductor. Furthermore,

---

Protesters demand political asylum for whistle-blower Edward Snowden during a Chaos Communication rally against governmental monitoring and surveillance in Hamburg, Germany on December 28, 2013. (David Fischer Baglietto/Demotix/Corbis)

other electric components like resistors, capacitors, and diodes can be made using the same process and materials.

1960s   Moore's law is recognized to denote this huge process in circuit fabrication, named after Gordon Moore, a pioneer in the integrated circuit field and the entrepreneurial founder of the Intel Corporation. Though accepting these advances in hardware technology, the question of how to hook up and share the data between computers remains. Also during this period, the revolutionary packet-switching technique invented by Leonard Kleinrock gains popularity among more computer users, and Paul Baran at the Rand Institute begins researching how to use packet switching for secure voice over military networks.

1969   The Advanced Research Projects Agency Network, or ARPAnet, is created to be the initial cross-continent, high-speed computer network built by the U.S. Department of Defense as a digital communications experiment. ARPAnet allows artificial intelligence researchers in dispersed areas to exchange information with incredible speed and accuracy.

Also, the standard operating system UNIX is developed by Dennis Ritchie and Ken Thompson, researchers at Bell Laboratory. UNIX is considered to be a thing of beauty because its standard user and programming interface assists users with computing, word processing, and networking requirements.

The Internet's Adolescent Years: The 1970s and 1980s

1970   The civil rights and women's rights movements are in full swing in the United States, and at this time, only about 100,000 computers are in use.

1971   One of the forefathers of the Internet who worked on the ARPAnet, Ray Tomlinson, gives to society one of the greatest online communications gifts in Internet history: the @ symbol for email.

A Canadian professor at the University of Toronto named Stephen Cook publishes Cook's theorem, identifying a large class of computational search problems that at this time would take the largest, most powerful computers millions of years to solve. This theorem helps researchers make huge strides in the cryptography field, critical for secure online transactions.

1972   The National Center for Supercomputing Applications creates the telnet application for remote login, making it easier for users to log into remote machines.

David Boggs and Robert Metcalfe invent Ethernet at the Xerox Corporation, making it possible to connect computers in a local area network.

1973   The file transfer protocol is developed, simplifying the transfer of information between networked machines. During this time, American computer experts believe that the bigger the computer, the more powerful it can be. But in this year, a Canadian mathematician and business genius, Mers Kutt, goes against the mainstream and argues that smaller is better; he releases onto the North American market the world's first personal computer (PC). With just 8 kilobytes of memory, the PC costs $5,000 and gets its power from a small chip rather than from vacuum tubes.

1975   Americans Steve Jobs and Steve Wozniak start the Apple computer company using the simplistic and user-friendly BASIC computer language in their machines and placing the roots for the soon-to-blossom home use computer market.

Americans Bill Gates and Paul Allen start the Microsoft Corporation, producing innovative software products.

1976   Secure transactions using the Internet get a power boost because Whitfield Diffie and Martin Hellman create the Diffie-Hellman public key algorithms.

1978   Though the Internet is still missing a networking social club, two men from Chicago, Randy Suess and Ward Christiensen create the first computer bulletin board system (BBS), the root of modern-day online chat rooms.

The transmission control protocol (TCP) is split into the TCP and IP (Internet protocol), a critical event in the evolution of the Internet.

1982   California IT pioneers Scott McNealy, Bill Joy, Andy Bechtolsheim, and Vinod Khosla start the Sun Microsystems company, based on the assumption that UNIX running on relatively inexpensive hardware is a grand solution for a wide range of applications. As a result, the Sun networks start to replace older and less efficient computer systems like the VAX and other time-sharing systems that take up a huge amount of floor space in large companies and research universities.

On a happy note, Scott Falhman creates the first online smiley, ☺, and William Gibson coins the term *cyberspace*. Also, the simple mail transfer protocol is published, which relates to how email is transmitted between host computers and users.

1983   The telnet protocol is published, allowing individuals with UNIX to log onto other computers on the Internet.

1984   Computer hacker Eric Corley (a.k.a. Emmanuel Goldstein) starts *2600: The Hacker Quarterly* to give hackers a venue for expressing technical and political issues in the virtual world.

Steven Levy's popular book *Hackers: Heroes of the Computer Revolution* is released, letting those in mainstream society gain some key insights into what goes on in the then-secret Computer Underground. Also during this year, Fred Cohen uses the term *computer virus* to indicate a cyberspace vandal that corrupts or erases information stored on computers. In the business realm, the Cisco Systems company is started by a small number of scientists at Stanford University.

1985   The first Web site domain name is registered and assigned, American Online is incorporated, and the Free Software Foundation is started by Richard Stallman so that computer users can use, study, copy, change, and redistribute computer programs as a means of promoting the development of free software. This is the year that the term *hacker* is introduced into mainstream society to indicate a well-meaning individual who enjoys learning the details of computer systems and how to stretch their capabilities.

1986   The term *criminal hacker* is used in the British press when Robert Schifreen and Steven Gold break into a text information retrieval system operated by BT Prestel; they leave a message for his Royal Highness the Duke of Edinburgh on his network mailbox.

U.S. Congress passes the controversial Computer Fraud and Abuse Act as a means of preventing fraud aimed at or completed with computers. The Internet Engineering Task Force starts to act as a technical coordination forum for individuals working on ARPAnet, the U.S. Defense Data Network, and the Internet core gateway system.

1988   Robert Morris, a U.S. graduate student, accidentally unleashes onto the Internet the first Internet worm. As a result, the Computer Emergency Response Team/CERT Coordination Centre is created at Carnegie Mellon University to coordinate communications among homeland security experts during emergencies.

1989   Herbert Zinn ("Shadowhawk") is the first minor to be convicted in the United States as a violator of the U.S. Computer Fraud and Abuse Act, after he cracks the American Telephone and Telegraph computer network and that of the U.S. Department of Defense—getting him nine months in prison and a fine of $10,000.

In Germany, a group of hackers called the Chaos Computer Club make international headlines after they exploit the U.S. government's computer network and sell the operating system source code to the Soviets. During this year, only about 90,000 computers are linked to the Internet.

The Internet's Adult Years: 1990 to the Present

1990   Tim Berners-Lee and Robert Cailliau develop the protocols that become the World Wide Web, a browser-editor that looks very one dimensional. Then the browser is renamed

Nexus to stop the confusion between the software program and the more abstract information space that is spelled World Wide Web (with spaces between the words).

During this period, tech-savvy individuals can finally afford to buy PCs similar in power and storage to those of the clunky computers of the 1980s, but the software for these PCs remains expensive.

1993   There are more than 1,000,000 computers linked to the Internet.

1994   Two Stanford University students named David Filo and Jerry Yang start a cyber guide in a campus trailer to track their interests on the Internet, the start of the Yahoo! (Yet Another Hierarchical Officious Oracle) search engine.

1994   The term *hacktivist* becomes a reality when individuals squash the U.S. government's highly controversial Clipper proposal, which would have placed strong encryption (the technical process of scrambling information into something unintelligible) under the government's control.

1995   Jeffrey Bezos launches the first online bookstore, later to be known as Amazon. Also this year, Microsoft releases its Windows 95 software product, making software prices more affordable for home PC owners.

1996   The World Wide Web now has 16 million hosts. Also in this year, the National Information Infrastructure Protection Act is enacted in the United States, amending the Computer Fraud and Abuse Act to enhance the power of this law.

1998   In the United States, the Digital Millennium Copyright Act is passed as a means of coping with emerging digital technologies and their unlawful disabling or bypass by tech-savvy individuals in the mainstream.

1999   The Melissa virus is created by David Smith and released onto the Internet, infecting millions of computer systems in the United States and Europe and costing at least $80 million in damages to computers worldwide. Also in this year, the Gramm-Leach-Bliley Act is passed in the United States to provide limited privacy protection against the sale of individuals' private information following mergers of financial institutions and insurance companies.

2000 There is worldwide panic about data losses resulting from Y2K computer glitches—which, as it turns out, never did happen. Also this year, the world learns about Canada's hacker headline maker Michael Calce "Mafiaboy"—showing the world the damage that can be caused by denial-of-service attacks. Through his exploits, Mafiaboy brought down high-profile Web sites like Amazon, eBay, and Yahoo!

2001 The fears of a "cyber apocalypse" arises as hackers attack a computer system controlling the distribution of electricity in California, an attack said to have originated in China's Guangdong province. Also in this year, users started playing games online, and massively multiplayer online role-playing (MMORPG) becomes popular.

2003 The CAN-SPAM Act is passed by the U.S. Senate to regulate interstate commerce by placing limitations and penalties on the transmission of spam (defined as "junk mail" delivered to online users without their permission).

2004 In January, the Recording Industry Association of America begins legal pursuits against U.S. netizens for swapping songs without paying royalties to the song artists, after tracking at least 500 song swappers by their IP addresses.

2005 Fears of Internet censorship begin to appear when the world learns that China is actively blocking Internet content perceived by authorities to be immoral or violent in nature. China closes more than 12,000 Internet cafes to prevent netizens of all ages from viewing so-called offensive material.

Also in this year, cyber wars become a media headline catcher; in March a cyber war breaks out between Indonesia and Malaysia over a dispute regarding the Ambalat oil fields in the Sulawesi Sea. Within 24 hours, the Web site of Uniersiti

Sains Malaysia is under cyberattack and plagued with aggressive anti-Malaysian messages with an Indonesian twist.

Elsewhere around the globe, five hackers belonging to a group called Oxlfe Crew in the Netherlands are found guilty of disabling a number of Dutch government Web sites, in their efforts to protest against recent cabinet proposals that they do not like. This incident is the first time that anyone in the Netherlands is convicted of such a cybercrime.

In China, which is getting a growing reputation for censoring Internet content, a newly released search engine called Baidu.com is publicly traded, creating high hopes for the 37-year-old founder Robin Li to become a high-tech billionaire. As Li is having a press conference outlining his hopes of becoming very wealthy, Chinese authorities shut down another two Internet sites popular among academics, journalists, and civil rights activists. One of the two serves as an online discussion group to report on anticorruption protests in a southern village around Beijing, and the other services the ethnic Mongolians.

2006   News headlines become dominated by the emergence of botnets—large numbers of computers that are commandeered by hackers and marshaled for personal gain.

Also, by year's end, the world hears about Internet censorship occurring in places like Iran. Authorities shut down citizens' access to some of the world's most popular Web sites, like Amazon, YouTube, Wikipedia, and *The New York Times* to impede "corrupting" foreign films and music and to purge Iran of Western cultural influences. When users try to open the filtered Web pages, they see this message: "The requested page is forbidden." At this time, Iran is listed by Reporters Without Borders (RWB) as being one of 13 countries branded as an "enemy of the Internet." The reason cited by RWB is that Iran not only has rampant state-sanctioned blocking of Web sites but also often intimidates and imprisons bloggers.

2007   Reports of Internet censorship continue to mount. The Burmese (Myanmar) junta try to shut down Internet and telephone links to the outside world after a stream of blogs and mobile phone videos capture dramatic scenes on the streets of Burma. Immediately, cyber cafes are closed by the authorities and mobile phones are disconnected. Although at this time less than 1 percent of the Burmese population have access to the Internet, and only 25,000 people have email addresses, certain clever netizens capitalize on loopholes by evading the official firewalls. The netizens seek access to the Internet by connecting to embassies, foreign businesses, and nongovernmental organization networks where Internet access is not so tightly controlled.

Also in this year, an attempt to force search engine Google to stop censoring its search results in content-repressive countries is rejected by the company shareholders. During this year, the world learns that the government authorities in Belarus, Burma, Cuba, Egypt, Iran, North Korea, Saudi Arabia, Syria, Tunisia, Turkmenistan, Uzbekistan, and Vietnam regularly restrict content on the Internet.

2008   Georgia and Russia briefly go to war online when distributed denial of service (DDoS) attacks bring down Georgian Web sites. The media pinned Russia as the obvious perpetrator.

Also during this year, Anonymous, a nebulous collection of hacker cells and splinter groups that coordinate their activities, targets the Church of Scientology. Apparently, the church's secretive, controlling nature runs counter to the hacker collective's views and values—which they want the online community to know and appreciate.

2009   U.S. president Barack Obama criticizes the Internet censorship that has been taking place in China since at least 2005, as he gives a speech to students in Shanghai. The president also speaks about the importance of the value of freedom of expression and political participation to the approximately 400 students gathered. The Chinese officials reject the U.S. request that about 1,000 students be invited to attend President Obama's talk and that it be broadcast live nationwide.

2010   The Facebook virus called Koobface shows the world that social media are now vulnerable to hack attacks; when this virus infects a computer, it sends a lurid message to the computer owner's friends, tricking them into downloading malware.

WikiLeaks is once again in the news for acquiring and publishing over 250,000 American diplomatic cables, ranging from unclassified to secret documents. A U.S. Army soldier named Bradley Manning downloaded the materials while stationed in Iraq and then turned them over to Julian Assange and the folks at WikiLeaks. WikiLeaks then releases the materials for worldwide transmission to *The New York Times* and *Der Spiegel*. The release of these cables causes massive controversy and embarrassment for the U.S. government because of the sensitive nature of the information. Companies providing funding and infrastructure for WikiLeaks—such as PayPal—pull their support. As a consequence, hacker cells worldwide begin DDoS hack attacks against the financial service providers to punish them for their actions. The controversy over these documents leads some authorities in the United States to call for the arrest of Assange, and even his execution.

2011   The Symantec IT security firm announces that there are at least 286 million malware variants in circulation worldwide—many of which have the potential to expose personal data on the Internet.

2012   In January, two U.S. bills—SOPA in the House and PIPA in the Senate—are designed to stop the piracy of copyrighted material over the Internet on Web sites based outside of the United States. Once word about these gets circulated among the online masses, on January 18, the largest online protest in the history of the Internet occurs. Small and large Web sites "go dark" in protest of these two pieces of legislation that could profoundly change the Internet.

Also, in this year, Julian Assange faces charges in Sweden, where he is wanted for questioning by authorities about sexual assault allegations. Assange fears that Sweden will extradite him to the United States to face charges related to the WikiLeak's disclosure of the secret cables. Assange, therefore, views himself as an information freedom fighter who deserves and is granted asylum in the Ecuadorian embassy in London in June.

2013 Assange remains on the lam and holed up in the embassy when he decides to run for a Senate seat in his homeland of Australia in September, and to this end, he releases onto the Internet a video making fun of Australian politicians. Ecuadorian president Rafael Correa chastises Assange, noting that as a matter of courtesy, Ecuador will not bar him from exercising his right to be a candidate, as long as he does not make fun of Australian politicians over the Internet.

On June 4, the court-martial of U.S. soldier Bradley Manning begins in the United States. This case illustrates the delicacy between national security during war and the role of the Internet and hackers in overriding established rules of information disclosure to the public. On the opening day of the trial, Manning confesses to being the source for the vast archives made public by WikiLeaks. By mid-June, prosecutors present evidence that Manning's leaks compromised sensitive information in a range of categories, including techniques for neutralizing improvised explosives and the naming of troop movements. By mid-August, Manning takes the witness stand and apologizes to the American people, saying that though he did what he did, he did not believe that his actions would cause harm. On August 21, Manning receives a sentence of 35 years in prison, the longest sentence handed down in a case involving a leak of U.S. government information.

On June 9, a 29-year-old past undercover CIA employee named Edward Snowden—a self-pronounced information freedom fighter—announces that he is the main source of recent disclosures in the United States about top-secret National Security Agency surveillance programs tracking phone and Internet messages around the globe with the objective of thwarting terrorist threats. Within 24 hours of this news, U.S. politicians like Dianne Feinstein of California accuse Snowden of committing "an act of treason" and say that he should be prosecuted accordingly. Snowden flees to Hong Kong and later to Moscow seeking asylum. On August 13, Snowden thanks Russia for granting him temporary asylum for one year. Immediately, U.S. lawmakers call for some form of tough retaliation against Russia, such as boycotting the Winter Olympic Games held in Sochi—a boycott that never happened in 2014.

Access Controls   The physical or logical safeguards preventing unauthorized access to information resources.

Account Harvesting   This term is often used to refer to spammers, individuals who try to sell or lure others through email advertising or solicitation. Account harvesting involves using computer programs to search areas on the Internet to gather lists of email addresses. Newsgroups and chat rooms are great resources for harvesting email addresses.

Actus reus   One of the four elements on which Anglo-American law bases criminal liability. This element means a criminal action or a failure to act when one is under a duty to do so.

Algorithm   A set of rules and procedures for resolving a mathematical or logical problem, much as a recipe in a cookbook helps baffled cooks to resolve a meal preparation problem. In computer science, an algorithm usually indicates a mathematical procedure for resolving a recurrent problem. IT security professionals are concerned with cryptographic algorithms—those used to encrypt, or encode, messages.

American Civil Liberties Union (ACLU)   Members work in courts, legislatures, and communities to defend and maintain

The login screen for the Facebook application on an iPhone 4s. (Editor77/Dreamstime.com)

individual rights and liberties that the U.S. Constitution and various U.S. laws guarantee citizens.

Anonymous A collection of hacker cells that coordinate their efforts, to some degree, in online chat rooms. The cells have brought down the Vatican's Web site, teased cabinet members in numerous countries when their political messages were controversial, and released cracked emails dealing with sensitive information regarding the U.S. government. This group of hackers seems to embody a culture of creative disturbance in the pursuit of chaos, justice, and retribution.

Anti-virus Software Detects viruses and notifies the user that the virus is present. This type of software keeps a database of "fingerprints," a set of characteristic bytes from known viruses, on file.

ARPAnet The first transcontinental, high-speed computer network built by the U.S. Department of Defense as an experiment in digital communications.

Attendant Circumstances One of the four elements on which Anglo-American law bases criminal liability. This element means the existence of certain necessary conditions. With some crimes, it must be proven that certain events occurred, or certain facts are true, for a person to be found guilty of some crime.

Authentication A user's legitimacy to enter the network information—typically a password, a token, or a certificate.

Blacklist Lists of Web sites that the Web filter's creators have designated as being undesirable; these tend to change over time, so most companies marketing this kind of software offer updated lists free of cost.

Blockers Term given to governments that block a large number of politically relevant Web sites and certain social media platforms. Term also includes governments that place considerable resources into hiring people with the talent and technical capacities to identify "offensive" content that should be blocked.

Blog Actually a short form for Weblog, a blog is like an online personal journal, such that online users can post thoughts or comments. Blogs usually have links to other Web sites. They are increasingly becoming popular ways of sharing social and political issues.

Blogosphere   Blogs on the Internet within a specific jurisdiction, such as the American blogosphere or the Chinese blogosphere.

The Budapest Convention on Cybercrime   A convention that came into effect on July 1, 2004—the first global legislative attempt to set standards on the definition of Internet-related crime and develop policies and procedures to govern international cooperation in order to combat it. The treaty was to enter into force when at least five states, three of which were members of the Council of Europe, ratified it.

Bulletin Board System (BBS)   The BBS, the precursor to the Internet, was a computer system that ran software to allow users to dial into the system using a phone line. The users could then download software and data, upload data, read news, or trade messages with other online users. It was popular from the 1970s through the early 1990s.

Censorship   Refers to tactics used by government authorities to block access to certain Web sites for online users within that jurisdiction.

The Censorware Project   Formed in 1997 with the mission of educating people about Web-filtering software and practices, their Web site features a series of investigative reports on the major filter programs and commercial applications available on the market.

Channel   An established communication link through which a message travels as it is transmitted between a sender and a receiver.

Chat Rooms   Online "rooms" allowing many users to engage in real-time, text-based chats.

The Citizen Lab   Located at the University of Toronto in Ontario, Canada, the Citizen Lab's mission is to advance research and development aimed at the crossover between digital media, human rights, and IT security on a global basis. By using experts in fields like political science, sociology, computer science, engineering, and graphic design, the participants are motivated to collaborate with other research centers and organizations to monitor, analyze, and determine the impact of political powers in the virtual world and to promote Internet openness.

Cloud Computing Basically speaking, any company's or government agency's data and applications running on the Internet. That means that everything is stored on servers at a remote location and can be accessed from any Web browser anywhere around the globe.

Conflict/Security Web Filtering Filtering content belonging to Web sites relating to wars, skirmishes, overt dissent, and other conflicts either within a nation or in some other nation.

Council of European Convention on Cybercrime The first global attempt of its kind to set standards on the definition of cybercrime and develop policies and procedures governing international cooperation to combat Internet crime.

Crackers Often called *hackers* in the media, crackers are individuals who break into other computer systems without authorization to commit crimes. Believed to be motivated by malintent, crackers are also labeled network hackers or net-runners.

Criminal Trespass A legal term indicating that someone has entered or remains in an area in which that person does not have legal access.

Critical Elements As in land-based crimes, for cybercrime to exist, four elements must be present: *actus reus* (the prohibited act or failing to act when one is supposed to be under duty to do so; *mens rea* (a culpable mental state); *attendant circumstances* (the existence of certain necessary conditions); and *harm* resulting to persons or property.

Critical Infrastructure Critical infrastructure according to the USA PATRIOT Act of 2001 included the following critical infrastructure sector and resources: chemical systems;

emergency services; information technology; postal and shipping; telecommunications; and transportation systems (including buses, flights, ships, ground systems, rail systems, and pipeline systems). Nuclear power systems are also part of this label.

Cybercrime   A crime related to technology, computers, and the Internet that causes harm to property or to persons.

Cyber terrorism   Unlawful attacks and threats of attack by terrorists against computers, networks, and the information stored within computers when done to intimidate or coerce a government or its people to further the attacker's political or social objectives.

Cyber cafe   A business where consumers pay a price to use computers so that they can gain legal access to the Internet for a given period of time.

Cyberspace   Composed of hundreds of thousands of interconnected computers, servers, routers, switches, and fiber optic cables. It allows a nation's critical infrastructure—telecommunications, energy, banking, water systems, government operations, and emergency services—to function well for society. In short, cyberspace is the virtual *nervous system* of the global economy.

Distributed Denial-of-Service (DDoS)   Web servers can handle only so much traffic, beyond which the network crawls or crashes. DDoS is one way of shutting down a network, which is bombarded with traffic from all directions. This can be done with a botnet, using which an attacker relays a signal that causes thousands or more infected computers to bombard a targeted Web server. There is also a volunteer attack, whereby Internet users use software like the Low Orbit Ion Cannon, which turns computers of willing users into generators of traffic. The multiple origins of the attack make DDoS attacks difficult to defend against.

Electronic Frontier Foundation (EFF)   An organization that started in the summer of 1990, primarily as a reaction to threats against free speech. Located in the United States, the EFF continues to defend parties whose rights in cyberspace are believed to have been infringed. Often, the EFF becomes involved in defending hackers charged of computer crimes.

Email   An electronic system, like the Internet, using which a message is sent from one party to another.

Facebook   A social networking Web site. Employers are concerned about social Web sites like Facebook for two main reasons: they think that employees' productivity will be adversely affected and that if they use mobile devices for corporate use to log onto Facebook, critical company information may be leaked though a social network.

Firewalls   Designed to allow only safe content through and prevent everything else from entering the network; firewalls may be either software or hardware.

Fixes or Patches   Updated system software, created by computer security experts to close security gaps discovered in software after it has been released into the marketplace.

Forum   Online discussion groups allowing users with similar interests to exchange messages through the Internet. Forums are also known as newsgroups.

Forum Trolling   Spies who linger in chat rooms or a forum so that they can read the posts of online users and then report their findings to the authorities.

Freedom House   An independent watchdog organization supporting democratic change that monitors the status of freedom in countries around the globe and assesses which ones are advocating for democracy, human rights, and Internet openness. This organization regularly publishes the report entitled *Freedom on the Net*.

Freedom of Information   A citizen's right to access information held by the government. In many developed nations, this freedom is supported as a constitutional right.

Hacker   A person who enjoys learning the details of computer systems and how to stretch their capabilities.

Hacktivism   Using the Internet to promote one's own political platform or mission.

Hypertext Transfer Protocol (HTTP)   A programming language used to transfer data over the World Wide Web.

ICT   Information and communications technologies that include hardware like computers and mobile devices.

Identity Theft   The malicious theft of and consequent misuse of someone else's identity.

Information Packet   A piece of data of fixed or variable size sent through a communications network like the Internet.

Intellectual Property (IP)   IP refers to the protection of creative products of the human mind like the protection of property. IP laws grant certain kinds of exclusive rights over these creative products, similar to property rights.

Internet   A network connecting computer systems.

Internet Censorship   When governments try to control online citizens' activities, restrict the free flow of information, and infringe on the rights of users.

Internet Enemies   Defined by Reporters Without Borders to be countries creating and maintaining the most censorious policies and restrictions on the Internet worldwide.

Internet Freedom   Protection of unfettered expression online.

Internet Usage Policies   Before giving them access to the company's Internet service, companies require employees to sign an Internet usage policy form, which has them agree they will be accountable for their online activities.

Intranet   An information system internal to an organization that is built with Web-based technology.

ISP (Internet Service Providers)   Internet service providers are companies providing access to the Internet for a fee;

typically, users who pay a fee for this service receive a software package, a user name, a password, and a telephone number to initiate a connection.

Keyword Blocking   Refers to a technique used by Web-filtering software; the software program scans a Web page as a user tries to visit it, analyzes the page quickly to determine if certain keywords exist, and blocks users' access to that page if that Web page is found inappropriate.

Limits on Content   The filtering and blocking of certain Web sites, as well as other kinds of online censorship and self-censorship.

Listserv   An online subscription to some topic of interest.

Mens rea   One of the four elements on which Anglo-American law bases criminal liability. This element means a culpable mental state.

Microblog   A kind of blog allowing online users to publish short text updates that are distributed to a large number of online followers. One such site is Twitter.

Nascent Blockers   Term given to governments that appear to be at a crossroad; though authorities impose politically motivated censorious blocks, the blocks tend to be sporadic, and the blocking system is far from institutionalized.

Net Neutrality   Refers to a so-called level playing ground where ISPs allow access to all content without favoring any particular Web site.

Netizen   Someone who is actively engaged in the Internet—a sort of virtual world citizen.

Non-blockers   Term given to governments not yet at the stage of systematically blocking politically relevant Web sites, although the authorities may have already restricted online content, especially after noticing the critical role that online tools play in overturning the political "status quo."

Obstacles to Access   Infrastructural and economic barriers to Internet access.

OpenNet Initiative (ONI)   An organization dedicated to letting the public know about Web filtering and surveillance policies globally.

Piracy   Copying protected software without authorization.

Political Web Filtering   Blocking content belonging to Web sites that include views counter to the respective countries' policies regarding the Internet and allowable content. This category includes Web site content related to human rights, religious movements, and other causes of a social nature.

Privacy   The state of being free from unauthorized access.

Privacy Laws   Laws dealing with the right of individual privacy, critical to maintaining the quality of life that citizens in a free society expect. Privacy laws generally maintain that an individual's privacy shall not be violated unless the company (or government) can show some compelling reason to do so— such as by providing evidence that the safety of the company (or of the nation) is at risk.

Protocol   A set of rules governing how communication between two programs has to take place to be considered valid.

Psiphon Software   A Canadian software application that is sometimes put into use in censorious jurisdictions to bypass Internet censors that have been put into effect by government authorities. Therefore, citizens in censorious nations can view Internet content that is deemed to be "inappropriate" by the authorities.

Public Knowledge   An agency whose mission is to promote openness of the Internet and the public's access to knowledge, as well as creativity through *balanced copyright* (defined as maintaining and protecting the rights of online consumers as they use innovative technology in a legal fashion).

Real Name Registration   In some jurisdictions, online users wanting to post a comment first have to complete a registration form that collects information like the user's real name (and not some moniker) or the user's contact phone number or address.

Reporters Without Borders (RWB)   Concerning itself with Internet censorship, this association keeps a list of "Internet enemies" and maintains a record of journalists and netizens who have been killed as well as imprisoned—often without a fair trial.

Security   Being protected from adversaries, particularly from those who do harm—unintentionally, or otherwise—to property or a person. IT security issues include but are not limited to authentication, critical infrastructure protection, disaster recovery, intrusion detection and network management, malicious code software protection, physical security of networks, security policies, the sharing of rights and directories, and wireless security.

Social Engineering   A deceptive process whereby crackers engineer a social situation with the purpose of tricking others into allowing them access to an otherwise closed network.

Social Networking Site   A Web site allowing users to create public profiles and form online relationships with others. Examples include Facebook, MySpace, and Orkut.

Social Web Filtering   Filtering content belonging to Web sites that focus on sexuality, gambling, drugs, and other social-cultural issues that a country's authorities may find "offensive."

SOPA and PIPA   Two U.S. bills designed to stop the piracy of copyrighted material over the Internet on Web sites based outside of the United States.

Spamming   To send unsolicited emails for commercial purposes or with the intent to defraud.

Surveillance   Governments intercepting online communications as a way of, allegedly, preventing terrorist attacks.

3G   Third generation of mobile communication technology, allowing high-speed Internet access for mobile phone users.

Trademark Law   Governs disputes between business owners over the names, logos, and other means used to identify products and services in the marketplace.

Trans-Pacific Partnership Agreement (TPP)   An agreement sought by the big media lobbyists pushing for trade agreements with copyright measures that are far more restrictive than those currently required by existing treaties or legislation in the United States, Canada, and elsewhere around the world. Feared by the Open Internet activists, the TPP was seeking the rewriting of the global rules on IP enforcement to give the big media new powers to lock online users out of content and services; seeking more liabilities to be forced upon ISPs so that they do a better job of policing netizens' online activities; and giving the big media companies stronger powers to shut down Web sites and remove content deemed to be "offensive."

Trust   A complex concept studied by scholars from a number of disciplines, defined to be present in a business relationship when one partner willingly depends on an exchanging partner in whom one has confidence. The term *depend* can take on a number of meanings, including the willingness of one partner to be vulnerable to the actions of the other, or the expectation that one partner will receive ethically bound behaviors from the other partner. IT security issues involving rust center on maintaining trust in online, or e-commerce, transactions.

Video Sharing   Uploading video clips online for others to see. The practice of video sharing can take place through paid Web-hosting sites or through free Web sites like YouTube.

Violations of Users' Rights   Placing legal protections and restrictions on online activities, watching over the Internet's content, overriding principles of online privacy, doling out penalties for online activities deemed to be "inappropriate" or "offensive," and engaging in imprisoning, physically attacking, or harassing online users whose activities are deemed to be "immoral," "offensive," or beyond established community standards of tolerance within a jurisdiction.

Virus A computer program that replicates itself by embedding a copy of itself into other programs.

Web Filtering Filtering content belonging to Web sites offering tools like email, instant messaging, language translation applications, and those aimed at circumventing censorship.

Web 2.0 The so-called second generation of the Web, it refers to advanced graphical features, greater interactivity by online users, and various online services like video sharing, social networking, and blog hosting.

Wi Fi Wireless technologies providing an Internet connection for such devices as computers and mobile phones within a given physical or geographical location.

WikiLeaks Founded by Julian Assange in 2006 to provide an outlet to cause regime change and open information sharing, this Web site is controversial. It has published materials related to the Church of Scientology, Guantanamo Bay, military strikes, and classified documents around the world. The Web site is most famous for its acquisition and publication of over 250,000 American diplomatic cables, ranging from unclassified to secret documents and tied to U.S. Army soldier Bradley Manning.

World Intellectual Property Organization (WIPO) A law and protection agency set up to protect intellectual property rights. This international organization promotes the use and protection of IP—creative outputs in all fields, including science, technology, and the arts—most of which are available for posting online.

About the Author

Bernadette H. Schell is well published in the hacking and IT domain. She has coauthored books such as *The Hacking of America* (2002), *Cybercrime* (2004), *The Internet and Society* (2007), and *The Webster's New World Hacker Dictionary* (2006). In December 2011, Dr. Schell's chapter on the fictional character Lisbeth Salander as a hacker appeared in the recently published book *The Psychology of the Girl with the Dragon Tattoo*. She has also coauthored two books with Dr. Tom Holt—*Corporate Hacking and Technology-Driven Crime* (2011) and *Hackers and Hacking* (2013). Currently the vice-provost at Laurentian University in Barrie, Ontario, Canada, Dr. Schell was formerly the founding dean of business and information technology at the University of Ontario Institute of Technology (UOIT) in Oshawa, Ontario, Canada.